MEN, MASCULINITIES & SOCIAL THEORY

EDITED BY
JEFF HEARN & DAVID MORGAN

London
UNWIN HYMAN
Boston   Sydney   Wellington

Published by the Academic Division of
Unwin Hyman Ltd
15/17 Broadwick Street, London W1V 1FP, UK

Unwin Hyman Inc.,
955 Massachusetts Avenue, Cambridge, MA 02139, USA

Allen & Unwin (Australia) Ltd,
8 Napier Street, North Sydney, NSW 2060, Australia

Allen & Unwin (New Zealand) Ltd in association with the
Port Nicholson Press Ltd,
Compusales Building, 75 Ghuznee Street, Wellington 1, New Zealand

First published in 1990

British Library Cataloguing in Publication Data

Hearn, Jeff
    Men, masculinities and social theory. – (Critical studies on men and masculinities).
    1. Masculinity
    I. Title   II. Morgan, D. H. J. (David Hopcraft John) *1937*–
    III. Series
    305.31

    ISBN 0–04–445658–1
    ISBN 0–04–445657–3 pbk

Library of Congress Cataloging in Publication Data

Applied for

Typeset in 10 on 12 point Bembo by Nene Phototypesetters Ltd
and printed in Great Britain by Billing and Sons, London and Worcester.

Contents

9   The significance of gender politics in men's accounts
    of their 'gender identity'   *Alison Thomas*   143

10 Masculinity, identification, and political culture
    Barry Richards   160

11 Male perception as social construct   *Leonard Duroche* 170

12 Doing masculinity/doing theory   *Wil Coleman*   186

PART 4   COMMENTARIES

13 The critique of men   *Jeff Hearn and David H. J. Morgan* 203

14 The new men's studies: part of the problem or part
    of the solution?   *Joyce E. Canaan and Christine Griffin* 206

15 Men, feminism and power   *Victor J. Seidler*   215

    Bibliography   229

    Author Index   246

    Subject Index   251

Series Editor's Preface

Gender is one of the most pervasive and taken-for-granted features of our lives. It figures strongly in the make-up of all societies. Yet it is easy to see that gender may also create problems – in terms of power, oppression, inequality, identity and self-doubt.

The growth of modern feminism and the associated development of women's studies have brought a deep questioning of women's social position. At the same time feminism and women's studies have provided continuing critical analyses of men and masculinities. In a rather different way the rise of gay liberation and gay scholarship has shown that previously accepted notions of sexuality and gender are no longer just 'natural'. This has led to a recognition that the dominant forms of men and masculinities are themselves not merely 'natural' and unchangeable. In addition, inspired particularly by important research in women's studies and the need for a positive response to feminism, some men have in recent years turned their attention to the critical study of men. These various focuses on men are clearly very different from the traditional concern with men that has characterized the social sciences, where in the worst cases men have been equated with people in general. Thus men and masculinities are not seen as unproblematic, but as social constructions which need to be explored, analysed, and indeed in certain respects, such as the use of violence, changed.

This series aims to promote critical studies, by women and men, on men and masculinities. It brings together scholarship that deals in detail with the social and political construction of particular aspects of men and masculinities. This will include studies of the changing forms of men and masculinities, as well as broader historical and comparative studies. Furthermore, because men have been domi-

[ix]

nant in the writing of social science and production of malestream theory, one area of special interest for critical assessment is the relationship of men and masculinities to social science itself. This applies to both the content and 'results' of previous social research, and to the understanding of social theory in all its various guises – epistemology, ideology, methodology, and so forth.

Each volume in the series will approach its specific topic in the light of feminist theory and practice, and where relevant, gay liberation and gay scholarship. The task of the series is thus the critique of men and masculinities, and not the critique of feminism by men. As such the series is pro-feminist and gay-affirmative. However, this critical stance does not mean that men are simply to be seen or understood negatively. On the contrary, an important part of an accurate study of men and masculinity is an appreciation of the positive features of men's lives, and especially the variety of men's lived experiences. The series includes a range of disciplines – sociology, history, politics, psychoanalysis, cultural studies – as well as encouraging interdisciplinarity where appropriate. Overall, the attempt will be made to produce a series of studies of men and masculinities that are anti-sexist and anti-patriarchal in orientation.

Finally, while this series is primarily an academic development, it will also at times necessarily draw on practical initiatives outside academia. Likewise, it will attempt to speak to changing patterns of men's practice both within and beyond academic study. Just as one of the most exciting aspects of feminism is the strong interrelation of theory and practice, so too must the critical study of men and masculinities and change in men's practice against patriarchy develop in a close association.

Acknowledgements

This volume arises from the conference, 'Men, masculinity and social theory', held in 1988 under the auspices of the Sociological Theory Study Group of the British Sociological Association. We would like to thank the members and officers of the Theory Group, the British Sociological Association Publications Committee and the British Sociological Association Executive Committee for facilitating the production of this book. We also would like to thank Richard Kilminster, Convenor of the British Sociological Association Sociological Theory Study Group, and Tim Piggott, formerly University of Bradford Conference Officer, for their assistance and advice in organizing the conference; Alan Carling for his willing help at the conference; and Mike Milotte, formerly of the British Sociological Association, and Gordon Smith, of Unwin Hyman, for their support in the publication of this volume. We also would like to thank Sue Moody for typing parts of the manuscript.

Chapter 5 is a substantially revised version of an article, first published in *Industrial Relations Journal* 20, no. 3, Autumn 1989, published by Basil Blackwell, parts of which are reproduced here by kind permission of the editor and the publisher.

Chapter 8 is a revised version of an article first published in *Social Theory and Practice* 14, no. 3, Fall 1988, and is reproduced here by kind permission of the editor and the publisher.

Contributors

Harry Brod is the editor of and contributor to *A Mensch Among Men: Explorations in Jewish Masculinity* (Crossings, 1988) and *The Making of Masculinities: The New Men's Studies* (Allen & Unwin, 1987). He has been active in the National Organization for Changing Men, and currently teaches Gender Studies and Philosophy at Kenyon College, Gambier, Ohio.

Joyce E. Canaan is a temporary lecturer on Women in Society in the Sociology Department at the University of Liverpool. She recently (1989) finished her PhD thesis, 'Individualizing Americans: the making of middle-class teenagers' (Anthropology Department, University of Chicago), which explores middle-class gendered subjectivity during secondary school. Her recent paper 'Is 'doing nothing' just boys' play?: integrating feminist and youth sub-culture perspectives on working-class masculinity' (in S. Franklin *et al.*, *Off Centre, Feminism and Cultural Studies*, Unwin Hyman, 1990) explores some contradictions and ambiguities in one form of working-class masculinity.

Cynthia Cockburn is a researcher and writer in the Department of Social Science and Humanities at The City University, London. Her publications include *The Local State* (Pluto, 1977), *Brothers* (Pluto, 1983), *Machinery of Dominance* (Pluto, 1985), and *Two-Track Training* (Macmillan, 1987).

Wil Coleman has research interests in ethnomethodology, sociological theory, the sociology and philosophy of language, texts, and textual analysis. At the moment of writing these biographical details he is completing a doctoral thesis entitled 'Language and social life' at the University of Manchester. A mature student, he entered higher education after working, among other things, as a chef.

[xiii]

Leonard L. Duroche teaches German, comparative literature, and humanities at the University of Minnesota, Minneapolis. Since 1979 he has been studying father–son relations in literature and changing images of men and masculinity in literature and society. His current research focuses on gendered space, the rise of modern homophobia, and male narratives.

Tim Edwards is a research student at the University of Essex, currently investigating the psychological and emotional impact of AIDS on the gay community. He previously completed a masters' degree on gay and sexual politics and these are his main interests as well as counselling and psychotherapy. He presently lives independently with two other gay men in Colchester.

Christine Griffin has been involved in the Women's Liberation Movement since the late 1970s. She is currently working at the School of Psychology, University of Birmingham, teaching social psychology. Much of her research work has concerned gender, 'race', and class relations in young people's experiences of the 'transition to adulthood'. Her publications include *Typical Girls?* (Routledge & Kegan Paul, 1985).

Jalna Hanmer is Co-ordinator of the MA/Dip Women's Studies (Applied) and Senior Lecturer in Social Work at the University of Bradford. She is a co-editor of *Women, Policing and Male Violence: International Perspectives* (Routledge, 1989), *Women, Violence and Social Control* (Macmillan, 1987; Humanities Press, 1988), and co-author of *Women and Social Work: Towards a Woman-Centred Practice* (Macmillan, 1987; Lyceum, 1989), *Well-Founded Fear: A Community Study of Violence to Women* (Hutchinson, 1984), *Man-Made Women: How New Reproductive Technologies Affect Women* (Hutchinson, 1985; Indiana University Press, 1987), and managing editor of *Reproductive and Genetic Engineering; A Journal of International Feminist Analysis*.

Jeff Hearn is Senior Lecturer in Applied Social Studies, University of Bradford, where his teaching includes courses on men and masculinities. He has been involved in men's groups and other anti-sexist activities since 1978. He is author of *Birth and Afterbirth* (Achilles Heel, 1983), co-author of *'Sex' at 'Work'*, author of *The*

Gender of Oppression (both Wheatsheaf/St Martin's Press, 1987), co-author of *Studying Men and Masculinity* (University of Bradford, 1988), co-editor of *The Sexuality of Organization* (Sage, 1989), and member of the Violence Against Children Study Group, *Taking Child Abuse Seriously* (Unwin Hyman, 1990).

Michael S. Kimmel is Assistant Professor of Sociology at the State University of New York at Stony Brook. He is the author of *Absolutism and Its Discontents* (Transaction, 1988) and *Desperate Hopes: Revolution in the Sociological Imagination* (Polity, 1990), and the editor of *Changing Men* (Sage, 1987), *Men's Lives* (Macmillan, 1989), and *Men Confront Pornography* (Crown, 1990). He is the editor of a series on 'Men and Masculinity' at Beacon Press, and the co-ordinating editor of a 'Research Annual on Men and Masculinity' at Sage. He is currently working on a documentary history of pro-feminist men in America, 1770–1990, and a book about the relationship between gender and sexuality.

David H. J. Morgan is currently Senior Lecturer in Sociology at the University of Manchester. He is the author of a variety of publications on the Sociology of Gender and the Sociology of the Family, including 'Men, masculinity and the process of sociological enquiry' in H. Roberts (ed.) *Doing Feminist Research* (Routledge & Kegan Paul, 1981), *Social Theory and the Family* (Routledge and Kegan Paul, 1975), *The Family, Politics and Social Theory* (Routledge & Kegan Paul, 1985), and the forthcoming *Discovering Men*, to be published in this series.

John Remy was born in 1947 into a working-class family in Hull. After studying painting at Hornsey College of Art, London, where he took part in the famous sit-in of 1968, he became involved in a wide range of radical movements. He is now an active member of the Scottish Green Party. For many years he had a 'bi-gendered' identity, and lived for eighteen months fulltime in the female gender. He is now living happily as a man.

Barry Richards lectures in the Department of Sociology at the Polytechnic of East London. He was previously a clinical psychologist. He is managing editor of the interdisciplinary journal *Free Associations*, the editor of two collections of papers on psychoanalysis and politics, *Capitalism and Infancy*, 1984, and *Crises of the Self*, 1989 (both Free Association Books), the author of *Images of Freud: Cultural Responses of Psychoanalysis* (Weidenfeld Dent, 1989) and of many articles on the psychological professions and on the social relations of psychotherapy and psychoanalysis.

Victor Jeleniewski Seidler is Senior Lecturer in Social Theory and Philosophy in the Department of Sociology, Goldsmiths' College, University of London. He has written *Kant, Respect and Injustice: The Limits of Liberal Moral Theory* (Routledge & Kegan Paul, 1986), *Rediscovering Masculinity: Reason, Language and Sexuality* (Routledge, 1989) and *A Truer Liberty: Simone Weil and Marxism* (with Larry Blum) (Routledge, 1989). His book *Love and Inequality: The Moral Limits of Modernity* will be published by Macmillan in 1990. He was a founder member of Achilles Heel, a journal of sexual politics and socialism.

Alison Thomas has an interdisciplinary background, with a first degree in social and political sciences and a PhD in social psychology (on the social construction of gender and identity). She now lectures in Psychosocial Studies in the Sociology Department of the Polytechnic of East London.

Sallie Westwood teaches at the University of Leicester and has conducted research in Ghana, India, and Britain. She is the author of *All Day Everyday: Factory and Family in the Making of Women's Lives* (Pluto, 1984) and co-editor with Parminder Bhachu of *Enterprising Women: Ethnicity, Economy and Gender Relations* (Routledge, 1988). Currently she is researching in the area of racism, gender relations, and mental health.

CHAPTER 1

Men, masculinities and social theory

JEFF HEARN
& DAVID H. J. MORGAN

The conference

This volume arises from the conference, 'Men, masculinity and social theory', held on 16 and 17 September 1988 at the University of Bradford, under the auspices of the Sociological Theory Study Group of the British Sociological Association. The proposal to hold this conference was made two years earlier, at the BSA Sociological Theory Study Group conference on 'Feminist theory' held at the University of Leeds in September 1986. When we agreed to go ahead and organize the Bradford conference, we imagined it might turn out to be a fairly small gathering, largely of enthusiasts and specialists. In the event the response to the call for papers was much greater than we expected; in addition to the fourteen papers presented, we had eight other offers (seven from men, one from a woman), which we could not include in the programme. Of those fourteen papers, ten are published here,[1] in most cases in a revised form, together with one other paper (Ch. 8) from one of the conference speakers.

The response, in terms of offers of papers, inquiries, and partici-pation indicated that there is a good deal of current sociological interest and activity in the study of men and masculinities. Just over a hundred people (approximately forty-five women and fifty-six men) attended, coming from a wide variety of back-grounds and positions within and outside sociology, and from a variety of countries, including Australia, China, Ireland, Israel, Norway, the United States, and West Germany. There were, however, only a small number of black participants. A relatively high number of people came from outside academia, including those from trade unions, teaching, social work, community work, probation, psychotherapy, public sector research, and unemployment, as well as from journalism and publishing.

The papers presented were spread between four plenary sessions and seven smaller group discussions. All the plenaries were chaired by women; originally one of them was to be chaired by a man, but he had to withdraw through illness. Five of the smaller groups were chaired by men; two by women. There were also at least two meetings of the Women's Caucus, and one meeting of a men's group. After the final plenary an informal open forum was held on some of the issues raised in the conference, particularly around the gender politics of academic change. This was attended by slightly fewer than half the conference participants, and chaired by David Morgan. To complete the picture, we need to add that while these details may appear to some 'irrelevant', we include them as giving some information on the social structuring of public discourse, a matter of major political and theoretical importance.

The history/herstory of the conference

The Bradford conference and the Leeds 'Feminist theory' conference before it had of course their own herstory. And while the search for origins always entails an engagement with the arbitrary, it is convenient to begin this story with the organization of the annual conference of the British Sociological Association on the theme of 'Sexual divisions and society'. This was held at the University of Aberdeen in 1974, and two volumes of some of the papers were subsequently published (Barker & Allen 1976a, 1976b). These books have come to be seen as landmarks in placing feminist critiques onto the professional agenda of sociology in the United Kingdom. The Aberdeen conference also highlighted the need to attend to sexism in sociology itself, and at the annual general meeting there two working parties were set up, on the Status of Women in the Profession, and on Social Relations Associated with Sex and Gender. These were in due course re-formed to become the BSA Committee on the Equality of the

Sexes, which in turn produced the bibliography, *Sociology Without Sexism* (BSA Sub-Committee on the Equality of the Sexes, n.d.). This carried out surveys of the employment of women sociologists in 1978–9 and the marginality of women in sociology in 1982–3. The committee's 1981 survey of sociological theory courses found no evidence of the systematic inclusion of gender issues or feminist theory.

Meanwhile, the BSA Women's Caucus was formed in 1974; and this was followed by the decision to create space for its meetings at future BSA conferences. In 1978 the BSA summer school was on 'Feminism and sociological research', and in January 1979 the BSA and the then Social Science Research Council co-sponsored a conference on methodology, at which these issues were prominent. The 1982 BSA annual conference, held at the University of Manchester, again placed the gender theme centre stage, under the title 'Gender and society'. The two conference volumes (Gamarnikow *et al.* 1983a, 1983b) brought together a selection of small-scale empirical studies and more general societal analyses, from the eighty or more papers presented. Both these volumes and those from the Aberdeen conference dealt explicitly with the problems of the neglect of gender within mainstream sociology, and the interface between that malestream and sociologies informed and inspired by feminist theory and practice. At the 1982 conference, there was also a small meeting of a men's group (Hearn *et al.* 1983); similar meetings have taken place at some subsequent conferences. In 1984 the BSA Equality of the Sexes Committee decided 'to assess how much progress had been made since 1974 in the development of teaching on gender, in the incorporation of gender issues into all areas of sociology teaching and in dealing with sexism in sociology departments' (BSA Standing Committee on the Equality of the Sexes, 1986, p. 348). The survey was carried out at the end of 1984 and published in 1986.

Throughout all these developments a number of BSA study groups, especially those on Sexual Divisions, Human Reproduction, and Medical Sociology, have continued to organize conferences either around the themes of gender and feminism, or in which those themes figure prominently. Similarly, the period under discussion has seen a gradual institutional growth in courses on women's studies, often despite a very difficult financial and political climate. For present purposes the most important initiative

[3]

amongst the study groups was, as already noted, the 1986 Socio-logical theory conference on 'Feminist theory'. This seemed to represent a further stage in the interrelation of feminism and sociology, with the institutional recognition of the importance of gender issues in social theory. From this the decision to organize the 1988 Bradford conference was an attempt both to continue discussion on feminist scholarship in the context of sociological theory and to focus on the developing critical study of men and masculinities.

Discourses on men and masculinities

Much sociology and sociological theory has been implicitly about men, without explicitly saying so. A number of sociological fields, for example, criminology and the study of juvenile delinquency, have a long tradition of the study of men and masculinity. Furthermore, in the 1950s a number of significant sociological texts were published on men, in several cases written by women, prior to the growth of Second Wave feminism. Just as feminist scholar-ship has demonstrated that 'woman', 'women', and 'femininity' are socially and historically constructed, and thus problematic, so too has it demonstrated the problematic nature of 'man', 'men', and 'masculinity' (for example, Delphy 1977, Chesler 1978, Friedman and Sarah 1981). Then there has been, often in association with gay liberation, the growth of gay scholarship and studies on homo-sexuality and gay men. Much of this has comprised detailed socio-historical research into the social construction of the 'male homosexual' (for example, Weeks 1977). While gay research un-doubtedly has major implications for the deconstruction of men (Carrigan *et al.* 1985), it has not always addressed 'men' and 'masculinity' as its explicit topic. Some of this work has been criticized for its neglect of feminist critiques, especially around sexuality and power (Stanley 1984).

From the late 1960s, there developed alongside the Women's Liberation Movement (WLM) and the Gay Liberation Movement (GLM), in a number of western countries, a small but identifiable series of groups and networks of 'men against sexism'. In some cases, and particularly in the United States, these have sometimes been seen as a 'movement' of their own. These networks have

[4]

generated a variable and irregular literature, in the form of news-sheets, journals, and autobiographical and political writings. A relatively early example of a book from this social context is *Unbecoming Men* (Bradley *et al.* 1971), recording the personal experiences of five men in a consciousness-raising group. Mean-while, more academic studies of men and masculinity were de-veloping from a mixture of largely sex-role culturalist sociology, social psychology, and some 'men's movement' writing. The obvious landmark text for this strand is Pleck and Sawyer's (1974) edited collection, *Men and Masculinity*. By the late 1970s this kind of sociological and psychological work together with literary and historical studies on men were being referred to in the United States at least, as 'men's studies'. In the United Kingdom, the landmark text was Tolson's (1977) *The Limits of Masculinity*, which developed an economic class analysis of postwar masculinities. By now there were courses on men in universities and similar institutions,[2] networks of scholars in North America and Europe, the *Men's Studies Review* based in the United States, numerous special issues of journals, a number of recently produced textbooks and readers, and at least five bibliographical studies on men and masculinity (Grady *et al.* 1979, Massachusetts Institute of Tech-nology Humanities Library 1979, August 1985, Ford & Hearn 1988, Treadwell & Davis n.d.). Some indication of the internationalism of these concerns can be gauged from the high level of interest at symposia on these questions at two recent major conferences: 'Men's response to the feminist challenge' at the Third International Interdisciplinary Congress on Women, Trinity College, Dublin, July 1987 (Hearn 1987b); and 'Men in gender studies' at the Joint Congress of the German, Austrian and Swiss Sociological Associ-ations, University of Zurich, October 1988 (*Männer in der Gesch-lecterforschung* 1988).

This limited institutionalization of these recent studies on men and masculinities has generated further controversy, not least because of the danger of this being used against the interests of women, now or in the future. These controversies operate at various levels and in various arenas. There are worrying issues around the gender/sexual politics of the allocation of scarce re-sources for teaching and research, and legitimate fears that 'men's studies' will become yet another variation on a well-established patriarchal theme. Then there are the uses and impacts of different

[5]

social science traditions on the study of men, particularly differences between positivism and critical theory, culturalism and structuralism, and increasingly modernism and postmodernism (Hearn 1989a, 1989b). To some extent these kinds of differences have become mapped onto differences between North American and European approaches to the study of men. In this sense the study of men reproduces tensions between North American and European traditions found in other branches of social science. One of the many implications of feminist critiques is a deep questioning of the possibility of being simultaneously a man, a positivist, and a critic of men. Such debates have been reproduced in uncertainties around the very naming of this area of study. As noted, the term 'men's studies' is favoured by some, and has been used particularly in the United States; others favour 'male dominance studies', 'the critical study of men', and so on; our own position on some of these questions is outlined in Chapter 13.

Men, masculinities and theory

The critical study of men and masculinities is clearly not just a question of institutional development; it is also very much a series of developments in relation to theory and theorizing. This is to be seen in a wide range of ways and through a variety of sometimes contradictory themes. In this section we spell out some of these themes, and in so doing introduce some of the questions that are examined in the papers that follow. One of the most important themes that runs through some of these papers and which certainly informs many of the recent writings about men is the relative invisibility of men, as an explicit focus in research and sociological theory. For example, this is noted in the paper by Kimmel (Ch. 6), and in the contribution by Duroche (Ch. 11), where he notes the relative absence of analysis of the male body. This argument is, of course, somewhat paradoxical. Feminists have justly argued that the central theoretical concerns and the general orientations to research have been dominated by the concerns of men (see Hanmer, Ch. 2). Research has often been about men, conducted by men and for men; where research has been carried out on women, it has often been by men and has reflected men's versions of the world. The term 'malestream' has been developed to describe the

[6]

numerical and ideological domination of men and their concerns within sociology (O'Brien 1981). Feminism has, clearly, challenged this male dominance although the impact has been somewhat uneven.

Moreover, if there has been an invisibility of men in sociological and other research this may not be entirely accidental. As Kimmel (Ch. 6) notes, the invisibilities of men may serve men's interests, keeping their activities apart from critical scrutiny, by other men as well as by women. Many men's fraternal institutions have indeed been dedicated, directly or indirectly, to the preservation of men's secrets (Remy, Ch. 3). Hence, when we write about the invisibility of men within sociology we are writing about an invisibility constructed through and within a wider framework of male dominance. Studies which are routinely about men, in that men constitute the acknowledged or unacknowledged subjects, are not necessarily about men in a more complex, more problematized, sociological sense. They tend to be resource rather than topic. Studies of social mobility, for example, may be about men for methodological reasons or administrative convenience but they are rarely, if ever, about men in the sense that researchers believe that such studies might make any contribution to the sociology of gender or the critical understanding of men and masculinities.

Such an adjustment of focus, seeing texts which routinely use men as subjects as also telling us something about men and masculinities, can itself be a critical exercise since it problematizes what is routinely taken for granted (Morgan 1981, 1990). However, we should not overstate this question of invisibility. For the most part, as has been argued, we are talking about the invisibility of men within 'malestream' sociology. Feminist research and theory, while it has been by women and for women, has never been just *about* women. A consideration of such issues as pornography, sexual harassment and violence against wives, or such concepts as patriarchy, sexism and reproduction, should serve as reminders that men have always been under critical consideration within feminist scholarship. It is likely that the recent articulated development of studies of masculinities has made some significantly new contributions, to certain aspects of fatherhood and to men's bodies and sexualities, for example, but the theoretical (as well as the political) inheritance from feminist writings should always be remembered (Stanley 1990; Hanmer, Ch. 2).

[7]

This volume deals with issues of theory, an area where for the most part questions of gender and masculinity have been even less visible than in some other sections of sociology. The links between theory and gender may be understood in at least two ways. In the first place, we may focus on the process of theorizing gender – in this case with specific reference to men and masculinities – and on the ways in which existing theoretical approaches may contribute to, or possibly inhibit, our understandings of the substantive gender issues. For the most part the contributions to and the discussions at this conference focused upon this aspect of the exchange between theory and gender, in other words upon the problems of theorizing men and masculinities. But we may see the relationship in the opposite direction, that is, from gender to theory. In this case, questions may be asked as to the extent to which and the ways in which various discussions and debates around gender issues might contribute to the reformulation of sociological theory and provide a critique of the practice of theorizing itself. This theme is somewhat muted in this present volume, as it was at the conference, but deserves more attention in this introduction.

Feminist theorizing has confirmed the socially constructed and gendered nature of social theory itself in its various forms, as epistemology, ontology, methodology, sociology of science, science, and so on (for example, Harding & Hintakka 1983, Harding 1986, 1987). Such problematizations of social theory have often drawn together major structural questions of power, and very immediate issues of practice, of how sociology and the social sciences more generally should be done. They have also necessarily prompted a growing interest in the relationship of social theory, men, and masculinities. The questions raised range from the impact of men's power upon the historical development of social theory, to the connections between masculinities and dominant conceptions of rationality, to ethical and political problems in researching by men and on men. Thus the relationship of social theory, men, and masculinity has implications not only for social theory in a generalized way but also for the full range of malestream sociological activities and traditions.

The need to theorize gender, in particular to theorize men and masculinity, arises largely because of the dangers of reification, essentialism, and reductionism that arise when using such categor-

[8]

ies as 'women' and 'men', 'femininity' and 'masculinity'. In some cases, for example, there may be a danger of importing taken-for-granted understandings of masculinity – men as competitive, striving, future-oriented and aggressive – into our analyses or re-analyses of existing texts. Preliminary moves in the business of theorizing of men and masculinity have been to argue for the socially constructed nature of these entities and for a pluralizing of the terminology such that we talk of 'masculinities' rather than of 'masculinity'. These moves are not, as some of our contributors recognize, without their own difficulties and dangers, although they would seem to be necessary preliminary moves in this theoretical undertaking.

This is not the place to provide a complete stocktaking of the sociology of gender and of masculinity. It is worth noting, however, that the actual use of the term 'gender' is still relatively recent within sociology and that the sociology of gender (as opposed, say, to the narrower study of sex roles) is not a well established area. Given this, it is impressive how much progress has been made. Feminist research and the analysis of gender/sexual stratification have already made substantial contributions to a sociology of gender, although it would not be wise to consider these as equivalents. Some recent work in the analysis of men and masculinities (for example, by Hearn 1987a, Connell 1987) has placed considerable emphasis upon theoretical considerations. Clearly, however, much more remains to be done, perhaps especially in the analysis of micro-gender processes and the ways in which these might be related to wider structural processes. Accordingly, several of the papers in this volume refer to the 'agency/structure' debate within sociology (Cockburn, Ch. 5; Edwards, Ch. 7; Coleman, Ch. 12).

Two particular examples of the need to theorize gender in general and masculinity in particular may be provided in the linked areas of the sociology of the body and the sociology of sexuality. Several of the papers in this volume do, indeed, refer to and discuss these topics. The study of the body has, like the sociology of men, made considerable strides in recent years, perhaps more on the theoretical front than on the empirical front (Foucault 1980, Turner 1984). Clearly, such studies have been influenced by feminist research and other studies on gender although it remains the case that many such studies, particularly of men and masculinities, remain somewhat disembodied. It is as if the conventional mapping of the nature/culture distinction on to women/men (Ortner 1974) has been carried over into the study of men and masculinities. Yet many of the central concerns of men and masculinities are directly to do with bodies – war and sport are two obvious examples. We need to elaborate theoretical links between constructions of the body and bodily processes in society (including denials or margin-alizations of bodily processes) and constructions of gender and gender identities. How far, for example, are popular accounts of 'body language' a reflection of and a reification of men's interests and concerns? We need to direct the study of gender and masculini-ties away from the ideological and the cultural, narrowly con-ceived, and towards the bodily without falling into biological reductionism. We can see some moves in this direction in the present volume in, for example, Duroche's linking of issues to do with perceptions of sound and smell to themes of class and gender, historically located (Ch. 11), and in Brod's discussion of porno-graphy as it affects men or is supposed to affect men (Ch. 8). Elsewhere, Connell has provided some interesting clues as to possible developments in the sociology of the body as applied to men (Connell 1983, 1987).

The sociology of sexuality is certainly closely connected with the sociology of the body (although it is not the same thing) and it is also a central concern of the recent developments in the study of men and masculinities. However, as Edwards (Ch. 7) points out, some of the theoretical links between and distinctions between gender and sexuality have not always been fully explored. Sexuali-ties are clearly implicated in the constructions of gender and indeed vice versa. Notions of hegemonic masculinity (Carrigan *et al.* 1985) are bound up with hegemonic sexualities as several of the papers in this volume emphasize (for example, Cockburn, Ch. 5; Edwards, Ch. 7; Kimmel, Ch. 6). The use of terms of stigmatized sexualities ('poof' or 'wanker') in encounters between young men may illustrate the interplays between the two. The links and inter-connections are clear enough; indeed so much so that there may be a danger of importing relatively fixed notions of sexualities just as there may be dangers of constructing relatively fixed notions of masculinities. Perhaps we need more theoretical discussion not only of gender salience (see Thomas, Ch. 9), the range and kinds of situations and encounters in which gender may be of greater or

[10]

lesser significance, but also of 'sexual salience'. Socially prescribed 'rights' to sexuality, for example, are not uniformly distributed and may be denied or severely restricted to certain groups or categories such as the young, the old, the disabled, or the mentally ill. If we are to provide links between gender and sexuality, it should be to an understanding of sexuality that has been informed by perspectives, such as those of Foucault, which seek to problematize the very deployment of the term 'sexuality' itself.

A major theme, therefore, in the processes of theorizing gender is that of deconstruction, of breaking down artificial unities of genders and sexualities. As has been said, one influential line of argument has been not simply to write of 'masculinities' in the plural but to attempt to examine relationships between masculinities within a given society, including relationships of dominance and subordination. Generally speaking, the concept of 'hegemonic masculinities' addresses itself to these issues, pointing to the dominance within society of certain forms and practices of masculinity which are historically conditioned and open to change and challenge. Thus today such a model might be white, heterosexist, middle-class, Anglophone, and so on. This implies that men too, within a society that may be characterized as 'patriarchal', may experience subordinations, stigmatizations or marginalizations as a consequence of their sexuality, ethnic identity, class position, religion, or marital status. The interplay between hegemonic and subordinate masculinities is a complex one, but should serve to underline the fact that experience of masculinity and of being a man are not uniform and that we should develop ways of theorizing these differences. In the present volume Westwood (Ch. 4) examines the complex interplays between masculinity, ethnicity, and class in the context of a society structured by racism as well as by patriarchy (see also Cockburn, Ch. 5). Similarly, issues of gay men and sexualities (especially in the context of concerns abouts AIDS) are examined by Edwards (Ch. 7) and Kimmel (Ch. 6). Their accounts of the 'clone', for example, highlight some of the complexities involved in the social construction of masculinities and sexualities.

Linked to this overall emphasis on deconstruction there is a common desire to overcome a variety of dichotomies. These have been widespread within sociology and have their own significance in the development of the discipline. However they can also be seen

[11]

as misleading and reificatory. Here we would include distinctions between nature and nurture, nature and culture, and between biology and culture; these are all distinctions which inform another central distinction between 'sex' and 'gender'. While this distinction has clearly been important in getting the sociology of gender off the ground, it has also presented further difficulties, particularly in so far as it leaves the biological 'sex' element of the distinction and its links to gender relatively undertheorized. An important point of departure is to see these distinctions as being themselves historically situated. In different ways, the papers by Edwards (Ch. 7) and by Duroche (Ch. 11) make contributions to this debate.

Of course the major dichotomy that pervades discussions of gender is that between women and men. Whilst the distinction is important in terms of gender/sexual politics and the analysis of power relations within society as well as being an important aspect of the ways in which most people order their everyday lives and understandings, it is not an unproblematic distinction. For example, a structural analysis of patriarchy, based upon distinctions between men and women, may not immediately translate into everyday practices. Indeed, unexamined and continued use of the everyday categories 'women' and 'men' (as, for example, in the routine analysis of quantitative data 'by sex') may have the effect of reproducing the power structures that gave rise to these distinctions. A theoretical analysis of gender must provide for the critical examination of the everyday deployment of the term 'men', 'women', 'femininity', and 'masculinity', and the occasions of their deployment (see Coleman, Ch. 12).

As well as the discussions, already mentioned, dealing with issues of class (Cockburn, Ch. 5), sexuality, and ethnicity, there are other ways in which we can look critically at the distinction between 'men' and 'women'. Thomas's discussion of 'gender salience' (Ch. 9), for example, sees variation in the degree to which men (and women) see their gender as something which is central and clearly defined in their everyday lives and understandings. From a different perspective, Richards (Ch. 10) shows how the Freudian tradition may be seen as generating three variations on the father/son relationship rather than a single model and that these might be deployed to examine variations in masculinities.

It should be stressed that such attempts to overcome or to criticize the everyday taken-for-granted assumptions about men and women should not be allowed to take away the critical edge that developed through the analysis of patriarchy and sexual politics, specifically addressed by Hanmer (Ch. 2), but also clearly the point of departure for several of the other papers. Both an understanding of diversity and a recognition of the whole are required in order to elaborate a critical analysis of masculinities. Perhaps this may best be achieved if we allow the critical examination of the distinctions between women and men to feed back into a critical examination of other dichotomies which are part of the deep ideological structure that maintains gender inequalities – especially those between biology and culture, and between sex and gender.

This may also apply to other dichotomies as well, for example that between the public and the private, one very much implicated in systems of patriarchy and one which has its own cultural histories (Duroche, Ch. 11; Westwood, Ch. 4). Another distinction, that between agency and structure, is, as has already been noted, addressed by several of the papers here. While it can be argued that a major sociological project is to find ways of providing for the interplay between such distinctions, it may also be argued that the very setting up of the problem in these terms is problematic. It may be problematic in that it may perpetrate distinctions which have their own history and which may have their particular impact on the present social and gender order. The topic of pornography, addressed in varying ways in the contributions by Brod (Ch. 8), Hanmer (Ch. 2), and Kimmel (Ch. 6), for example, raises all kinds of theoretical difficulties. Does the distinction between agency (men as producers and users of pornography) and structure (pornography as a form of gendered speech, pornography as a multi-million enterprise exploiting women) help or hinder the analysis of this topic, one which is clearly so crucial in the understanding of the construction of genders and sexualities in contemporary society, and one which is at the heart of gender/ sexual political debate. A critical examination of the distinction between agency and structure may be necessary in order to develop further the critical analysis of masculinities and of the diversities of men's responses, including the ways in which some men are themselves beginning to provide (for) a critique of the gender order of which they themselves are a part.

There are, in addition, a variety of more specific theoretical issues and contributions made in these papers. There are, for example, the varying conceptualizations of the terms 'patriarchy' and 'fratriarchy' developed in the papers by Brod (Ch. 8) and Remy (Ch. 3). In the process of theorizing men and masculinities, we find a variety of overlapping and contrasting traditions being drawn upon: feminisms, Marxism, phenomenology, symbolic inter-actionism, ethnomethodology, structuralisms, psychoanalysis, social psychology, and so on. However, the papers do not simply draw upon existing theoretical traditions; they also make contri-butions to these traditions. One aspect of this, a feature directly or indirectly of all the papers included here, is the critical analysis of theorizing and the process of theorizing themselves.

One central aspect of this is an understanding of theory as itself being an experientially located activity, and not simply as some-thing which goes on inside people's (mostly men's) heads. When we argue that feminism is a point of departure for the critical examination of men and masculinities we do not simply refer to a set of ideas or theories but to the experiences of women as they confront patriarchal structures and sexist practices (see, especially, Hanmer, Ch. 2). Similarly, and yet simultaneously *not* similarly, we are concerned with the experiences of men as we/they live and work in a world which includes the theories and practices of feminisms. Here we are restating the obvious point that theories do not simply exist within a closed world of theorizing (although the structure of academic life may sometimes make it seem like that) but exist in response to individual and collective experiences, human needs, and historical changes; in the broadest sense, theories have a material base or material bases. However, experience itself is not just something which is direct or unmediated; it is itself shaped by and given meaning by theories, latent or manifest, lay or professional, acknowledged or unacknowledged. We wish to ex-amine this circuit, this interplay between theory and experience as it applies to particular issues of men and masculinities.

Here, one or two general points may be made. First, as has already been stressed, the main influences have been the impact of feminisms and a growing sense of perceived 'crisis' on the part of men, partly although rarely straightforwardly in response to, or as a consequence of, the development of feminism. Of course, the idea of 'crisis' is the complex outcome of a historically situated set of influences and circumstances. It is almost certainly not evenly distributed throughout society and it would seem that many men,

[14]

at all social levels, find little that is problematic about their gender or about the gender order in general (Brittan 1989). However, it would be wrong to say that this sense of crisis, or at least unease, is simply confined to intellectuals or sociologists. As Thomas (Ch. 9) points out, at least some theoretical traditions argue for a deep-rooted male insecurity and these may be given particular content and meaning by particular historically situated experiences. Richards (Ch. 10) provides some illustrations of how this process might be seen and understood.

While there are clearly some experiential roots in the recent developments in studies of men and masculinities, it should be stressed that the relationships between experience and theory are not the same for men as for women. This point is made forcefully by Hanmer (Ch. 2) and reinforced in Thomas's social psychological account (Ch. 10). Thomas notes that even where men are developing a consciousness of their gender identity and a desire to challenge gender ideologies, the basis of these desires often appears to be more in terms of abstract principles or general political programmes than direct experience. This lack of equivalence between women and men in these respects should always be stressed and may indeed be generalized. Superordinates, whether in terms of gender, class or race, are not routinely called upon to theorize their own situations in either a sociological or mundane sense, except perhaps in order to provide legitimations of their superordinate position (see Goode 1982). In the normal course of events, men, elites, or ruling classes generally have no more need to theorize their situations than fish need to theorize about water; yet even saying that does not quite ring true, for there are also numerous contradictions, disjunctures, ambivalences, uncertainties, and just temporary wonderings in the ordinary lives of men which need to be acknowledged too.

Women, therefore, have every right to be sceptical about and critical of many aspects of the recent ways of studies of men and masculinities. How much of this will have the unintended consequences of providing yet another set of legitimations or justifications on the part of men remains to be seen, although we should always be aware of such possibilities. Yet, as Segal (1989) has argued, it would be unfortunate if all these developments in the critical study of men and masculinities, together with all the attempts on the part of men to confront and to change their own practices, were to be rejected.

[15]

Hence, many of these papers show how the study of gender might contribute to the study of theory by providing a particular, and central, example of the relationships between experience and theorizing. It is to be hoped that the critical studies of men and masculinities will not simply draw upon existing theoretical traditions but will also provide for a general critique of the process of sociological theorizing. Some specific examples may be found in the present volume. Cockburn (Ch. 5) shows some of the ways in which a consciousness of gender issues may lead to the critique of and reformulation of organization theory (see also Hearn & Parkin 1987). Brod (Ch. 8) re-examines the class concept of alienation and shows how this might be given new depth by a more gender-sensitive perspective. And, from a somewhat different perspective, Coleman (Ch. 12) casts a critical eye at the whole business of doing theory and doing masculinity. This kind of scepticism about existing theoretical traditions and the practice of theorizing, whether it arises out of the experiences of actual men and women in relation to the feminist challenge or from some other source, will undoubtedly be needed if the critical interplay between gender and theory is to continue and to develop.

One final point may be worth mentioning in this section. The growth of critical studies on men and masculinities that this volume reflects is not to be confused with the alleged development of the 'new man'. This 'new man' is supposed to demonstrate a wider range of domestic involvements, a wider range of emotional responses and a greater willingness to criticize his own practices. Most of these recent texts, in common with many of the papers in this volume, are sceptical of this formulation and point instead to the relative lack of change on the part of men in many areas. Hanmer's (Ch. 2) sober reminders about violences against women and the growth of reproductive technologies and Kimmel's (Ch. 6) account of men's 'risktaking' in relation to AIDS provide two examples, while Thomas (Ch. 9) sums up much recent research when she talks about the masculinization of women being unaccompanied by much corresponding feminization of men. Certainly critical, theoretical discussion of men and masculinities must address itself to the forces making for relative lack of change as well as the forces making for change. However, there are some reasons for optimism as are illustrated in Cockburn's references to some of the more positive aspects of equal opportunities legislation (Ch. 5) or Richard's consideration of some potentially positive features of Freudian theory (Ch. 10). Indeed the conference itself and papers such as these are positive signs which show the possibilities for the beginnings of debates between women and men around issues of gender inequalities and exploitation. It is unlikely that these debates will be easy and, as the present volume indicates, will not achieve any ready or artificial synthesis. Nevertheless, the fact that these debates are taking place at all is a reason for some guarded optimism.

The volume

The previous section has pointed to some of the ways in which parallels and contrasts can be drawn between the papers. While the links are numerous, we have found that the papers can usefully be arranged in three broad groupings – around power (as the overarching and most pervasive issue), sexuality (as question of specific importance, arguably the basis of gender), and identity and perception (as topics of growing interest at the intersection of sociology, social psychology, and psychoanalysis). Each of these three parts of the book thus provides a range of papers around one of these themes; yet even within each section a consensus is not to be found.

Part 1 includes papers on men's exploitation of women (Hanmer), patriarchy and fratriarchy (Remy), racism and black masculinity (Westwood), and men in organizations (Cockburn). In Part 2 there is a synthetic paper on sexual dysfunctions, pornography, and AIDS (Kimmel), as well as papers on homosexuality (Edwards) and pornography (Brod). This grouping is thus clearly also about power, domination, and violence, and indeed these connections are important aspects of the analysis of men's sexualities. Part 3 is made up of papers on gender identity (Thomas), psychoanalysis (Richards), perception (Duroche), and ethnomethodology (Coleman). The final part of the book includes three short responses to the issues raised at the conference (Hearn & Morgan, Canaan & Griffin, and Seidler).

Notes

1   The papers given at the conference but not included here were as
    follows: Harry Brod, 'From patriarchy to fratriarchy: adventures in the
    making of masculinities'; Terrell Carver, 'Private men/public theories:
    the case of Marx and Engels'; Georg Brzoska & Gerhard Hafner,
    'Men's studies in Germany'; and Michael Opielka, 'Men's studies in
    Germany – Defining a new discipline or expanding a middle-aged one?'
2   The first of these courses was in the United States in the mid-1970s; by
    1984 there were still only forty. According to Bliss by 1986 there are
    over a hundred such courses in the United States alone. A recent report
    suggests that by the end of 1989 there were more than two hundred
    courses 'dealing with some aspect of the male experience' in colleges
    and universities in the United States (Wiegand, 1989). An invaluable
    collection of syllabuses of such courses is that by Femiano (n.d.).

Part 1

POWER AND DOMINATION

CHAPTER 2

Men, power and the exploitation of women

JALNA HANMER

As an academic area, Men and Masculinity or The Study of Men arises out of a history, or herstory, of women raising the issue of gender and gendered issues. The concerns of this chapter are how we reached this point and where we are˝and where we can go with this new field of study. It begins with the origins of women's studies and why these are relevant to The Study of Men. How these two fields differ from each other and the challenges coming from women's studies for the development of The Study of Men follows. Two examples are used; one from work on violence against women and the other from work on science and technology.

The feminist scholarship that developed out of the Women's Liberation Movement in the early 1970s gave collective meaning to these types of individual experiences by applying the concepts of domination, oppression, exploitation, ideology, to women's experiences. The most oppressed of all conditions is to have no words to explain the feelings and predicaments one is experiencing, while the belief systems of dominant culture and intellectual life deny its reality.

For example, as an adolescent and young woman I tried to understand why men and women were never really friends. Sociology at Berkeley provided no answers to an existential reality I observed in my own situation, that of family members, and everyone else I knew. In the 1950s the proudest boast of the Berkeley sociology department, one they used to prove that they were

[21]

first-rate, was that they had never employed a woman. Women students were given to understand that they could take under-graduate degrees and even study for doctorates, serve as research assistants in exceptional circumstances – and *that is all*.

While not on any syllabus, students at Berkeley in the 1950s with intellectual interests in the social world read Simone de Beauvoir's, *The Second Sex*. Published in English in the early 1950s, it seemed to offer an explanation for a natural condition, the 'otherness' of women. It was much later that the 'problem with no name', began to be explored (Friedan 1963). Prior to the Women's Liberation Movement both in the United States and in Britain, new work on the condition of women in marriage and families began in the 1960s (Friedan 1963, Gavron 1966). But it is with the student movement, the New Left in Britain, the civil rights movement in the United States, the anti-imperialist struggles in both countries, that the new scholarship on women began to take shape. Marge Piercy's, 'Grand Coolie Damn' (1970) records the distillation of women's experience in SDS (Students for a Democratic Society) that led to separate Women's Liberation Movement organizing in the States which subsequently came to Britain. This early history in Britain is recorded by Sheila Rowbotham in *Beyond the Fragments* (1979).

The late 1960s and early 1970s saw a rich outpouring, like a released dam, of comment, polemic, and search for explanations. There were some wonderful writings that slammed into men and social relations between men and women. SCUM Manifesto (Society For Cutting Up Men), for example, has been reprinted recently (Solanas 1968, 1988). These new works drew on personal experience while the bibliographies of early published work in-cluded some academic citation.[1] But the relationship between the Women's Liberation Movement and academic women really flowed in the opposite direction. From the beginning of this wave of feminism scholarly work on women and the relations of men and women drew on the previously silenced voices, and presences, of women. The fundamental questions that we continue to explore today were raised in richly amusing and breathtakingly imperti-nent, very angry but largely ephemeral pieces written for Women's Liberation Movement conferences, newsletters, papers. In Britain these publications were produced on the understanding that readers were only to be women, but over the years the ideas have found their way into print via established publishers. In these works men were named as at least partly, if not totally, responsible for the exploitation and oppression of women.

Women in academic life then took these questions:

(1) Have women always been oppressed?
(2) What is oppressing women? Children, childbearing, marriage, capitalism, the family, and men, were dominant focuses.
(3) How can the oppression of women be overcome? While this is not a question usually addressed by academic women directly, implicit within many analyses lies a policy direction.

I remind us of this rich herstory, as it is the origin of the study of men as well as of women and all too often ignored in the academic writing called men's studies (Brod 1987). Too many books mention feminism, without citation, and move on in the usual way to cite another man whose work is as intellectually derivative of these origins as his own.

The lack of citation is as true for work that is based on an implied naturalist base for heterosexuality as that which challenges this approach by raising the relevance of gay liberation and homosexuality between men. It was the Women's Liberation Movement that recognized the centrality of sexuality to women's experience, to our relationships with men, to our relationships with other women, to social theory. The classic article which summarizes eloquently and pithily this understanding is 'Compulsory heterosexuality and lesbian existence' (Rich 1980). Adrienne Rich describes heterosexuality as a system of social relations, a social institution, whose hegemony is so nearly total that it can be described as compulsory. Men studying men and in gay studies owe their understanding of the social nature of heterosexuality to the Women's Liberation Movement. The lack of recognition and citation of feminist work is an issue for radicals, liberals, heterosexuals, and gay men who study men.

This is an aspect of where we are, and always have been. Making women invisible is the ideological project of male domination, that is, scholarship in the intellectual and personal control of men. Disappeared women, male the generic person, male angst, the human condition, is where the Women's Liberation Movement and its child, women's studies, came in. We at the bottom of the pile see it with a clarity that social dominants, that is, men, because

[23]

you/they are social dominants, obviously cannot. In practice this means that women scholars have to read both what women and men write, while scholarly men continue to need to read only each other, their ideological dominance within the disciplines maintained by the social practices and structures of the old boys' network. This explains the origin of the importance women place on acknowledging other women's work, of using first names to identify women in bibliographies, of networking amongst women. Women know that the high point of ideological domination is to silence or ignore the intellectual contribution of those with different questions and, therefore, different concerns and answers.

There are two fundamental issues that in reality are never separate; the first is the political meaning of studies on men and women, and the second is the theoretical project. For women's studies scholars a baseline question is what is the relationship of the study of men to women's scholarship, to the recognition and commitment to undertake academic explorations that will provide an understanding that can be used to improve the personal and social conditions of women?

Women's studies is about a great deal more than just 'adding women on' to existing knowledge (Harding 1986, 1987); in the joke of Mary O'Brien the process of commatizing women; that is, 'social class comma women comma blacks comma gays comma youth and so forth' (1982, p. 1). This is, of course, the easiest way to conceptualize the relationship between the study of men and women as it assumes a parity. The current tendency to describe women's studies as the study of femininities and men's studies as the study of masculinities is based on this assumption. As Harry Brod explains:

> The most general definition of men's studies is that it is the study of masculinities and male experiences as specific and varying social-historical-cultural formations. Such studies situate masculinities as objects of study on a par with femininities. (1987, p. 2).

While the purpose of this definition is to overcome the presentation of generic man as universal norm in traditional scholarship, it also serves to make women disappear as their reality cannot be subsumed under the rubric, the study of femininities. This redefinition

[24]

of women's studies in order to further its presumed complementarity with men's studies reduces women's studies to the academic
equivalent of identity politics.

'The personal is political', the rallying cry of the Women's
Liberation Movement, is an epistemological stance on how the
world is to be understood and changed. This stance is not simply
concerned with individual experience of femininity or masculinity
in interpersonal relationships, but with a broader canvas, that of
social structure. Through experience women found social structure, for example, while a rapist is an individual man, the state is
composed largely of men, particularly at the top, operating a
criminal justice system that does not protect women. With the
construction of knowledge the marginality of women is not
superficial, but inbuilt into language, methodologies, approaches,
concepts, subject divisions, hierarchies of disciplines.

Men cannot be added onto existing conceptualizations either, as
women's studies challenges academic orthodoxies. It is grossly
inadequate to describe the task as:

> In inverse fashion to the struggle in women's studies to
> establish the *objectivity* of women's experiences and thereby
> validate the legitimacy of women's experiences *as women*,
> much of men's studies struggles to establish the *subjectivity* of
> men's experiences and thereby validate the legitimacy of men's
> experiences *as men*. (Brod 1987, p. 6).

To bring women into social theory is to dislocate men from its
centre. This process has epistemological ramifications that challenge positivism with its dualities of objectivity and subjectivity,
and complementaries.

While all of social science can be said to be about studying
ourselves, traditional epistemology requires a distancing from the
subject matter under investigation. But an acknowledgement of the
closeness of self to the researched upon, an acknowledgement of
the self as part of that under study, is central to women's studies
scholarship. Objectification disappears, even though the exact
experiences or area of research do not precisely correspond with
one's own life history. Feminist scholars are developing a new
epistemology in which the connectedness of women in the social
order in relation to men is recognized as well as the differences

[25]

between women. In this situation poor scholarship matters more. In the social sciences we are surrounded with less than adequate scholarly work, but in women's studies and the relation of the study of men to it *it matters*, because what is at stake is the positive transformation of women's lives or women's liberation as it used to be called. The inseparability of the political and the theoretical is understood in the gut, so to speak.

The Women's Liberation Movement began with a critique of men. They were always present, explicitly and implicitly. To reduce women's studies to the study of women and the differences between us is to deny our origins. The study of men needs to take these early insights and views on board. Those who study men need to reference the work of these women, even though it may be an anathema, and dismissed as polemic or man-hating or just political, because this work is about men as well as women.

But as we are all aware, how men are to be theorized has been a major source of disagreement among women. This dispute can be recognized in the study of men in equally divisive ways. I note a tendency amongst those who study men that, if women's scholarship is acknowledged, it is *some* women academics, some so-called *types* of feminism, that are recognized, but not all. Some women are apparently elevated into the male scholarly world by being identified as asking questions and providing theory judged relevant to the study of men.

While Harry Brod's work (1987) is perhaps the grossest example of this process, another was provided by Michael Kimmel at the conference (see Ch. 6). His talk on sexuality included a swingeing attack on the work on pornography by Andrea Dworkin (1981, 1988) and Catharine MacKinnon (1982, 1983, 1987). His positivist argument was that experimental research on the effects of por-nography on men of exposure to sexual violence against women was short-term and therefore Dworkin and MacKinnon are wrong and to be dismissed – and anyway neither of them are sociologists![2] When challenged it was obvious that he did not consider the impact on women of pornography and the multi-billion-dollar industry as factors to be considered in his theoretical calculations. Michael Kimmel's conference presentation was not only divisive in relation to women's scholarship but it also provides an example of the male liberationist thrust of men's studies.

In this volume Michael Kimmel acknowledges that feminist

work on pornography has had some impact on the conceptualizations of the men who research on it, but there is a firm adherence to a psychological experimental method of research on men as constituting real proof of the effects of pornography on women. His work is positivist in orientation, both methodologically and conceptually. The impact on women of pornography and its social meaning more generally cannot be proven solely by studying men in laboratory-like conditions (Bart & Jozsa 1980, Kappeler 1986; Minneapolis City Council Public Hearings, 1988).

I teach a feminist theory course and it is theoretically interesting to consider who is left out and how women are defined or typed. Sometimes those who are left out are said to be not very nice, or dying, or dead, or non-existent nowadays (Bouchier 1983). Their analyses are misrepresented or perhaps simply not understood. I am, of course, referring particularly to analyses in which men are viewed as a class, with class interest based on the continuing exploitation of women. Specific issues can become dominant in the critical discourse on the relation between men and women in differing historical periods and cultures. Pornography is playing such a role today; as Catharine MacKinnon explains, pornography is gendered speech (1987).

Women are so accustomed to being blamed for everything that is wrong; it is usually the wife or the mother, especially the mother, who is at fault. And women are so used to being found inadequate and inferior by learned men, and an occasional woman, via our hormones, brain structure and intelligence, our emotions, our biological difference. In brief, biology establishes inferiority while social relations establish blame.

But men are not accustomed to being held responsible for anything negative about themselves either individually or as a social group. It must be a deep blow to the psyche to read women who are critical of men; even an insult. Men say it makes them feel defensive; it seems so unjustified to be attacked or criticized for one's biology or gender or misuse of social power. But even though it is those who have *no right* to set the terms of the debate, to demand an accounting, that is, women, we cannot be dealt with by dismissal or misrepresentation – at least not yet.

I wish to be publicly associated with the perspective that is denied and exorcised – and is attacked with the most potent of words, essentialism. Any theories which posit that men, all men,

[27]

have common interests and benefit as a gender from the continuing social subordination of women, all women, are attacked with the charge of essentialism. It reminds me of a small boy with a wooden sword after the dragons that live in dark places, or is it envy, the male hysteric, the inability to allow women any place where men are excluded? (Braidotti 1987).

Women's scholarship has led to an epistemological critique of dominant ways of knowing. Sandra Harding (1986) speaks of feminist epistemologies, empiricist, standpoint, and postmodernist, as women seek to understand women's experiences as a resource to generate scientific problems, hypotheses, and evidence, and to design research for women that places the researcher in the same critical plane as the research subject. It is contradictory to argue that politicized inquiry can increase the objectivity of inquiry only if the epistemological stance is a belief that research can be value-free, neutral, without a point of view, objective. This epistemological stance has served men well. It has enabled men to retail their views as the only view, as the knowledge of humankind, and to render women invisible. Only social superordinates can utilize in their favour this way of knowing the world; their so-called objectivity is the emergent quality of their position as social superordinates.

Because those bound in hierarchical relationships do not share the same reality, feminist epistemologies do not see men's views and women's views of the world as equal or relative. Silence or laughter, is this the final core that so enrages men in feminism or, as Kamuf (1987) writes, fem*men*inism? Like the pea in the walnut shell game, now you see it, now you don't; wherever the theoretical attack on (dare I say the words of the unspeakable, the unknowable, the root of the envy?) *radical feminism*, the women throw in caveats, if not direct challenges, like bouquets of some unknown reality whose essence eludes comprehension. The silence and the laughter grow in proportion to the flailing about of 'there is no woman', 'no man', 'no gender', 'no difference' (Jardine & Smith 1987, Moore 1988). The Study of Men cannot avoid these epistemological issues.

In these most interesting exchanges, radical feminism becomes essentialist for those who attack, as if there were only *one* radical feminism. Radical feminism is misrepresented as unitary. Radical feminism along with revolutionary feminism is very far from the reified definition developed within the literature of femmeninism, more neutrally described as men's studies. At its most extreme, radical feminism is not just wrong analysis, but something to blame, the reason, even, for the problem between men and women (Jardine & Smith 1987). Men are finding ways around women's analyses of how men personally hold and express power. To claim that radical feminism is essentialist is to ignore radical feminist materialist writings in which it is the systemizing of women's subordination that is under analysis (for example, see Delphy 1984, Friedman & Sarah 1982, Hanmer & Maynard 1987, 1989, Hanmer, Radford & Stanko 1989, Jeffreys 1985, MacKinnon 1982, 1983, 1987, O'Brien 1981, Barry 1979).

To misrepresent radical feminism to be about femininity – to conflate feminism, woman, women, femininity – is a theoretical travesty. Co-opting femininity as a strategy by men to meet the criticisms of radical feminism does not begin to come to grips with their arguments. There is a liberalism here, as well as bad faith or poor scholarship, that 'men's studies' needs to address in order to become The Study of Men.

To conceive of the study of men to be about liberating men is to have little interest in any area of social analysis that seriously critiques men as men, as part of the problem, not just to women and each other but to society and our continuation as a species. There are aspects of this philosophical position in approaches that are far from crudely concerned with personal liberation. I refer in particular to the use of role theory and socialization theory, however critical the stance taken. To use role and socialization theories, particularly widespread in the American approaches to the study of men, is to limit the area of study to the individual or to attempt to explain social formation and processes through the study of individuals. This is inherently flawed theoretically, but critical work in men and masculinity studies is beginning (Carrigan et al. 1985, Connell 1985, 1987, Stoltenberg 1990).

For women, women's studies involves the recognition of social powerlessness, not just victimization, but survival, under difficult and unequal conditions. For men the problem is different. The study of men involves the recognition of the use and misuse of social power that accrues to the male gender, of recognizing benefits even when none are personally desired. These basic patterns are obviously not uniformly experienced by all women or

[29]

by all men, and they are historically and culturally specific. As we all know, race, ethnicity, culture, religion, age, sexuality, social class, and many other factors mediate personal experience, but biological sex and its associate, gender, remain major social stratifying as well as individually possessed qualities for all of us.

I do not wish to imply that the study of men is monolithic. Exploring differential power amongst men is beginning by examining race, class, and sexuality in relation to masculinities and social power (for example, Rutherford 1988, Mercer & Julien 1988, Kimmel & Messner 1989). One thread of challenge is provided by gay studies and critiques of heterosexuality. But what does this challenge to a monolithic view of men's studies mean in terms of the relation of the study of men to women's studies; of men to women?

Gay men share with heterosexual men the relationship to reproduction in the three senses in which feminist scholarship has developed this term; biological, domestic labour, and cultural transmission (Edholm et al. 1977). Gay men, like heterosexuals, benefit from the construction of the labour market and the private–public divide in which women have socially devalued tasks without monetary compensation or without monetary compensation at anywhere near the same level as men. The personal relationships of gay men with this serf-like group can be non-existent, personally hostile, or friendly. Even though gay men face discrimination in society, it does not reduce the structural and personal privilege their maleness gives in relation to women.

As we all know, the gendered role of women consists of providing care for anyone who needs it, both in the so-called private sector and the public labour market. The material conditions of being a woman, unlike those of being a man, do not allow escape from the demands of co-operative functioning. While men and women would benefit from a less competitive social system, the situation facing women is one of conflicting demands. Women bear the social contraction between the growing stress on individual competitiveness and women's role in maintaining social cohesion through caring more heavily than men. Whether homosexual or heterosexual, men need only adopt a competitive posture to fulfil gender expectations dominant in western societies.

Women are primarily oppressed as women, whether lesbian or heterosexual, but gay men are oppressed as sexual deviants. While gay men are seen by the sexually dominant group as deviants, traitors, queers, sexual perverts, sexual predators, and child molesters, heterosexual men are unwilling to put themselves into these categories. But many women experience heterosexual men as sexually deviant; as queer, sexual perverts, sexual predators, and child molesters (Saunders 1985). This paradox arises out of the power of heterosexuality as a social system: *the* social system for the control of women. The men who identify with it are protected from exposure; their social dominance results in almost total individual protection from social knowledge, ostracism, or prosecution for sexual and other crimes against women (for example, Russell 1984, Hanmer & Saunders 1984, 1987, Kelly 1988, Stanko 1985, Hanmer *et al.* 1989, Edwards 1989).

Sexual variation between men can be accommodated within this system of sexual domination, although men are deemed traitors for not participating fully in the daily maintenance of heterosexuality as a social system. But the control of the sexual expression of women is a fundamental aspect of our social subordination. Sexual distancing from men is an act of rebellion against a system of subordination characterized by hierarchy, objectification, submission, and violence.[3] It is dangerous, it carries a personal price, but all women are in danger of being accused of this crime. As MacKinnon (1979) explains, the woman who too decisively resists sexual overtures is accused of being 'dried up' and sexless or lesbian. To be woman identified, to prioritize women over men in any way whatsoever, runs the risks of this confrontation with those who hold heterosexual power, that is, men.

The importance of all these issues to the study of men can be illustrated through any area of feminist scholarship. But I will use two examples because they are areas in which I work. The first is known as violence against women, and the second is the new reproductive technologies and genetic engineering.

Violence against women

With Sheila Saunders I have recently completed research into how the police respond to interpersonal crime against women (1987). This study in West Yorkshire involved interviews with the police (forthcoming), the welfare agencies providing services for women, with women, with lawyers, monitoring of reports of crimes against women and the criminal justice system generally in three daily West Yorkshire papers, and the monitoring of a few selected court cases of men charged with violent crimes against girls and women. I then agreed to discuss the study and the policy recommendations with community forums set up by the Police Authority in the five district council areas that make up the old West Yorkshire county. These are primarily composed of men, and the Chief Constable was awaiting their views. I also spoke to local authority sex advisory groups and women's committees where the audience was largely of women.

The Deputy Chief Constable and I were like a travelling roadshow, appearing at a number of these venues together. The gendered understanding of women's experience observed in the formal research was replicated in exchanges at these meetings. By and large to men, women deserved it, wanted it, needed it, would do nothing to help themselves, would not leave abusing men, and would attack you if you tried to intervene to help them – so why bother? Women spoke of trying to get away, of leaving, of undeserved attacks, of unwanted attacks, of unneeded assaults and abuse, and of not being able to find anyone to help. But this is not about identity and consciousness only, but a social system that enables men and women to have very different personal and institutional experiences both as service providers and as individuals in marriage.

If I had not spent years in Women's Aid, the refuge movement for women who leave home because of violence, these opposing viewpoints would be difficult to understand. As Jessie Bernard (1972) explains, we have 'his marriage' and 'her marriage', and with policing and community services for women we also have 'his state validated response' and 'her state permitted response', as most police are men (91% in West Yorkshire) and most women–centred voluntary services are provided by women. Women helping women rediscovered violence against women and the practical activity of providing refuges exposed the various ways in which the state comes into contact with individual women. The social services, housing departments, the police, medical services, the courts, lawyers, the social security system are all central to defining how a woman is seen and what she can expect in the way of assistance, and in shaping her experiences and the legitimacy of her demands. While many women work in these agencies, their management is almost exclusively male, as are those who determine the legal framework of these agencies. In the UK women have had some impact on altering services provided by local authorities through women's political and professional actions, while those with a national power base remain less affected.

By and large, policing is a state activity which does not treat the abuse of women in their homes as crime, but as a peace-keeping activity. The aim is 'to cool out and get out'. The so-called domestic, which identifies the usual place of women's assault as well as the relationship between household members, is distinguished from what is called 'real' crime which, if interpersonal, is seen to take place elsewhere and amongst strangers. The criminal victimization patterns of men and women are very different. Women are much more likely to be physically and sexually assaulted in their homes or very near them – in the garden, on the footpath, in the street immediately in front of their homes – than are men. Women are much more likely than men to be assaulted sexually and physically by men they know, and the closer the relationship the more likely assault is. Men are almost always safe in their own homes, but many women are not, both when children and when adults. Assaults on men more easily fit the police criteria of 'real' crime. I am not arguing that men receive a good policing service, but that men have gendered interests in common that are expressed through the definition of 'real' crime, and when faced with a woman complaining about male behaviour (Edwards 1989, Hanmer & Saunders 1984, 1987, Hanmer et al. 1989, Hanmer & Maynard 1987).

With interpersonal crime against women there is a relationship between age and vulnerability, with younger women more at risk than older, but other demographic or personal correlates have not been substantiated. Our samples of women were stratified by class, and class does not make a difference to rates of interpersonal assault, nor is it likely do race, ethnicity, or religion. How are we to understand types of masculinities in this area of social research?

Why do men beat their wives? The feminist theoretical position that has emerged from paying close attention to women's experiences is that they do it because they can get away with it. In the words of the old music hall joke: 'Do you beat your wife?' 'Of course, I can't beat anyone else's!' It is not that they all *do*, but that they all *can* should they wish to. *Vis-à-vis* the state nothing will happen to you if you do, and even if you seriously injure your wife it is unlikely that much will happen to you. Most men only abuse their wives and children although a small number of men use violence against others more generally, which is more likely to result in state intervention. Deviance theory does not really help us as we are talking about Mr Anyman. Theories of masculinity or femininity are less than helpful given the widespread dominance, backed up by law and various state sectors responsible for its implementation, of men in marriage and families.

While far from the only data that suggest men want marriage as it is more than women, the police concern that to intervene would break up the marriage – and this is the *worst* possible outcome imaginable – demonstrates another common interest between husbands and male police officers, almost all of whom either are or will become husbands (Parliamentary Select Committee 1975). One question could be: why are there differences between men's and women's behaviour in marriage? But much more interesting questions for women who want the world to improve for women concern how particular social institutions, for example, police, housing, and welfare, respond to gender, and where can policy and practice be challenged? Is the study of men going to take this on board? The study of men conceptualized solely as the study of personal identity, of masculinities, is too narrow to do so.

Another strand of work on violence against women is a focus on recurring images, such as the ideological presentation of the so-called domestic killing of women as understandable given a wife who taunts her husband or lover, or the 'sex fiend' who preys on innocent young women; and on recurring patterns, such as the multiple murders of wives and children followed by flight or attempted suicide or suicide, or multiple murders of women and children generally (Cameron & Fraser 1987, Caputi 1988, Jouve 1986). An area I want to look at, when strong enough, which is coming I think, is the death and serious injury of children while on access visits to fathers. That happened to my oldest child. Like other women I live with experience and knowledge that needs to be deindividualized, rendered visible, and reintegrated into society. I make no apology for this because as a feminist scholar, and to refer back to the comments on epistemology, I work on the assumption that through subjectivity objectivity is achieved.

[34]

The dimensions of social privilege that adhere to the male gender and the ways in which these are acted out in relation to women and children in the family could be the basis for research questions for both the study of men and for women's studies. And there are many other areas: pornography, harassment and violence at work, child sexual abuse, to name a few categories in that area called violence against women and children.

Reproductive technologies and genetic engineering

My second example to illustrate how the study of men needs to develop in order to take on the questions and theoretical perspectives of women's studies is in the area of human reproduction. The new reproductive technologies, such as artificial insemination, in vitro fertilization, sex determination, foetal diagnosis and surgery, genetic testing of embryos and foetuses, the mapping of the human genome – to name a few of the present projects applied to humans – when coupled with proposed technologies such as cloning, ectogenisis, genetic manipulation of sex cells – will lead to a reorganization of human reproduction. This has profound implications for women and men as individuals, based upon their sex/gender, and for social life generally. Control over the reproduction of life, including human life, is assuming greater commercial, agricultural, manufacturing, and military importance and could restructure the relations between men and women.

Let me discuss this in a more down-to-earth way. A search-and-arrest operation by 200 officers on thirty-three objectives took place in the Federal Republic of Germany in December 1987 (*RAGE* 1987). It was primarily directed against women who have critically examined questions of genetic and reproductive technology and included a number of sites, such as the homes of intellectuals and academics, business premises, and the gene archive in Essen. The operation was conducted in the usual way: streets sealed off, no search warrants, officers who force their way into premises with firearms at the ready. Scientific material relating, for example, to human genetics, prenatal diagnosis, research work into genetic technology was seized, also radio and video recordings, postcards, address lists of seminars, personal address books, notes, alarm

[35]

clocks, and other objects. 'Extreme condemnation' of genetic technology was cited as the criterion for the seizure of documents.

One of the arrested women was investigating the so-called cholera trials in Bangladesh, said to be immune system research using drugs to combat a particularly virulent strain of cholera. The research involves the World Health Organisation, and on investigation the funding for the trials seems to be related to the Swedish Defence Department and the United States government, with results intended for the government of South Africa (Akhter 1986, Naser 1986, Radio Ellen 1987). The Swedish woman journalist who tried to investigate in Stockholm is not in jail, but was given heavy flak from her government. The Bangladesh people, read women, who are trying to investigate allegations of indifference by the researchers to severe side effects in the 84,000 women and children who were used as experimental subjects which resulted in one death of an 11-year-old girl, are trying to determine exactly what this research is about and for whom, and are seeking help from the west to do so, are meeting a blank wall in their male-military-dictatorship-led country where military hardware deliveries are said to be tied to fulfilling population policy norms, read the mutilation of women's bodies.

Here we have everything, science at the coalface, industry through the pharmaceutical companies, the military, imperialism, the exploitation and oppression of women and girls (men could not be found to take part in these experiments), racism, classism, the state, you name it. Genetic engineering of pharmaceuticals, control of population or disease, their use as warfare technology, begin as socially located decisions, no ivory towers here, in which state interests intermingle with those of commerce, consumers (particularly the military), and professional groups whose livelihoods depend upon the outcome. Most of these decisions makers, researchers, scientists, company owners, and investors, are men. The researched-upon are those whose social position is the weakest, Third World women living in a military dictatorship, as are those who are demanding accountability, the women of the First and Third Worlds. This is gendered from every angle. The study of men will have to expand to breaking point to begin to take issues and situations such as this on board. Feminist scholars and activists are doing so, as women's studies is the study of women in relation to men in a sexual hierarchy in the social world.

[36]

Naming the study of men

Because of the liberationist tinge and the implied parity with women's studies, the term men's studies received critical discussion at the conference on Men and masculinity. It was agreed by a majority of those present that another term must be found to express the desired transformative task inherent in the study of men. The exclusion of women from academic recognition is the starting point for women's studies. It is interdisciplinary and demands the transformation of academic knowledge. The study of men, however, has a different starting point, as human knowledge, academically rendered, is already by and large men's studies. There can never be parity in any obvious way, so until a better suggestion comes along I propose to speak of The Study of Men while continuing to use the term women's studies.

But I welcome 'men's studies' even though it is not clear what is meant by this term. Naming the issues and problems to be examined may have to come first. Until it is clearer what The Study of Men entails it may not be possible to name this field of study correctly. An agreed term will not surface in our consciousness.

But however it progresses I support the development of the field now called 'men's studies', because it is historically necessary and for what it might become – useful. I support it, whatever the quality of its output, because it has something to offer women's studies and feminism. If men write self-serving apologia, do not recognize feminist scholarship, restrict their questions, use inadequate theoretical perspectives, try to split feminist academics and theory by accepting some and rejecting the rest, it will sharpen the critique of men and male class privilege. If occasionally research and writing on men contribute to our understanding of how men gain, maintain, and use power to subordinate women, then we have more positive material for women's studies and feminism.

I expect men's studies to be used against women's studies in the sense that if funding is available for research, teaching, action, employment, and promotion it is likely to go to men, for men, or for the promotion of analyses that do not fundamentally critique the social power of men. So what is new about that? For example, the recent initiative suggested by the ESRC (Economic and Social

[37]

Research Council) is on gender relations rather than, as they put it, the narrower field of women's studies. Women's studies has never received any substantial attention from the ESRC even though it has been the major growth area for theory in the social sciences for the past fifteen years in Britain. The men who dominate the committees of the ESRC, as with everything else that has power and resources, have managed almost completely to ignore the most intellectually challenging, practically relevant, area of social science theory.

I found this a very difficult paper to write. Many were the times I wished I had not agreed to take part and queried why I had and what I could say. Perhaps it goes back to the early days of Women's Liberation where women were entreated to not spend their energies on men as this impeded the development of the Movement, of relationships between women, of the political cause for women. But the problem of men demands women's consideration.

The conference on Men and masculinity illustrates a qualitative change in the institutional development of the study of men in Britain that can only be welcomed. Scholars on women and women scholars have created a small space where men as generic, men as theoreticians of humanity can be challenged. It is usual for academic institutions and scholarly areas to proceed as if this small space does not exist. The Study of Men helps to make this space a little larger. Naming men, as *men*, as *one* of *two* genders, can never be all bad.

Notes

I wish to acknowledge the women of the women's movement and women's studies without whose existence this article could never have been written. In particular I would like to thank Mary Maynard and Sheila Saunders for reading drafts and reassurance, and Pauline Bart and Diana Leonard for last-minute helpful comments. This article was originally presented at the first plenary session of the conference.

1 To cite these works and their interconnection fully is a project in its own right. For example, Robin Morgan in *Sisterhood is Powerful* provides a three-part bibliography:

   (a) the earlier work that influenced this wave of feminism;
   (b) a list of magazines, publishing groups, individual article reprints on women's liberation literature available in 1970;

(c) a 'drop dead list' of work deemed particularly insulting, hostile and detrimental to women.

A limited selection of early work that I remember as providing the ideas, the changed consciousness of women's lives and their relationship to men – all available by 1975 – is:

Allen, Sandra, Lee Saunders, & Jan Wallis (eds) 1974. *Conditions of Illusion: Papers from the Women's Movement*. Leeds: Feminist Books.

Benston, Margaret 1969. The political economy of women's liberation. *Monthly Review* **21**, 13–27.

Birkby, Phyllis, Bertha Harris, Jill Johnston, Esther Newton & Jane O'Wyatt (eds) 1973. *A Lesbian Feminist Anthology*. New York: Times Change Press.

Brownmiller, Susan 1975. *Against Our Will: Men, Women and Rape*. Harmondsworth: Penguin.

Bunch, Charlotte & Nancy Myron (eds) 1974. *Class and Feminism*, Baltimore, Md. Diana Press.

Chesler, Phyllis 1972. *Women and Madness*. New York: Doubleday.

Comer, Lee 1974. *Wedlocked Women*. Leeds: Feminist Books.

Covina, Gina & Laurel Galana (eds) 1975. *The Lesbian Reader: An Amazon Quarterly Anthology*. Oakland, Calif.: Amazon Press.

Dalla Costa, Mariarosa 1972. *Women and the Subversion of the Community*. Bristol: Falling Wall Press.

Davis, Elizabeth Gould 1971. *The First Sex*. New York: Putnam.

de Beauvoir, Simone 1949 (in French). *The Second Sex*. London: Cape, 1953.

Delphy, Christine 1970. *The Main Enemy*. Available in English (mimeo) Edinburgh, 1974. Subsequently published as a Women's Research and Resources Centre pamphlet in 1977 and in *Close to Home*, London: Hutchinson, 1984, 57–92.

Densmore, Dana (n.d.) *Sex Roles and Female Oppression*. Boston, Mass.: Free Press.

Diner, Helen 1965. *Mothers and Amazons: The First Feminine History of Culture*. New York: Anchor/Doubleday, 1973.

Ehrenreich, Barbara & Deirdre English 1973. *Witches, Midwives and Nurses*. Glass Mountain Pamphlets. New York: Feminist Press.

Ehrenreich, Barbara & Deirdre English 1974. *Complaints and Disorders: The Sexual Politics of Sickness*. Glass Mountain Pamphlets No. 2. New York: Feminist Press. London: Compendium.

Figes, Eva 1970. *Patriarchal Attitudes: Women in Society*. London: Faber.

Firestone, Shulamith 1970. *The Dialectic of Sex: The Case for Feminist Revolution*. London: Cape, 1971.

Firestone, Shulamith & Anne Koedt (eds) 1970. *Notes from the Second Year: Women's Liberation*. New York: Radical Feminism.

Freeman, Jo 1970. *The Social Construction of the Second Sex*. Pittsburgh, Pa: KNOW.

Friedl, Ernestine 1975. *Women and Men*. New York: Holt, Rinehart & Winston.

Gavron, Hannah 1966. *The Captive Wife*. London: Routledge & Kegan Paul.

Gornick, Vivian & B. K. Moran (eds) 1971. *Women in Sexist Society: Studies in Power and Powerlessness*. New York: Signet.

Griffin, Susan 1971. Rape: the all-American crime. *Ramparts* **10** (3), 26–35.

Johnston, Jill 1973. *Lesbian Nation: The Feminist Solution*. New York: Simon & Schuster. (The chapters of this book were sold in duplicated form prior to this edition.)

Klagsbrun, Francine (ed.) 1973. *The First Ms Reader*. New York: Warner.

Koedt, Anne & Shulamith Firestone (eds) 1971. *Notes from the Third Year: Women's Liberation*. New York: New York Notes.

Koedt, Anne, Ellen Levine and Anita Rapone (eds) *Radical Feminism*. New York: Quadrangle.

Leacock, Eleanor B. 1972. Introduction to F. Engels, *Origin of the Family, Private Property and the State*. New York: International Publishers.

Lonzi, Carola 1970. *Sputiamo su Hegel*. Milan: Scritti di Rivolta Feminile. Available in English (mimeo) London, 1972.

Matriarchy Study Group (n.d.) *Menstrual Taboos*. London: Matriarchy Study Group.

Millett, Kate 1970. *Sexual Politics*. New York: Doubleday.

Mitchell, Juliet 1966. The longest revolution. *New Left Review* **40** (Nov./Dec.), 11–37.

Mitchell, Juliet 1974. *Pyschoanalysis and Feminism*. London: Allen Lane.

Morgan, Robin 1970. *Sisterhood Is Powerful*. New York: Vintage.

Morgan, Robin *c.* 1972. *Monster,* a pirate edition necessary because the poem about Ted Hughes and the death of Sylvia Plath, 'Arraignment', scared off established publishers.

Morgan, Robin 1976. *Going Too Far: The Personal Documents of a Feminist*. New York: Random House. In the early 1970s these articles circulated in the WLM before being published as a collection.

Myron, Nancy & Charlotte Bunch (eds) 1975. *Lesbianism and the Women's Movement*. Baltimore, Md: Diana Press.

National Women's Aid Federation 1975. *Battered Women Need Refuges*. London: National Women's Aid Federation.

NY Radical Women 1968. *Notes from the First Year*. New York: Redstockings.

Psychology and Women Seminar, Cambridge-Goddard Graduate School 1972. *Women and Psychology*. Cambridge, Mass.: Feminist Studies Program. An annotated bibliography which structures the field from a women's liberationist viewpoint.

Radical Education Project (n.d.) *I am Furious (Female)*. Detroit, Mich.: Radical Education Project.

Radicalesbians 1970. Woman–identified woman. Reprinted in *Lesbians Speak Out*. Oakland, Calif.: Women's Press Collective, 1974.

Redstockings 1975. *Feminist Revolution*. New York: Redstockings.

Reiter, Rayna (ed.) 1975. *Toward an Anthropology of Women*. New York: Monthly Review Press.

Rosaldo, Michelle Zimbalist & Louise Lamphere (eds) 1974. *Women, Culture and Society*. Stanford, Calif.: Stanford University Press.
Rowbotham, Sheila 1972. *Women, Resistance and Revolution*. London: Allen Lane.
Rowbotham, Sheila 1973. *Women's Consciousness, Man's World*. Harmondsworth: Penguin.
Rule, Jane 1975. *Lesbian Images*. New York: Doubleday.
Solanas, Valerie 1968. *SCUM Manifesto*. New York: Olympia. London: Phoenix, 1988.
Tanner, Leslie B. (ed.) 1970. *Voices from Women's Liberation*, New York: New American Library.
Tax, Meredith 1970. *Woman and Her Mind: the Story of Daily Life*, Boston, Mass.: New England Free Press.
Ware, Celestine 1970. *Woman Power: The Movement for Women's Liberation*. New York: Tower.
Weisstein, Naomi (n.d.) *Psychology Constructs the Female or, The Fantasy Life of the Male Psychologist*. Boston, Mass.: Free Press. Revised and expanded 'Kinder, Kuche, Kirche as scientific law: psychology constructs the female' in Robin Morgan 1970. *Sisterhood is Powerful*. New York: Vintage.

In Britain the first academic discipline to respond to the new wave of the women's movement was sociology. The British Sociological Association's annual conference in 1974, on Sexual Divisions in Society, resulted in two volumes:
Leonard Barker, Diana & Sheila Allen (eds) 1976. *Dependence and Exploitation in Work and Marriage*. London: Longman.
Leonard Barker, Diana & Sheila Allen (eds) 1976. *Sexual Divisions and Society: Process and Change*. London: Tavistock.

2   Catharine MacKinnon is a Professor of Law at York University, Toronto, and Yale University, and Andrea Dworkin is a well-known writer whose academic background is in the discipline of English.
3   Subordination is a social-political dynamic consisting of several parts.
    The first is that there is a hierarchy. There's somebody on the top and somebody on the bottom – it's very simple. It's not a complicated hierarchy. We're on the bottom of it.
    The second element of subordination is objectification. That is, the person is dehumanised, made less human than the person – whoever it is – who is on the top. And the person who is on the top becomes the standard for what a human being is. The consequences of being turned into an object are very significant because nobody needs to treat an object the way they need to treat a person.
    The third element of subordination is submission. When people on the bottom of the hierarchy have been turned into objects by those who have power over them, then their behaviour becomes submissive. It doesn't just become submissive when a direct order is given, but it's a characteristic of oppressed people that they can anticipate the order.

The fourth element of subordination is violence. Whenever you see a social situation in which violence is widespread – so widespread that in fact it's normalised – they you know you already have the other three existing elements solidly in place. (Dworkin 1985).

CHAPTER 3
Patriarchy and fratriarchy as forms of androcracy

JOHN REMY

In this chapter I outline a paradigm by means of which the system of men's power can perhaps be better understood. Particular attention will be given to identifying the institutions upon which I believe this system is based, and to describing their morphology and how they work. An exposition of my theory requires the introduction and explanation of a nomenclature adequate to convey the ideas under discussion.

The corporate system of androcracy

The theory is based on the premise that, from a gender-political point of view, the current social order may be characterized as *androcracy*, or 'rule by men', and that this system takes two forms: *patriarchy* ('rule of the fathers'), and *fratriarchy* ('rule of the brother-(hood)s'), both of which are predicated on the institution known as the *men's hut*. The higher status which many women have achieved in the economically better-off countries in recent years and the succession of a small minority into leading positions in society does not yet justify a substantial revision of this formulation. Androcracy does not depend for its functioning merely on the whims and caprice of individual patriarchs, or even on the existence of the family. Though these are undoubtedly key factors in the pattern of male domination, to focus on them as the paramount institutions of this system is to fail to realize that what we are dealing with here is, above all, a *corporate* form of organization.

In western society, androcracy has generally held sway for about 5,000 years. An exhaustive study of early and pre-classical cultures in the Mediterranean more than a century ago led the Swiss anthropologist, J. J. Bachofen (1861), to conclude that androcracy had been preceded by *gynocracy*, implying the hegemony of women. Bachofen, in common with most subsequent researchers into this area, interpreted this to mean *matriarchy*, or 'mother right', though there are indications that what one might call *sororiarchy* ('rule of the sister(hood)s') also sometimes played a role. Amazonism may be an example of this (see Diner 1965).[1]

Patriarchy and fratriarchy

Since the coming of the Second Wave of feminism, the word 'patriarchy' has been used to describe the system of men's rule as a whole. It is unfortunate that a term which signifies a particular form of a phenomenon should come to designate the phenomenon *in toto*. The word androcracy, which contains no such ambiguities, is preferred here when alluding in a general sense to the system of men's rule. Patriarchy traditionally meant the primacy of the father in kinship, and by extension an authoritarian and often antiquated yet paternalistic form of government, as well as 'the rule of the elders', the 'wise old men'. The term is used here to embrace all these meanings and their spiritual, biological, social, and political ramifications, as well as to cover the whole familial mode of androcratic domination. Bearing in mind the hypothesis of the primacy of corporate institutions in the system of male power, it is necessary to emphasize that patriarchy, like fratriarchy, is above all a *social* phenomenon, though this often tends to be obscured by the atomization of the nuclear family. The ultimate seat of power of the father/husband always lies *outside* of the home, since he is a member of the *patriarchate* which meets in the *patriarchal men's hut*.

Fratriarchy[2] is a mode of male domination which is concerned with a quite different set of values from those of patriarchy. Although the *fratrist* can be expected to share all the common assumptions about matters such as the origin of life in the father, together with the whole ideology which springs from this, he is

[44]

preoccupied with matters other than paternity and parenting, raising children, providing for a wife and family, and acting as guardian of a moral code. Unlike patriarchy, fratriarchy is based simply on the self-interest of the association of men itself. It reflects the demand of a group of lads to have the 'freedom' to do as they please, to have a good time. Its character is summed up in the phrase 'causing a bit of bovver'.

Fratriarchy implies primarily the domination of the *age set* (of which more in a moment) of young men who have not yet taken on family responsibilities. Marriage frequently gives rise to divided family loyalties on the part of the groom. His duties towards his family often conflict with his allegiances towards his fraternity 'buddies'. Many men attempt to preserve something of the atmosphere of the stag night well into middle age. Some, to put not too fine a point on it, simply never really grow up, and remain psychologically trapped in the *fratriarchal men's hut* for the rest of their lives. In rebellion against female values, particularly those associated with the mother, and frequently against those of the father, too, the fratriarchal fraternity, or *frat* to avoid a tautology and adopt an appropriate colloquialism, usually has a markedly delinquent character, including a penchant for gratuitous violence. The form of domination to which it gives rise relies heavily on methods of intimidation and not infrequently on outright terror.

Männerbund, *men's hut, age–sets, rites de passage, fraternity, blood brotherhood, and secret society. Rediscovering the language of a forgotten tradition in the social sciences*

A concept which well encapsulates the corporate nature of androcratic institutions, and without which the notions of patriarchy and fratriarchy as used here cannot be adequately understood, is what early German social scientists concerned with this area knew as the *Männerbund* (literally 'men's league'). The terms *male bond* and *fraternity* closely approximate to it. Unfortunately none of these terms, or synonyms for them, have yet found their way into the standard vocabulary of gender studies. This is perhaps surpris-

[45]

ing, since the concept of the banding together of individuals into corporate bodies is surely integral to any understanding of systems of domination.

The primary seat of power in androcracy, and its organizational fulcrum, is the *men's hut* (sometimes called 'men's house'). This is the place where those males who have earned the right to call themselves *men*, or are in process of attaining this emblem of privilege, gather. It has a much higher profile in contemporary society than does its female counterpart, the *women's hut*, this being a measure of the degree of male domination of institutions, as well as the fact that women still tend to spend more time at home than men. The men's hut is the building or space in which the men meet, talk, work, and play. It is the pivot of their domination. The amount of power they possess naturally depends on a number of factors, including class and ethnic status, but every member of the men's hut without exception is a member of a socially dominant gender. The men's hut can also refer to the association of men itself, an example of this being the way the word 'lodge' is used by, for example, the Freemasons, or Britain's all-male National Union of Mineworkers. It can be any size, from a small coterie to a large army. It may well embrace all males of a community over the age of puberty.

The importance of this institution has hardly yet begun to be appreciated, in spite of its being known to social science for almost a century, ever since the pioneering studies of Dr Heinrich Schurtz (1900, 1902), and Hutton Webster (1908). These two scholars, the one a German and Curator of the Bremen Museum, the other an American and Professor of Sociology and Anthropology at the University of Nebraska, researched this same social form during the same period, each in complete ignorance of the other's work. Both agreed about the primary function of the men's hut as the place where the young men of a tribe are initiated, and where they reside until they marry, frequenting it on a part-time basis thereafter. However, while Webster viewed the hut as being under patriarchal control, with the bachelors living under the tutelage of the tribal elders, Schurtz stressed the *autonomous* character of the age-set (*Altersklasse*) of youths. This essentially fratriarchal emphasis had a powerful appeal in Germany among those who were searching for a social-scientific validation for their belief in the cultural superiority of the band of young warriors. Thirty years after his death, Schurtz's theories were being enthusiastically embraced by a growing number of young Nazi intellectuals.[3]

Schurtz's influence, however, was felt far beyond the ranks of extreme right-wing academics. It permeated all the main schools of anthropology in the German-speaking countries. The distinction which Schurtz drew between associations based on 'natural kinship', such as the family and the clan, and those based on 'fictitious kinship' (künstliche Verwandtschaft), such as the Männer-bünde, and particularly his view that the modern state was created by the latter, found ready acceptance not only among the followers of Richard Thurnwald (1932), a tireless investigator of male associations, a keen Nazi, Honorary Professor of Ethnology, Ethnopsychology and Sociology at the University of Berlin, and the leader of the Functionalist school in Germany, as well as among adherents of the theory of the cultural circle (Kulturkreislehre) elaborated by Leo Frobenius (see Jensen 1933), but also by members of Professor Wilhelm Schmidt's Vienna-based Kulturhistorische Schule (Schmidt 1935, pp. 88–9), who were persecuted by the Nazis and forced into exile. Prominent sociologists such as the corporatist theoretician, Othmar Spann (1930, pp. 438, 444), who was tortured by the Gestapo, also recognized the importance of the concept of the Männerbund, and in 1922 Herman Schmalenbach (1922) published a definitive paper in which he consolidated the place of the Bund concept in the taxonomy of German sociology as a designation for a social form to be set beside R. H. Tönnies' Gemeinschaft and Gesellschaft. In spite of Schurtz's transparent misogyny, too, his scornful dismissal of female bonding as a 'pale imitation' of that of the men, providing nothing but opportunities for idle chatter and malicious gossip (Schurtz 1902, pp. 17–18), and his bitter opposition to the women's movement, he also had a not insignificant influence on feminist scholarship before the Second World War. The anthropologist Ida Lublinski (1933, p. 92), for instance, believed that the essentially masculine-separatist nature of the lifestyle of the men's hut, which contrasted so markedly with that of the mother clan, and whose importance Schurtz had been the first to grasp, had been decisive in the overthrow of matriarchy, as well as in the genesis of patriarchy. The idea that the male played a biological role in conception, she contended, had been born in the men's huts, many of which were adorned with phallic carvings.

Only in Germany, however, has gender bonding been studied on

[47]

a systematic basis, and even here interest waned dramatically after 1945. Moreover, such works as did appear from time to time in other countries tended to find a significant resonance only in Germany. This was true, too, of Webster's work. There are, I believe, reasons for this which are related to the way in which an aggressive and highly visible type of male bonding, which eventually took a *fratristic*, fascistic form, came to dominate life in Germany. I shall deal with this further in a work now in progress which has the provisional title *The Erection of the Nazi Men's Hut: The Antifeminist Gender-Politics of the Männerbund in Germany, 1900–1945*. The decisive defeat of this most extreme form of fratriarchy as a would-be world-conquering force had ramifications in the realm of those academic disciplines which had been instrumental in giving rise to such an ideology in the first place. The same is true of what was known as 'racial studies' (*Rassenkunde*).

It is to be hoped that a revival of studies of the *Männerbünde* might arouse interest in this area among supporters of the contemporary women's movement. With some notable exceptions there has been surprisingly little interest from this quarter in the study of men's associations, though this situation may now be changing. Barbara Rogers' recent *Men Only: An Investigation into Men's Organisations* (1988) is a landmark in this regard. Other important contributions in this field in the last few years have included Cynthia Cockburn's *Brothers: Male Dominance and Technological Change* (1983) and Valerie Hey's *Patriarchy and Pub Culture* (1986). These works are all studies of the men's huts, but suffer from the lack of a nomenclature of the type adopted by the Schurtzian school. What has still to be grasped, however, is *the degree to which an extra-familial, extra-patriarchal impulse is at work in many men's associations*, which gives rise to what we have decided to call fratriarchy.

The few feminist or pro-feminist writers of the last twenty years who have been aware of the men's hut have included Kate Millett, who referred to 'the men's house culture of the Nazi *Männerbünde*' in her *Sexual Politics* (Millett 1971, p. 167), the anthropologist Silvia Rodgers (1981), who in an engaging study has described the House of Commons as resembling the men's houses of tribal societies, and last but not least my close friend Keith Mothersson, who has most imaginatively applied the concept to the modern workplace, in his 'Industry as a men's hut' (Paton 1977).[4]

[48]

The men's hut traditionally rigidly excludes women. This reflects its function, as already noted, as the actualization of the desire for separation from women and children and their world. But entry to the hut is not automatic, even for adult males. A *man* in this context is someone who has been awarded an honorific title bestowed on those who, being of male biological sex, have passed the requisite *rites de passage*, a precondition for becoming a fully-fledged member of the masculine community. This most apposite and evocative of expressions was coined by the Dutch ethnologist and Professor of Ethnology at the University of Neuchâtel, Arnold van Gennep, in 1909.[5] It has mainly been used in religious studies and by social psychologists. Such rites subject the candidate to a series of tests, often involving terrifying and painful ordeals. Usually taking place around the age of puberty, they mark the culmination of a long period of education and socialization. Their passing confirms that the young man has 'proven himself', that his gender identity has been confirmed.

Webster grasped the implications of this social definition of manhood when he recited how an elderly Australian aborigine visiting a neighbouring tribe was forced to cower among the women and children since he was forbidden to congregate with the men. The reason for this was that the 'old patriarch' belonged to a tribe which did not have initiation ceremonies and hence was regarded by his hosts as 'never having been made a man' (Webster 1908, p. 25). Such a story is not without its humorous aspect, though one should not underestimate the amount of humiliation involved. This is in fact a common feature of androcratic initiation rituals, as well as being one of the hallmarks of the fratriarchal way of life. Judging by the frequency with which the refrain 'Join the Army; it'll make a man of you' is still heard, this notion of male adulthood retains as much currency as ever.

With the assumption of a common purpose and a tightening of the bonds between its members, often symbolized by an oath of loyalty, the men's hut may become a formal *fraternity*, in taxonomic terms a parallel social form to the *sorority*, the sisterhood of the women's hut. A particularly close, and closed, form of fraternity, is a *blood brotherhood* (see Hocart 1970, pp. 185 ff.). This is founded upon the experience of the members of the fraternity undergoing a special ceremony involving the collective symbolic shedding of blood, as may happen most strikingly in war, as well as in the more

[49]

mundane setting of, for example, a boy scout hut, where the lads may take it in turns to nick their forearms with a penknife, allowing the trickle of blood which issues from the wound to mingle with that of every other member of the circle. This archaic custom superficially echoes the menstrual synchronicity which can occur among groups of young women who bond very closely or live in close proximity.

Secrecy also has an important part to play in the androcratic men's hut. It goes hand in hand with the separatist impulse and the exclusivity which is usually involved. It is an easy step for the fraternity, particularly if it is a blood brotherhood, to develop into a full-blown *secret society*. This was the expression which Webster used to describe this whole culture complex. The terms 'fraternity' and 'secret society' are often used interchangeably. All the expressions used in this section are, indeed, different ways of describing the same phenomenon. The order in which they have been enumerated here indicates, above all, progressively more tightly bonded and disciplined forms of organization.

Family and fraternity

The father/husband, unlike the son, has *two* seats of power: the family home and the men's hut. Thurnwald's observation that the husband, although the legal head of the family, which he was correct to view as essentially a *matrifocal* institution, and its protector, is nevertheless 'chiefly a member of the men's society, which in relation to the women leads its own life' (Thurnwald 1932, p. 10) may at first sight appear an exaggeration. Yet the more one considers it the more it has the ring of truth about it. After all, most married men are absent from home for a large part of the time. Much of this is likely to be spent in an organized workplace, and it is from this men's hut that the husband will derive his main social identity. In addition, he may also frequent the golf club, the Masonic lodge, the local pub, or the bookie's.

The life of the married man is likely to be a schizophrenic one, since he has a foot in two very different worlds. *The family and the fraternity have quite different ethical codes.* An example of this double standard drawn from personal experience should illustrate this. Some years ago I worked in a warehouse alongside a man who used

[50]

four-letter words in practically every sentence. When I asked him if he used such foul language in front of his wife and family he looked at me aghast. Gritting his teeth and clenching his fist, he exclaimed in a menacing tone: 'Of course I f---ing don't. Any f---ing geezer that come [sic] into my house f---ing swearing, I'd murder the f---ing c--t'. He did a karate chop in the air. The use of a special language, though not necessarily an obscene one, is another important feature of life in the men's hut.

Modus operandi *of the frat*

The men's hut in an androcratic society must be understood primarily as a unitary institution. Nevertheless, conflicts between its patriarchal and fratriarchal variants, or between the values represented by the respective modes of behaviour which these symbolize, can be just as bitter as those between family-centred and fraternity-centred codes. Conflict, it hardly needs to be said, is a hallmark of almost all male associations.

Although the origins of the men's hut appear, both in a historical sense (as Ida Lublinski believed) and in a generational sense, to be closely associated with what we have called fratriarchy, it must not be imagined that every last boys' club is a junior frat. A large number of the activities which preoccupy a group of lads, even if they do call themselves a gang, are, to be sure, perfectly innocuous. What concerns us here are those which involve displays of gender domination. As already mentioned, such domination can range from petty harassment to the vilest of crimes. The examples which follow show, interestingly enough, how the petty intimidation which is such a common feature of fratriarchy still takes place even when the stakes have been raised to involve full-scale terror. They are not intended to be a representative sample so much as to serve as illustrations of a potential which is all too frequently realized. What should be clear enough by now is that what confronts us here are not isolated outbreaks of aberrant behaviour but a *pattern* of corporate male aggression whose motifs have been repeated *ad nauseam*, often down to the last detail, from tribal times until today.

The separatist impulse may cause the frat to break away completely from the community, which it then proceeds to prey upon in parasitic fashion. The 'brotherhood of terror' then arrogates to

[51]

itself a series of nefarious 'prerogatives', claiming the 'right' to demand with menaces, to plunder with impunity, to burn, rape, torture, and murder (Remy 1986a 1986b). It imposes a curfew and rules by means of what amounts to martial law.

Schurtz told of how the fraternities which proliferate in Melanesia and West Africa, and which have often become the supreme organs of political authority in these societies, would use terror on a systematic basis in order to instil fear into the population (Schurtz 1900, p. 116). He described how 'a terrorism of the most invincible kind emanated from the *Männerhaus*'. The primary targets were not other men, but the petrified women and children of the village. One such fraternity, the *Tamate* of Melanesia, would suddenly descend upon a community, their faces covered with hideous masks. They would block off all avenues of escape. Anyone attempting to flee would be considered fair game to be slain. Having declared the territory 'closed', they would 'permit themselves the greatest liberties', giving any woman or child that caught their eye a sound thrashing, and thieving anything that took their fancy. Woe betide anyone who should attempt to resist them or fail to show the terrorists, whose commands had the force of law, the 'respect' which they demanded.

One need venture no further than the boys' playground of the nearest school in order to witness similar instances of mob rule, complete with grotesque parodies of legitimate authority, though albeit not of a life-threatening character. The level of violence may be lower and the degree of fear less, but the content and direction of the behaviour is the same.

Corporate criminal activities of this kind, with their strong ritualistic element, are not confined to a particular culture or historical period. Otto Höfler, a keen student of Schurtz's work and a leading intellectual in the Nazi SS, turned to an account by the sixteenth-century Swedish clergyman Olaus Magnus (1555) to show that the Germanic peoples of what are now the Baltic states had known *Männerbünde* similar to those which Schurtz described in his comparative studies. These poor peasants suffered attacks on their cattle from marauding wolves all year round, but these caused not nearly as much damage as the havoc wrought by the *werwolves*, which Magnus recognized as men dressed in wolf skins. Thousands of these werwolves would gather at certain times of the year and hold initiation rites involving jumping over a stream or a wall.

[52]

Whoever failed the test would be given a good whipping. After dark fell the fratrists would turn their attention to the peasants. They would 'besiege people's dwellings ... with unbelievable ferocity, ... smashing the doors in, so as to destroy the humans and animals inside'. They would then make for the cellar of the cottage, break open the barrels and consume as much of the family's stock of home-brewed beer as they could manage. The level of their violence increased with their degree of intoxication (Höfler 1934, pp. 22–5).

Höfler claimed that these frats were cross-class associations, comprising both aristocrats and farm lads. The recent troubles in affluent parts of southern England involving middle-class *lager louts*, and the ongoing problem of football hooliganism, a mainly proletarian phenomenon, demonstrate, if further proof were needed, that drunken men's gangs exist among all social classes.

Höfler's observation that what had been overlooked in regard to the packs of werwolves was precisely what he considered to be the most important thing about them – their sociological phenomenology, the fact that they were a *Männerbund*, is equally true today. Whether one encounters the *drapesers*, the bands of young thieves of Afro-Caribbean origin who have mugged people, mainly women, at London's Notting Hill Carnival in recent years, or those who practice *wilding*, which involves 'gang bang' rapes of female joggers in New York's Central Park, or the guerrillas known as the *Tamil Tigers* who operate on the strife-torn island of Sri Lanka, and who, 'creeping out of the jungle well after dark', recently fell upon a defenceless village, 'clubbing and hacking to death thirteen victims, including five children' (Rettie 1988), the same social grouping is involved in each case.

Most of the long litany of crimes committed by the frat are, alas, soon forgotten, though the victims' loved ones continue to remember them and to grieve for them. Are the fruits of half a century of concentrated research, which can teach us so much about this phenomenon, to remain forgotten, too, or will we harness its rediscovery to the enrichment of a social theory which seeks to understand this omnipresent problem?

Notes

The published version of this paper has undergone a substantial reworking. Written under the name of Valerie Remy, it originally carried the rather unwieldy title of 'Patriarchy and fratriarchy as forms of androcracy spawned in the men's hut "womb"'. At the suggestion of the editors, the theme signified by the final word of the title was omitted. I dedicate this work to Kathleen Sild. She has given me much love and happiness and brought about a metamorphosis in me as complete as any transmutation of the alchemists and shamanesses of old. I wish to thank my friends Keith Mothersson, Jeff Hearn, Daphne Francis, Colin Archer, and Denise Arnold for all their help and encouragement during the writing of this work.

1 For a very readable synopsis of Bachofen's work see his *Myth, Religion and Mother Right; Selected Writings of J. J. Bachofen* (1967), with an introduction by the noted American writer on the philosophy of religion, Joseph Campbell. Helen Diner's *Mothers and Amazons* which was first published under the pseudonym 'Sir Galahad' in Munich in 1932, also has an introduction by Campbell. Terminologically, if in no other sense, sororiarchy is the female equivalent of fratriarchy.

2 I first began to use the term 'fratriarchy' around 1976 to characterize the form of organization of fascist gangs. Only much later did I learn that the Marxist-feminist anthropologist, Evelyn Reed, had used it in her *Woman's Evolution* (1975), albeit to signify something rather different, although there were certain points in common between our respective usages. Another contributor to the BSA conference, Harry Brod, presented a paper with the title 'From patriarchy to fratriarchy: adventures in the making of masculinities'. See also pp. 132–4.

3 Outstanding works in this genre were: Höfler 1934, Stumpfl 1936, and Wolfram 1936, 1938. All three men held doctorates and posts in academia, Höfler and Wolfram being awarded professorships during the course of the Third Reich. They were all Nazi Party members. Höfler and Wolfram were influential figures in the *Ahnenerbe* (Ancestral Heritage) section of the SS.

4 The article was written under the author's original name, Keith Paton. It is thanks to Keith that I first became aware of the term 'men's hut'.

5 *Les rites de passage* was translated into English and published by the University of Chicago Press as *The Rites of Passage* in 1964. An outstanding contribution to this theme is Bruno Bettelheim's *Symbolic Wounds: Puberty Rites and the Envious Male* (1955), in which the renowned child psychologist maintains that 'womb envy' plays an important role in such ceremonies. Brian Easlea (1983), with his theory of the 'pregnant phallus', takes a similar view, though not specifically in relation to initiation so much as *vis-à-vis* the men's association in general. This work has made an important contribution to our understanding of the psychology of fratriarchy.

CHAPTER 4

Racism, black masculinity and the politics of space

SALLIE WESTWOOD

This chapter is an exploratory and tentative attempt to grapple with some of the issues raised by the current discussions of masculinity. I did not set out to research masculinity in a substantive way nor to provide an ethnography of the lives of some black men in a provincial city. The research grew out of an earlier research project which reconstructed the history of a black youth project, a local *cause célèbre* in the mid-1980s. The men who are the subjects of this paper were politicized through the project and I came to know them through the research. At the same time I was teaching on an inner-city access course which also included some of the men involved in the youth project; others I knew through my own involvement with community politics in the city. The men who have contributed towards this paper have been involved with the process throughout. I am conscious, however, that it has, ultimately, been constructed out of an ongoing process of negotiation in which I, as a white female researcher with a university background, have sought to interpret the lives of black working–class men. I am aware of the limits of this encounter and the ways in which racism and sexism intervene in the research process.

There is no innocent ethnography and I am mindful of the critiques of white sociology generated by black critics like Lawrence (1982). Black people have been poorly served by a sociology and an anthropology which has contributed to the definition of black people as 'Other' through the silences on black people's lives and the racism of British society, or through the presentation of black people's lives as a form of exotica, or through the use of stereotypes which have framed the representation of black people through the fixity of the stereotypes (Bhabha 1983). That this has happened partly relates to racism within the social sciences which is suffused with the commonsense of the day and equally it relates, I would argue, to the essentialism of the subject in sociological discourses. My hope is that, by developing an alternative, non-essentialist account which places racism centrally in the analysis, previous errors will not be reproduced within this paper.

Feminist analysis has consistently made men and masculinity problematic and this has provided an impetus to the current interest in masculinity and the development of men's studies. Yet certain currents within feminism have also promoted an essentialist account of men and women, masculinity and femininity, positing a polarity between the two which often belies the lived experiences of women and men in their everyday realities. More materialist accounts have used Marxist analysis to generate a class theory of gender in which men share a position of dominance *vis-à-vis* women, and through their forms of dominance in both the public and private realm they are able to exploit women (Delphy 1977, Hartmann 1981). Black feminists have inserted a different agenda, one which speaks to difference and which insists upon the centrality of racism to our understandings of both masculinities and femininities in Britain (Joseph 1981, Parmar 1982, Carby 1982, Davis 1982, Hooks 1982, *Feminist Review* 1984, Bryan *et al*. 1985). Britain is a post-colonial and racist society and this is the context in which our understandings must be forged. Thus, an analysis of black masculinities must also move away from the essentialisms of feminism to a different terrain in which the essentialism of the subject is challenged.

Multiple selves

My task in this paper is to de-centre the subject and to de-essentialize black masculinity. The essentialism of the constructions that surround the black man and of black masculinity have given plenty of scope for racist accounts through stereotyping and the construction of black men as 'the Other'. For black men of African descent the stereotypes have been fixed on the body, on physicality, physical strength, and as a site for European fantasies about

[56]

black male sexuality. Orientalism has generated a different picture for men of Asian descent. The colonial designation of the 'martial races' of northern India produced an account of men of vigour and strength, fighting men who were at some distance from the wily oriental who, by being tied to conceptions of manipulation and wiliness, became feminized in the eyes of the white men of the colonial era. The fixity of these stereotypes places 'races', genders, motivations, and behaviours in such a way that they become naturalized and a substitute for the complex realities they seek to describe. It does not help to try and replace one set of stereotypes by another; the point is to dismantle all stereotypes and to move to a much more shifting terrain in which identities are not seen as fixed and cannot, therefore, become stereotypical.

No one understands this better than the men who are the subjects of this paper. They understand themselves simultaneously as Gujaratis or Punjabis, as Hindus, Muslims, or Sikhs, as Afro-Caribbeans or Jamaicans, and as black men, a politically forged identity in post-colonial Britain. They understand that they are legally British but not culturally British or English because, as Desh commented, 'British means white' and as Kuldip said with feeling 'Black people will never be allowed to be British'. Their identities have been forged in relation to the specificities of their cultural and historical backgrounds and yet they recognize commonalities with white working-class men because of their class position which generates both political and cultural overlaps related to them as men. But these identities are not separable; to be one does not deny the other. They are lived and experienced simultaneously which is why in any analysis we have to make sense of this. Identities are not finished products like the old socialization model would have us believe, rather they are constantly produced and thus a shifting terrain. However, shifting identities are not just freefloating; they are positioned within histories, cultures, language, community, and class. This suggests a lack of fixity and thus a politically uncomfortable position in which contingency matters. There are contradictions and coalescences between the cultural and the social, identity and difference.

Thus, Dollimore (1986, pp. 6–7), writing on homophobia and sexual difference, notes:

identity is a construction and, as such, involves a process of exclusion, negation and repression. And this is a process which even if successful, results in an identity intrinsically unstable. This is bad news for masculinity one of whose self-conceptions is stability, and whose function is to maintain it socially and psychically.

Thus, the crucial work of this paper is one of deconstruction and especially the deconstruction of 'black masculinity'. In this sense it is a political intervention against the stereotypes past and present of black men in Britain. These have not been helped by the earlier accounts of masculinity that concentrated upon the construction of 'the male role'. In their critique of this, Carrigan, Connell and Lee (1987, p. 80) comment: 'Let us be blunt about it. The "male sex role" does not exist. It is impossible to isolate a "role" that constructs masculinity or another that constructs femininity.' Accounts of masculinity tied to the notion of role, however, are in circulation and have specific consequences when the discussion turns to black masculinities. Franklin (1984, pp. 60–61) concludes his discussion in the following way: 'Black males tend to internalize a masculine role which can be characterised as follows: An emphasis upon physical strength, an expectation of both submissiveness and strength in women, angry and impulsive behaviour, functional relationship between men and women, and strong male bonding'. This is the culmination of an account which serves to pathologize and stereotype black men noting the difficulties they have in assuming the male role due to the forms of socialization, the black family structure, etc. It is an account which feeds on and feeds racist assumptions about black men, and while racism is crucial the problem also relates to the insistence upon 'the male role' against which all men must be measured. It is thus vitally important to offer an alternative conceptualization and Carrigan, Connell and Lee (1987) pursue this in their critique, suggesting instead the notion, which is not fully explored, of hegemonic masculinity to which other forms, especially homosexuality, are subordinated. I do not wish to pursue the discussion of Connell's treatment of hegemonic masculinity here (see Rattansi & Westwood 1989) but to invoke the ways in which he moves closer to a deconstructionist position when he, Carrigan and Lee comment (1987, pp. 88–9):

The history of homosexuality obliges us to think of masculinity not as a single object with its own history but as being constantly constructed within the history of an evolving social structure, a structure of sexual power relations. It obliges us to see this construction as a social struggle going on in a complex ideological and political field in which there is a continuing process of mobilization, marginalization, contestation, resistance and subordination.

Public spaces

In my own account I want to try to unravel the cross-cutting discourses on black masculinity in relation to the way in which they are played out in different spaces that are privileged. Discourses are constructed and elaborated and they too cross-cut the spaces. They are not mutually exclusive and are played out through the discursive practices that surround lived experience in specific spaces. There is, however, a materiality to the politics of these spaces. We find mutuality and contradiction, dominant and subordinate discourses, and the ways in which black masculinities are made, remade, and reworked as an essential part of the cultures of resistance of black people in Britain against the racism of British society.

Discourses as registers of masculinity are worked through in a variety of spaces and this chapter concentrates attention upon the public realm and only two sites within this, inner-city streets and football, the most public of public spaces. Like the world of family and household these are arenas of contested terrain, areas of struggle in which masculinities are called up as part of the fight against racism. To consider black masculinities as part of the cultures of resistance to racism is not to suggest that they are not in themselves contradictory. These areas, the streets and football, are important to consider because it is precisely in these areas that current stereotypes about black men have been generated and have become part of the commonsense racism of today.

Although this paper concentrates upon the public sphere the reader should be aware that this does not exhaust the fields for black masculinities, or the discourses on black masculinities, and does not suggest that these fields have pre-eminence and are in themselves privileged over the worlds of work and, most importantly, family and the home. On the contrary, the world of home and family is vitally important especially as a site of resistance to racism in British society. It is, however, an arena in which women have power and this is acknowledged by the men with whom I spent time. Although as black men they had power in the home as brothers, sons, husbands, and fathers they acknowledged that the domestic world was a power base for women in which they often had to defer to the power of women to define this realm. One example of this was the way in which many of the men would smoke cigarettes in the pubs and clubs but not at home because women in their families objected. It is also important to emphasize that the private–public dichotomy is not a real opposition; the public intervenes in the private world of the family and none more so than in the case of black families subjected to specific forms of state intervention (Westwood & Bhachu 1988) which often break up black families. Black families have therefore sought strength and unity as a form of resistance to racism in Britain (Mercer & Julien 1988).

For the black working-class men who are the subjects of this paper there is a powerful distinction to be drawn between the world of home and the world of the streets and the football pitch. I want to concentrate upon the latter because I am interested in the ways that masculinities are played out and validated not for home and family but for other men. The subjects of this paper are black working-class men not middle-class black men for whom the nuances of masculinity will be different but who will, I would suggest, still require a male audience for the validation of certain forms of masculinity. Women are not entirely absent from this public male world. They enter it through specific discourses on women which place women in relation to the home and domesticity and to romance and sexuality. The men who are the subjects of the lived realities presented here are also makers of discourses which is part of an engagement involved in the production of black, male, working-class identities. Thus, one man, Manjit, said of another, Bal, 'You see Sallie', he said, 'all this macho stuff from Bal, it's for the men. You should see him at home. He's a real romantic.' Manjit made this point in relation to Bal but in discussion he elaborated the view that it was pivotal for all the men, himself included.

In concentrating attention upon the streets and upon football in this account I am calling up not the masculinities of physical prowess, although this is part of the discussion, but the cultural politics of 'race' in which popular culture is a crucial site. Football is a vital part of this and while it has since its inception been tied to 'manliness and vigour' it can also be analysed in relation to cultures of resistance. It was the late C. L. R. James who understood the significance of sport as a terrain of political and racial contestation, and this is elaborated in his famous account of cricket, *Beyond a Boundary*.

Racism

Staples (1985, p. 20), writing on black masculinity, comments: 'In the case of black men, their subordination as a racial minority has more than cancelled out their advantages as males in the larger society'; and he continues: 'The issues of masculinity and race are too interwoven to separate at this time.' The men in this paper are acutely aware of the articulation between masculinity and 'race' and they see in racism an affront to black masculinity. As a counter to racism black masculinity is called up as part of the cultures of resistance developed by black men in Britain.

Racism in Britain is, as Cohen (1988, p. 63) notes, 'not something "tacked on" to English history, by virtue of its imperialist phase, one of its aberrant moments; it is *constitutive* of what has become known as "the British Way of Life"' (emphasis in original) or as Gilroy points out: 'Racism is not a unitary event based on psychological aberration nor some historical antipathy to blacks . . . It must be understood as a process.' (Gilroy 1987, p. 27) The process is elaborated in 19th-century discourses that have become part of the commonsense racism of English life (Cohen 1988). Generally, the process to which Gilroy refers is characterized by prejudice and discrimination against groups of people understood to share common racial heritages. Racism rests, in part, upon the mistaken belief that there are biologically distinct races in nature and therefore people have natural attributes determined by their racial origins. Implicit in racism is the idea that one race is culturally superior to another and is, therefore, justified in exercising political and economic hegemony.

To take this one step further we have to consider the forms of

[61]

racism and again Cohen's work is useful (Cohen 1988). He seeks to differentiate the forms of working-class racism by concentrating attention upon a reworking of the rough/respectable divide and by introducing gender as a crucial determinant. Cohen emphasizes 'the nationalism of the neighbourhood', that 'imagined community' to which loyalty is displayed and which invokes the politics of space as crucial to an understanding of the articulations between territoriality, masculinity, and racism. The defence of defined space as 'ours' is itself exclusionary, and the definition of imagined communities are themselves exclusionary acts; they exclude black people. Tolson (1977, p. 34) also emphasizes the importance of space and neighbourhood when he writes: 'The intense localism and aggressive style shape the whole experience of working-class masculinity.' He is writing of white working-class men but the intense localism is something shared by the black working-class men whose lives are discussed in this paper.

It is clear that the 'nationalism of the neighbourhood' is not confined to white men. In black areas it is appropriated and the inner-city space becomes 'our place' for black people and 'our streets' become the space to be defended against the incursions of white men and most especially the police. This takes me into the discussion of privileged spaces which begins with life on the streets.

The local context

The men live in a provincial city which has undergone major restructuring of its manufacturing base in the 1980s with high unemployment rates as a consequence. On current estimates 25% of the city population are black British with a large Asian population now settled in the city and a much smaller Afro-Caribbean presence. The men belong to these diverse communities and refer to themselves in relation to specific cultural and religious identities but also, as I have emphasized, as black men. They often remarked that Asians and Afro-Caribbeans were closer in this city than in London or Birmingham. The men have grown up in the same inner-city neighbourhood, attended the same schools, and as young men were all involved with the politics of a youth project in their locality which had a crucial role in forging black political identities. They also share experiences of racism and encounters with the police. Most of the men had had brushes with the law in their younger days and continued to be wary of the police.

Among a wide network of contacts there was, during the time of the research, a core group of fifteen Asian and Afro-Caribbean men who lived locally, met regularly, and were in close and fairly constant contact. They were a predominantly Asian group but Asian and Afro-Caribbean men were close friends. Half of this group were unemployed, several worked in manual jobs in local factories or for the city council, one man worked on a community project, and another for a trade union. They were in the 20–30 age group and a third were married or had longstanding partners; some had young children.

Their world is an intensely local world and their social life relates to the inner-city area which is their home. Moves outside this world might be made for weddings in nearby cities, for football tournaments and matches, or for the occasional visit to clubs in a town thirty miles away.

The streets

There is a long history of young working-class men being presented as 'dangerous' in official discourse and in the media (Pearson 1983). But this has of late become specifically racialized with young black men positioned within street life in particular ways, from the moral panics surrounding mugging and criminality explored by Hall *et al.* (1978) and Gilroy (1987) to the more recent accounts of the 'riots' in Britain. These latter accounts, both from the media and within official discourse, articulate a moral panic with the current crises in British society and the British state (Benyon & Solomos 1987, Solomos 1988). Black men are highly visible in relation to street life which is expressed through visual representations in the media and in the current discourses on law and order. What it means for their lives is that they are subject to 'the Empire of the gaze' or as Foucault (1979, p. 187) elaborates: 'It is the fact of being constantly seen, of being able always to be seen that maintains the disciplined individual in his subjection.' The 'disciplined individual', however, has many ways of resisting 'the Empire of the gaze' and the streets of the 1980s have borne witness to this in spectacular ways.

There are, however, many less spectacular strategies available with which to resist surveillance. Thus, life on the streets generates a series of discourses that relate to the importance of being streetwise, but these are not easily articulated because they are part of the commonsense of urban life for black working-class men. What is called up in relation to being streetwise is the ability to handle the dangers of street life, and this links masculinity, defence, and manly behaviour. Contrary to the popular views, however, that being streetwise privileges physical prowess and fighting acumen, it is essentially an intellectual, cerebral attribute. What is required as a context for being streetwise and being able to operate safely on the streets is an intimate knowledge of locality which all the men shared. Thus the links between territoriality and white working-class masculinity underlined by the work of Tolson (1977) and Cohen (1988) can also be seen in the lives of black working-class men.

The area with which I am familiar is one of contested terrain in the material sense of terrain. There are no longer white gangs like the 'ketchup gang' (whose 'trademark' was to beat up Asian men and then douse them in ketchup) or the National Front; latterly these have been routed from the area. But the state intervenes in the form of policing adopted for the inner city. The area is very close to the main city police station and the police can arrive immediately, as they did following a pub shooting. In seconds there were armed police on every corner, long before the ambulance arrived to attend to the injured man. However, this was an extraordinary event. What affects the lives of black men on a day-to-day basis is the level of routine harassment where they are stopped, searched, intimidated, and subjected to racially abusive name-calling and physical duress. The hostel, one outcome of the youth project with which the men were involved, is regularly raided, the doors smashed, and the residents taken from their rooms. These encounters with the police undermine the collective strength of black people and are seen by the men as an affront to black men as men.

Faced with the power of the police the men would say that it was vital 'to know how to handle yourself' and this meant everything but a physical response. As Dev commented, 'You have to stay cool and let them heat up'. Staying cool is essentially about maintaining dignity and control in a situation which very often denies both. It means remaining calm, signalled through a quiet voice and reasonableness in the face of what the men considered to be provocation. The quietness covers the necessity of staying mentally alert and agile. The men were conscious that their intimate knowledge gained from childhood of the local area was crucial to safety. All the men were wary of other parts of the city and especially the city centre late at night. It was dangerous and they did not voluntarily walk alone in the city up to and after midnight. It was not 'safe', in fact it was known to be hostile. The language of safety expresses the feelings of trust and being at home only in their part of town. 'Safe' was also applied to people, those who could be trusted, and to situations where the men felt at home.

An intimate knowledge of locality allowed the men to disappear quickly if there was trouble on the streets and to reappear at some distance, usually, from the police. The speed of disappearance meant an ability to run and this was marked by the tracksuits and trainers that the men wore which were also a symbol of their commitment to sport. Tracksuits and trainers are not just about the whims of fashion, they express something about the nature of street life and the importance of physical fitness.

The politics of the street as a clash between men in blue and men without uniforms is an old story of urban life, but the documented racism of the police (*Broadwater Farm Inquiry* 1986; Institute of Race Relations 1987) is a crucial element for black people generally and black men in particular. In addition, the police now have available an armoury of weapons with which to police the streets. The men were acutely aware of both the changes in tactics and technology and the ways that these were used. 'They try to wind us up so they can show off their hardware', said Amrit, and continued: 'but we're not stupid. We know their games.' Wiliness, not confrontation, was seen to be the best way to resist. The point was to outwit the police. 'You've got to use your brain and act fast', said Mark with a grin, 'the coppers don't have much brain or pace.'

Life on the streets, therefore, requires courage, wit, and knowledge. Even with this the men still had uncomfortable encounters with the police and in other parts of the city with white men. There were many incidents. One, for example, involved Kuldip late at night in a Chinese takeaway that was opposite a white working-class pub. While he waited for his order two white men attacked him, the women with them looking on. They grabbed his glasses and he responded by telling them 'to leave it alone'. He recounted

[65]

the incident with some surprise. 'I just swung my right arm at all four of them and then I left running as fast as I could up the street.' Kuldip's friends were shaken and angry and their response was to try and look for the attackers. But they were dissuaded by Kuldip: 'It happens', and the men all recognized the truth of this. The attack was not construed simply as a unique act of violence but as part of the pattern of racial attacks and therefore as an attack on black people in Britain. Thus the attack was politicized by the understandings brought to it and the men sought ways to fight back. Their views that areas outside their own were dangerous were confirmed and this incident prompted a long discussion on the lack of safety for black men in areas of the city and the city centre and added a very powerful dimension to my understanding of their intense localism.

Being streetwise is not only about negotiating the city, it is also about satisfying needs and demands through a very local network of goods and services. Thus the men could organize vans and drivers to take them to football matches or acquire some of the latest fashion gear cheaply, or get some assistance with welfare rights or housing. They could get their houses painted cheaply or electrical work done or a car fixed through a complex process of reciprocal relations which enabled them to earn some money, raise their standard of living, and have fun. When I lent some of the men my car for a football weekend it was returned the following week with a new MOT, my trade for the loan of the car. Being able to summon up and control access to resources directly is a mark of power and status and an acknowledgement of male control over the immediate environment. In this way it has a direct bearing upon masculinity and the power that a man can exercise in the group. Favours are traded and power is demonstrated by the range of favours owed to any one man. Within the group one man was pre-eminent and his advice and guidance was sought with legal and economic problems and this was traded against the skills he did not possess like driving. Thus, there was a micro-politics to the reciprocity set up within the economic system of the inner city.

Football

In a favourite pub in the locality a huge silver cup is passed around the bar. It is filled with Barcardi and coke, a gift from the Asian landlord, in celebration of the triumph of the Saints in the Sunday league. The cheer and high spirits are for football, not just any football but amateur football and the dominance of a black team of Afro-Caribbean and Asian players over the white world of soccer – a heady moment, relived by recalling the final and other memorable matches when black teams have carried off the cups. For despite the glamour of John Barnes and Ruud Gullit and the media coverage of black players, English football is well known for its banana skins and racist chants. The racism and the masculinity of white working-class men are welded into one by the articulations between a white working-class masculinity socially and ideologically constructed out of the post-imperial chauvinism of British society. Modern football, growing up as it did in the Victorian and Edwardian eras, is redolent with the politics of 'race'.

Racism, however, does not go uncontested in Britain, on or off the soccer pitch. Black men play soccer because they love the game but their entry into the game means that they are immediately involved in the cultural politics of 'race'. So much of the impact of this politics is missed if local amateur and semi-professional football is ignored. The lads, as they sometimes called themselves, were not city supporters and part of the reason for their lack of support was their view that the city team had not tried to recruit black players, despite the numbers of young Asian and Afro-Caribbeans who went for trials at the club. The team does have one black player but, unlike Arsenal, young black players are not filtered through the youth scheme so there are no local black players. Manjit's view was clear. 'A city with so many black people and no black footballers. Ask the manager why is that? We know why, it's racism, that's why.' The absence of Asian men from the national football scene is discussed by Rajan Datar. Writing in *The Guardian* (28 June 1989) he points to the passion for football among Bengali boys and comments: 'Frustrated by the lack of opportunities to play organised football, many young Asians are now involved in their own leagues. From Huddersfield to Hayes in west London new competitions are sprouting up to accommodate demand.'

The response from black footballers and supporters is a collective one, generated and sustained through the local level in the amateur sphere of FA football. Like cities up and down the country the town has a thriving amateur section with a proliferation of leagues

[67]

and knockout competitions in which black teams of Afro-Caribbeans, Asians, and those (which I know best) bringing Asians and Afro-Caribbeans together, are very prominent. Some of the black teams have grown out of the youth project in which the men were involved, others from community organizations and some from the Gurdwaras. The latter is an interesting way in which ethnicity, masculinity, and popular culture are fused. Some of the most fiercely contested tournaments in black football are those organized around the Sikh festival of Vaisakhi. It is celebrated in the temples and homes of Sikh people but also on the football pitch.

The teams and the prowess of black players are a collective statement about the power of black men to dominate in a sport where white men consider themselves superior. Consequently, matches between black and white teams are fought on and some-times off the pitch and old rivalries between city teams of black men and county teams of white men are renewed. It is a fiercely contested terrain because, as the black players and supporters say: 'White teams don't like being beaten by a black team.' It is, in effect, an injury to white masculine pride and a source of power and celebration to black masculine pride when white teams are beaten.

The game is a set of discursive practices in a discursive space. The game, at one level, is very formal, yet black players have a particular style and this is constructed by white players and supporters in the image of 'the other' as black footballers who are loud and aggressive and the oriental male who 'jabbers' a lot. The image of the half-mad Indian is set against the controlled stoic, the disciplined white footballer. Thus, white teams and referees complain about the lack of discipline and the behaviour of black teams and the FA boards that adjudicate complaints, discipline players, and allow entry into the higher leagues are all white. Bad behaviour and lack of discipline are invoked, the men believe, in an effort to keep their teams from moving up the amateur league. More insidious still is the way in which black teams in the city who have won their leagues (and won twice in one case) are not able to progress through into the next amateur league, the senior league, because the other teams must vote for the team to come in. White teams, the men insist, do not vote for black teams to enter their leagues. In fact, the attempt seems to be to ghettoize the black teams. Several moved into one of the leagues and started winning matches against white teams. The response from the white teams was to start leaving the league and from the FA board to catapault black teams, not of the same standard, into this league.

Romance and rivalry

There is a romance to football. It offers an arena in which men can work together and invoke loyalty and camaraderie while it also offers a space for the drama of performance where individuals can shine, and have status and acclaim. Equally men can exercise power as 'nifty' players through their mastery of the ball and the pitch which requires both physical dexterity and tactical prowess. Football represents for the men I know their own specific history. They can recount the events of football matches from one year to the next and time is measured in terms of who won what in any specific year: the time they went to Barking or to Derby, the local matches fought and won, and the cups and medals that they all have in their front rooms. Each story has its own drama, and the disastrous starts and the eventual triumphs are all recorded with real pleasure. It allows a space in which aspects of masculinity can be elaborated through the nuances of football: loyalty, brotherhood, collective responsibilities, status, and, of course, when things don't go well a man has to live with his own and his team's failures. It can be an uncomfortable and fraught space.

Football offers status through performance validated by other men and the chance to win and carry off the prizes in one very important area of life. It is part of the cultural politics of 'race' in Britain today and it is a politics deeply rooted in masculinity. The discourses on masculinity developed through the discussion of football and its history are also displayed when the men appear in the pub limping or on crutches with a variety of knee and leg injuries which are shown off with some pride like battle wounds. Injuries are recognized as the consequences of an active involvement with the game, as part of some daring play the effects of which can now be displayed and even celebrated.

The discourses on physicality, dexterity, and abilities in the game are linked for black players not just to 'manliness' and 'vigour' *per se*, but to loyalty and support. Supporters are important; 'It makes you feel good to have a big crowd with you' because the men generally expect the 'refs' to regard them differently from white players and it's important to have support on the sidelines when

[69]

appeals are being made. Later, the game is dissected in the pub, where missed chances and poor play are part of the analysis and lack of effort is judged, but not in public. Loyalty to the team is demanded, so when white teams try to poach individual black players, offering financial incentives to them to play in the higher leagues, the individual player is faced with a dilemma. There is also the political point that black players and supporters want access to the higher leagues for black teams not just for individual players.

The collective response from teams does not mean that individual performance is not rewarded. There are stars within the local teams and it is important to a man to be a good football player. But football is not seen simply as a display of physical abilities and therefore, as tied to the body. Thus when I talked to the men about what makes a good footballer the replies were swift and concentrated on 'vision'. Darren said: 'A good footballer has got to have vision. He's got to have ideas in his head and be able to read the game. Football is an easy game. The ball does the work for you but you have to have it in the head and in the feet.' It is not necessarily easy to articulate this passion for football; as Dev said: 'I can't explain football, deep satisfaction when I know I have played well and when we lose I am so miserable I keep going over it. There are bad losers and bad losers! But you've got to accept the losses. It's part of the game. You can't win every time.'

What is important to the politics of football in the teams that I know, however, is the relations between Asians and Afro-Caribbeans who play together in these teams, a legacy of the youth project teams. The men were very proud of their multi-ethnic teams, contrasting their teams with specifically Asian or Afro-Caribbean teams. In fact, their 'black' teams have created problems for them within black football. The Sikh festival tournaments declared that they were Indian events but the city teams that went to play had both Indian and Afro-Caribbean players and at one tournament in Coventry the officials wanted to disqualify the city team on the grounds that it was not an Indian team. The team would not compromise and eventually took the case to the FA who ruled that they could play a joint team which is what they now do. Their loyalty to each other and to the politics of forging a black identity from Asians and Afro-Caribbeans did not waver and they now play as they have always done, as a team of Asians and Afro-Caribbeans.

[70]

Players who do not perform well in the team are dropped and football managers exercise a ruthless power over the fate of men who are their friends. But their decisions are also public and subject to examination and analysis by the other men, who are not slow to offer advice and counsel the mangers of the teams about their players and their tactics. A good manager is one 'who can motivate the team and who has vision. He can develop tactics and determine strategies and in training he points out where they are going wrong. A manager has to be ruthless too, but fair with no favourites. He has to make the right decisions', said Luke when we were discussing managers. Thus, the manager is bound to the fate of his team and bears a large responsibility for them. He demonstrates his power through the players he can attract and keep and through their appraisal of him. As one of the managers said, 'Football is all about politics'.

It is a politics rooted in the cultures of resistance that have developed as part of the urban black experience in Britain. There is a collective mobilization through football that calls up black masculinities as part of the resistances that black men generate against the racisms of British society and by which they validate each other. It is a male space; women are not involved but the world of family and home is often present on warm days when the men bring babies and toddlers to the matches, caring for them while they watch the game and demonstrating as they do that even within the male world of football men too can call up very different black masculinities from those associated with the machismo world of the football pitch. The juxtaposition is an important visual reminder of the varieties of black masculinities and our understanding of them as shifting terrain.

Note

This paper would not have been possible without the generous support of the men whose lives are presented here. My warmest thanks to them all but especially to: Rashpal, Scratch, Ajit, Daljit, Hari, Burgess, Stuart, Trevor, Nittin, Yogi, Archie, and Raj. Thanks also to Ali Rattansi for reading and commenting on an earlier draft of this paper and to Dorothy Brydges for typing the paper.

[71]

CHAPTER 5

Men's power in organizations: 'equal opportunities' intervenes

CYNTHIA COCKBURN

King Kong was a rarity – and short-lived. The truly powerful hold power not individually but by means of organization and in organizations. This is how the power of class is exerted – in capitalist enterprises, armies, political parties, families. Power, however, has more than one face, and the powerful exercise their power in many different sets of interactions. Men wield power as men, and white people as such. The effects and the means are both individual and institutional. The situation that is produced is often called 'inequality', a term that does not sound too harsh to the ear in liberal society and seems to imply that people are stacked above and beneath each other in layers. It is a premiss of what follows, however, that inequality in organizations is at root a matter of dynamic relations of power.

During the 1980s many companies, public authorities, and other institutions have declared themselves 'equal opportunities employers'. They were prompted by the Sex Discrimination Act 1975 and the Race Relations Act 1976 and by the women's movement and anti-racist movement of that decade. Many activists entered the structures of politics and employment in the late 1970s and early 1980s. A few years of 'equal opps' effort then led to self-congratulation by some employers, disillusion on the part of many activists.

[72]

The purpose of this paper is to explore what the equal opportunities experience adds to our understanding of organizations. Equal opportunities (EO) invokes a system of organizational power that is, first, complex, with multiple sources and multiple effects (the subordination of women and ethnic 'minorities', for instance, as well as working-class groups). Second, it reveals organizational power as interacting with power systems lying outside the immediate structure of the organization. And, third, outcomes clearly result from an interaction between individuals (constituted only in part through work) and the structure and processes of the organization. I will examine some of the ways a white male power system reproduces itself over time, resisting interruption by equal opportunities strategies, and end with some thoughts about what seem to be some of the necessary conditions for EO to be a significant challenge to the power systems within organizations. I will draw on my own current research into the responses of managers and managed to 'positive action' for 'equality'.[1]

Whether you felt EO policies were 'succeeding' depended on what you held the aim to have been. The nature of managers' aims for EO depends partly on their role in the organization. Thus managers responsible for developing labour-market policies may favour more 'mothers' privileges' to attract women to remain at work or come back after having children; those concerned with selling, PR, or advertising may welcome women and black people in visible roles to encourage the black/female client; company lawyers may be concerned with keeping the enterprise within the discrimination law. Managers also vary, however, according to individual orientation: some male managers are frankly misogynist, for instance, while others are genuinely seeking a new kind of relationship with women and each other.

Among the targeted groups of EO besides are many different 'wish lists'. Some women, black and white, and some black men, would rather integrate and become invisible in the organization; others see self-identification as necessary to challenging power. Some want to see positive measures taken to change the balance of power; others deplore positive action because it sounds like favouritism.

In the course of the research I have come to feel that it is fruitless to categorize approaches to equal opportunities or to pose 'liberal' against 'radical' versions of EO as right or wrong. It is more helpful

[73]

to see equal opportunities as having an agenda of shorter or greater length.[2] At its shortest it may be no more than technicalities of recruitment processes. These may (depending on other factors) be useful steps towards change, or a damaging attempt to sanitize and contain the movement. At its longest, however, the equal opportunities agenda aspires to be a project for the transformation of power relations in organizations. The transformational project, while it necessarily includes access of more individuals of disadvantaged groups to positions of relative advantage, is not only about quantity. It is also qualitative, proposing the restructuring and resocializing of the organization, its purpose, and its behaviour. It is those who espoused the long agenda that have been most disappointed with the results to date.

'Equal opportunities' as a transformative project

What evidence is there that equal opportunities may be seen in such a progressive light? After all, its many failures have brought the very term into ill-repute among feminists and black activists. A few examples may help. First, in the area of positive action for sex equality, some employing organizations today (encouraged by standards emanating from the European Community) are offering fathers new leave provisions: paternity leave on childbirth, the right to share in the non-statutory element of maternity leave, family leave to look after sick dependants, career breaks, and part-time or job-sharing possibilities. The incidence of childbirth has always produced wildly diverging career paths for women and men. If the new provisions were to become genuine expectations on men, and if they were acted upon, this would produce a fundamental change in both the relationship of work to home and of men to organizations and careers.

'Equal pay for work of equal value', too, is a potentially transformative goal. It implies a change in what values are held to be important in an organization. Men's and women's traditional skills are not just any old categories; they are precisely to do with, on the one hand, physical strength, materials, and machinery; on the other with people, relationships, and care.

Evidence also arises in many individual women's aspirations for

EO. Frequently women I have interviewed have expressed the
hope that women entering management 'would not become surro-
gate men', would 'do things differently from men'. There is clearly
some idea here that women will not step into power without
problematizing it and modifying it. There is an implicit belief that
women's past experience has produced in them different values and
ways of doing things, that there is an interaction between the
individual and the structure or processes of the organization, and
that women as individuals can change the way power is wielded.

Many women and black people of both sexes are cautious or
even outright opposed on the question of 'positive action': special
training courses for disadvantaged groups, 'targeting' for certain
increased percentages in certain grades. This opposition to a purely
quantitative project at one level appears retrograde – for positive
measures are needed. But I believe it has to be seen as the product of
a contradiction. For women, black and white, not only want better
jobs, they also want better organizations. They fear it would be a
backwards step to acquire promotion by means that appear to make
the organization less 'fair'.

There is again a quantitative and qualitative issue in positive
action on ethnicity. Beyond recruiting higher percentages of employees of ethnic 'minorities', EO can also be about breaking the
white monoculture. In one organization where I made a case study
agreement had been won for Muslims to adapt their working hours
on a Friday to allow religious observance; in another Hindus had
become a majority of the staff and Diwali was celebrated as
wholeheartedly as Christmas.

Some organizations have adopted an equality policy for lesbians
and gay men. This seems to me to be purely and most significantly
a qualitative and transformative strategy. There has never been any
question of targeting homosexuals in terms of numbers. The
project is about nothing if not breaking down heterosexist culture
to enable gay people to identify themselves without disadvantage
or discomfort. It aims to expose the links between heterosexism
and male power.

A further clause in most equality policies concerns disability.
When equality for people with disabilities is taken seriously it can
modify the very definition of what is 'fit for work', substituting a
concept of 'work fit for people'. It extends to a broadly defined
policy on health and safety at work for everyone. It is especially

[75]

relevant to women who, after all, are considered for many purposes to be physically 'less fit' workers than men. It should invoke the issue of male career stress and burn-out.

Finally, at their best and unfortunately not often enough, equality strategies for disadvantaged groups are associated with class strategies. Some activists stress that all EO measures should benefit women in the lowest ranks as well as the high-flyers. But more, an EO policy may be associated with a levelling approach to grade and pay structure. This is the case for instance in some trade unions, including the National Union of Public Employees.

Some equality officers are quite conscious in adopting transformative goals. Thus one EO manager from a private-sector firm told me: 'I'm a socialist and a feminist. I believe in equality as such and my feminism is very much bound up with that.' She was not naive about how much or how fast it would be possible to change a capitalist enterprise:

> I was under no illusion as to the ethos and values that would pertain. But in spite of that, and knowing the danger equal opps might be an exercise co-opted to management interests, I felt it was important to address it the way I would have wanted in an ideal organization . . . that I shouldn't be fettered by what I knew the organization to be.

Power and its reproduction

An approach of this kind, equal opportunities at its longest agenda, clearly raises questions of *power*. The natural place to look for an understanding of power in organizations is that extensive body of work known as 'organization theory'. Unfortunately, however, conventional organization theory has almost all been devised from the point of view of those whose role is to control organizations – owners and managers. It has, besides, almost completely neglected issues of gender and race. To take just one example among many, Henry Mintzberg's authoritative and comprehensive *Power in and around Organisations* (1983) exhaustively categorizes and discusses the source and use of power in organizations without a single reference in the index to men, women, sex, or gender. By contrast, the power brought to view by equal opportunities strategies is a power which is complex and multi-faceted. It is not only managerial power over the managed. It is not even just class power – the power of owners of the means of production over those whose labour power they purchase. It is also male power through which men as a group dominate women economically, socially and sexually. And it is systemic white domination over people variously defined as black, of 'minority' ethnicity etc.

Conventional organization theory seldom considers the power within organizations, the power exemplified by top management, as an expression of power relations external to the organization. Hearn and Parkin (1983) have pointed out that critical organization theory in the Marxist tradition, while it does recognize the movement of (class) power across organizational boundaries, does not recognize the societal power systems of race and sex. Patriarchy is not one of its categories.[3]

The extraordinarily prolific literature of organization theory, which has been overwhelmingly the work of men, is thus unable to answer questions such as: how do class power and male power interact? how is such a complex power system reproduced over time? how is power reproduced both as lying in the same hands, and as the same kind of power – unshared (for instance), absolute, or arbitrary? It cannot analyse the varied forms of domination lived by working people who have many identities in addition to that of employee. Yet this multiplicity of identity becomes very clear the moment one listens to members of the disadvantaged groups speaking of their experience and needs.

Equal opportunities raises a further question about organizations: what is the relationship of individual attitudes, ideologies, and intentions to organizational structure and processes? Interviewing more than a hundred men I found many (but by no means all) expressing sentiments that imply resentment of women having sustained careers, being favoured by EO, and competing with men for professional and managerial jobs. Many (but again not all) white people show some prejudice against or distancing from people of ethnic 'minorities'. There is a profound and widespread dislike of homosexuality. (The disabled escape this hostility at the cost of neglect.) A thousand colourful quotations could be inserted here. Detailed evidence, however, is not the point. The question is: what is the relationship to actual institutional outcomes of this welter of ideas, some progressive and for change, others retrogressive and opposed to change on the part of the individual 'bearers' of the relations of power?

To try to get some purchase on the interaction between class and gender power (to limit ourselves here to just two facets of complex organizational power), and between individual agency and organizational behaviour, I will isolate a handful of processes that seem, from my observation of workplaces, to be among those that serve the reproduction of male power within a capitalist organization. These particular instances – which will be familiar to EO activists in many other organizations – are drawn from a large British private-sector retail firm with a chain of high-street stores and a network of distribution centres.

The first three illustrate male power interests apparently riding on or expressed through responses to economic (mode of production) phenomena, with the effect of subverting the EO policy and holding it to its shortest agenda.

(1) The 'main aim'

When raising questions of equality among white male managers I have met with a continuous reiteration of what I have come to call 'the main aim': what the organization is 'really here to do'. In the public sector it may be 'to run a cost-efficient service'. In business 'the bottom line' (a phrase in common use) is specified as profit. A transformative approach to EO of course proposes a deflection of resources either above the bottom line (as additional costs of production) or below it (diversion of profits) to improving the situation of disadvantaged groups.

In the retail firm in question a tussle had occurred between cost-conscious top management on the one hand, and on the other a socially-conscious board member in alliance with the company's EO manager, in which the EO principle competed with the 'main aim' over how much would be spent on extending maternity provision. Would the new generous leave provision be for all women, down to the lowest-paid manual worker or would it be for the middle and senior management grades in which the company had invested training? The cost difference was £300,000 a year. The 'main aim' won out. It was particularly ironical since the company prided itself on working with and in the community and on promoting 'the family' as 'this most important and fundamental unit of British society' through various sponsored events.

(2)   Autonomous labour market policy

A second mechanism is a detaching of EO from other company policies, to the detriment of the former. In this firm, while the EO activists and supportive managers had included in the code of practice the phrase 'we aim to benefit a wider workforce', the company was none the less meanwhile developing employment policies that seemed to be diminishing the chances of the local female manual and clerical labour force faster than EO could ever hope to improve them. There had been large-scale redundancies. It was anticipated that computer technology would reduce the demand for relatively unskilled labour yet more in coming years. There had been a strong move to part-time working in the interests of flexibility and productivity. Though some steps had been taken to harmonize the conditions of part-timers, they were still disadvantaged in pro-rata pay rates and excluded from the pension scheme. As one personnel manager put it, 'the biggest benefit you could give to women in the company would be to treat part-timers equally with full-timers'. There had been a significant move towards shift-working, to cover more efficiently the peak shopping hours. Finally there was a growing preference for temporary contracts. It is particularly ironical that the slowly increasing numbers of ethnic 'minority' employees were found most in jobs that symbolize the deterioration of terms and conditions: Saturday work in shops is an example.

These trends were of course not exclusive to the company.[4] The company was responding to developments in the economy. But when we add to them the fact that the equality principle had brought about, among other things, a recruitment of men into some 'female' jobs at the populous base of the firm, overall losses in job opportunities, security, and pay to the manual working women of this catchment area may well have been greater than the gains through EO.

(3)   The evasiveness of power

Power sometimes changes its location as women reach for it. Often women are given access to precisely the locations from which the real significance has recently leached away.[5] The instance of the store manager in the retail firm may stand as an example.

At one time it had been inconceivable in this firm that a woman could do the job of store manager. The former director had wanted

[79]

'pairs of trousers' on the retail floor. Even after the Sex Discrimination Act 1975 there had been an unofficial quota limiting women to 25% of store-manager recruits to this firm. In those days the store manager's job was the classic route to power. The executive committee comprised almost entirely ex-store managers who formed in effect a company elite. Recruitment to store management was considered important enough to be handled in head office.

By 1988, following positive action measures, 12% of store managers and 50% of trainees for this post were female. There were however fewer ex-store managers in top jobs in the firm and recruitment had been regionalized. The attitude to store management had changed. It was now acceptable that some managers settle in for long periods at that level. There was a move towards a new kind of smaller, more specialized highstreet store, to supplement the big department stores. While some progressive personnel managers saw the management of these mini-stores as a great new opportunity for women (which in a sense it was) others saw women's value as lying precisely in the fact that they were less likely to be ambitious, more willing to stay at this level and not crowd the promotion ladder.

Individual intentionality here was pushing and pulling; the company was responding to pressures of change in the retail trade; internal practices were modified; women were making short-term or local gains; but the significance of the gains was being simultaneously undercut.

In addition, this company like many others had been developing a crucially important computer facility. There had been a shift of power from the traditional, functional departments to the computer-controlling areas and staff, on whose skills the company was now very dependent. While women's numbers were increasing on the buying and merchandising side, it was in the computer division that, despite EO efforts, women were worst represented. The impulse here was economic and largely external to the firm, but the internal effects were gendered.

The remainder of the mechanisms I will describe are instances in which male power acts through culture and hence more clearly through individual men in relation to each other and to individual women. The first, however, has economic underpinnings, as I will show.

[80]

(4)   Leaving domestic ties to women

Improved maternity provision, brought about by EO activism, had brought about new possibilities, as described above, for men to respond to domestic ties, particularly those of parenting. Men I had found already ambivalent towards the new generosity of provision for women with children. On the one hand they felt it was 'fair enough', women should be helped to handle their double load. On the other they felt annoyed at the problems maternity leave and family leave created for them as managers with a task to administer or as colleagues inconvenienced by absent women staff. As to men themselves taking more responsibility for children and home life, however, here men were clearly united. Though they would certainly not say no to a few days off for a new baby, especially if this were to be provided as of right, there were very few men who would seriously consider taking a long 'paternity suspense' or career break to raise children.

The economic argument produced first and foremost to legitimate such a refusal was that men normally earn higher salaries than their female partners and that the family unit as a whole would suffer from such a choice. Other, more cultural, reasons were however introduced to buttress this case. Women's 'natural motherliness' was invoked. Some men said honestly that they were disinclined to prioritize home over work.

The effect however was the same. Men showed no signs of treating their careers as interruptible. Senior managers were certainly not encouraging junior males to do so. While this was so, however generous the maternity conditions, women would continue to compete, one hand tied behind them, with men both of whose hands were free to keep hold of power at work.[6] Paternity leave was a case of a provision being agreed by male managers under pressure from EO activists, implemented sketchily, and systematically ignored by the supposed beneficiaries whose individual ideas remained unchanged.

(5)   Defining when difference is legitimate

I met rather few men who approved of the idea of single-sex activity by women, or self-organized activity by ethnic groups. It was criticized as divisive, as 'us and them' behaviour. EO is often turned around: 'If you want to be equal you can't say you're different.' In fact of course many things in company life point to women as being different from men, even construct the difference, and the company gains by this difference.

For a start, there is a profound sexual division of labour which will take more than a few years of EO to dissipate. Women's traditional skills, used to advantage by the firm as throughout the economy, and relatively underpaid, are the basis of many of the key production and service functions of the firm. There are, besides, rigid dress codes. Trousers are not held to be appropriate dress for women in the company's shops and offices. Skirts and high heels are the convention. The acceptable style is feminine and neat, though it may be colourful. For men it is smart and universally grey: the standard suit, collar, and tie.[7]

Men socialize more with each other than they do with women colleagues. There is, for instance, an all-male golf society and many of the other sports and social activities are sites of male bonding activity.[8] As well as strengthening masculine culture, to which women are marginal or subordinate, they are a practical source of information and contacts. Yet when women, encouraged by the EO manager, called just one women-only meeting for women managers, the reaction by men was so negative that the chief executive felt obliged to order that it be held off-premises and out of office hours. Here top management, responding to individual men's feelings, deflected a proposed new institutional practice. And those feelings also acted directly to curb women's self-expression.

By such means an atmosphere had been generated in the firm in which women felt unable to consider dispassionately what they might gain from a supportive identity grouping, a little autonomy, a modicum of self-organization. What first sprang to mind always was the backlash that would ensue. What would the men say? Assimilation and invisibility for black people and for gays, too, is the price of white acceptance in the firm. Without self-organization of course there can be no social movement, no countervailing power. And EO remains safely within the frame of something given, not demanded.

(6) Organization sexuality
There is a regime of organization sexuality, actuated in dress, in social and interpersonal relations, and in work roles within the gender/sexual division of labour that contributes to the retention of power by men.[9] This mechanism works by asserting that women

[82]

are equally active partners in and equal beneficiaries of heterosexual sexuality. It obscures the fact that the asymmetry of power between men and women renders sexuality itself a factor in women's subordination. This is not to say that women themselves do not want to be sexual and to live and work in a sexualized environment. Most would ideally wish to do so. But the gender relations in which we are embedded ensure that we can seldom do so on terms that do not disadvantage us.[10]

The sexual regime also took two forms in the head office of this retail firm. One form was controlled by the traditionalist men. They were at best gentlemanly, at worst saw women as fitted only for kitchen and nursery. These men were puzzled by the ambitious and successful new women at work. They put down and marginalized those they could and were resentful of those they could not.

It was often said in the company that sexism and racism would die out naturally with the departure of such traditionalists. It seemed, however, that an alternative was replacing them, an inhospitable regime controlled by the newer modernist men, the technocrats and executives. Here the ideology was sexually 'liberated'. To be 'equal' women must tolerate, join in, and be prepared to retaliate in kind when sexual innuendo and jokes, the stock in trade of modern management, were deployed around them. Women were seen as spoilsports if they complained. While the old culture lodged in the ancient strongholds of buying and merchandising, sales and distribution, the new culture found a natural home in the new-style subdivisions of the firm: computers, public relations, design. Women may be good at their jobs, but socially they are continually wrong-footed by such a sexualized culture. To participate in power needs skill with a two-edged sword, for women find sexual dressing, sexualized behaviour, and repartee damaging to use.

The culture in question is of course not only objectifying of women, it is both implicitly and explicitly anti-homosexual. Men bond with each other by using women as symbolic, humour-laden material in their masculine discourse.[11] Since, however, there is always a danger of misconstruction of male closeness, proper patriarchal bonding must always assert heterosexuality and constitute the homosexual, as well as the woman, as 'other'. Women (both heterosexual and lesbian) and gay men thus have a common

[83]

cause in resisting the taken-for-granted heterosexist sexualization of workplace culture (Harrison 1985). Unfortunately many women do not recognize this commonalty.

(7) Shaping women's consciousness

Some controlling mechanisms are purely cultural and operate only at the level of individual and group, without institutionalization in the organization's rules and procedures. The following is an example. Most of the women managers I interviewed in the retail first were assertive of women's strengths, aware of women's disadvantage, and had many observations as to how the system worked to the gain of men. They liked working for an EO employer but they did not like to think they owed their advancement in any way to EO.

Yet it was women more often than men who made reference to the 'terrible jobs' of some women manual workers in the firm, the ghetto in which secretaries were 'stuck', and the 'rudeness' of some males to their inferiors. They felt women should try not to become like men as they climbed the ladder, but should continue to do things 'their own way'. Women were seen as having more common sense, being more efficient and practical, paying more attention to detail than men. Besides, 'women are more fun', women are 'more sensitive to people's needs', 'women have a third dimension'. Many women disliked the competitive games men play at work. So there was a latent project here for changing men and the way men wield power in organizations. They recognized that women are not all alike, yet they had the hunch that with more women at the top it could be 'different and *better*, yes'.

Yet also and overwhelmingly these women were not or said they were not feminists. To understand this we have to see what men were saying about feminism. I met few men in the company who did not use the term in a frankly pejorative way. Some felt, yes, there were a few 'feminists' in the firm and they were notable mainly for carping about minor details of behaviour (rejecting little courtesies). Such feminists were distinguished from the great majority of 'reasonable' women. 'Women's libbers' out there were portrayed as harsh, strident, demanding, uptight, aggressive, vociferous, dogmatic, radical, and overly ambitious. They 'can't take a joke', and they are zealots who wear crusading badges. The term feminism was commonly associated by men (and by women)

[84]

with being 'anti-men', with 'lesbianism', 'loony leftism', and 'extremism'.

Though women must ultimately bear responsibility for their own ideology and politics, the anti-feminist discourse of men has to be seen as a policing of women's consciousness and an important mechanism in the reproduction of male power.

Individual and organization

These few examples are a reminder that the theorizing of the equal opportunities project calls for an understanding of power as multi-faceted and complex, and as spanning organizational boundaries. The specific relationship of manager and managed may lie wholly within the organization, but it is graphically clear that the oppressions of race, sex, and class do not. The individual oppressed and the individual oppressor move in and out of the workplace carrying much of their power and powerlessness with them. Understanding EO, as the above instances have demonstrated, also enforces a concern with the relationship between individual agency and organizational structure. The powerful act both face to face as individuals (with a passing sneer about homosexuality, for instance), and through systemic processes (stacking recruitment interviewing panels with white men).

In this connection it is interesting to return to what is probably the most reputed theoretical work on the position of women in organizations, Rosabeth Moss Kanter's study of the corporation she called Indsco (Kanter 1977). *Men and Women of the Corporation* is a meticulous observation and analysis of power relations within an organization, focusing in particular on the relationship between managers and secretaries. Kanter discusses our very questions: the 'forces which lead the men who manage to reproduce themselves in kind; and the reasons for conformity pressures on managers'. Her answer, however, is that the causes lie uniquely in the structuring of the organization. What accounts for seeming 'sex differences' is the structure of relative power and opportunity. The 'problem of women and leadership' reveals itself as product of the bureaucratic structure that traps some people in 'downward spirals of ineffectiveness'.

For Kanter it is because of occupational sex segregation that men and women behave as they do. Thus women become parochial, timid and praise-addicted because their secretarial status is one of contingency, principled arbitrariness and fealty. Isolated men working in all-female situations she sees as experiencing just the same stresses and adopting the same strategies as 'token' women in male fields. My own research by contrast shows these situations to be asymmetrical, due to the different social value given to men and women, and to men's and women's work (Cockburn 1987).

In Kanter's study, while men's damaging attitudes to women are starkly demonstrated, men are seen as behaving as they do because of the nature of the organization they inhabit and their niche within it. Curiously absent is any sense that men and women are locked, indeed formed, in an unequal gender order that spans not only work but childhood, sexual intercourse, domesticity, street culture, leisure, and public life. There is no sense of how the organization historically came to take the damaging form it did. No sense of how white, heterosexual men come to be (as a group) at the top and to stay there, defining the organization's purpose, structure and procedures. Thus while Kanter's analysis appears at first as a progressive and helpful rescue of women from the charge of 'being their own worst enemies', it ends by letting individual men and systemic male power, a historic and society-wide project of control over women, off the hook of theory. In truth, I would argue, the societal gender order and society-wide systems of racial domination penetrate the workplace where individuals act as vectors of power across the boundaries between the organization and the outside world and to which individuals bring their own ideas, partly though not entirely generated outside the workplace, to influence organizational outcomes.

Organization theory has long suffered from a difficulty in bringing into a single analysis both phenomena at the systemic level and individual attitudes and intentionality. Structuralism and systems theory, the dominant paradigm this last twenty-five years, has neglected individual agency, without which sex and race issues cannot be understood. When counter-theories have recognized individual intentionality – and here David Silverman's well-known *The Theory of Organisations* may serve as an example – structure has tended to escape from view (Silverman 1970).

Silverman's approach none the less prepares an ideal opening for the insertion of EO. Thus he says:

[86]

an organization itself is the outcome of the interaction of motivated people attempting to resolve their own problems ... the environment in which an organization is located might usefully be regarded as a source of meanings through which members defined their actions and made sense of the actions of others.

This is clearly directly applicable to the issue of men and male power in organizations. Indeed he could be addressing 'positive action' policies when he suggests there is a negative correlation between the possibility of 'changing the rules of the game', and the 'attachment of actors to them'. In reality this work was written before equal opportunities policies came about and is blind to both gender and race. And structure, the systematization of power, is under-emphasized.

It has been from outside the theory of organization and management, in social theory, that the most sustained attempts have come to formulate the interaction between structure and individual intentionality. Anthony Giddens, in his 'structuration theory', for instance, proposes that:

structure is not as such external to human action, and is not identified solely with constraint. Structure is both the medium and the outcome of the human activities which it recursively organizes. Institutions, or large-scale societies, have structural properties in virtue of the continuity of the actions of their component members. But those members of society are only able to carry out their day-to-day activities in virtue of their capability of instantiating those structural properties. (Giddens 1987, p. 61).

This formulation seems a good beginning for understanding the way power generated in one institution can bear on another (the family on the enterprise, immigration law on the school), and the way individuals give power to and take power from institutional processes. It is interesting that R. W. Connell in his essay on gender and power, despite criticisms, commented of Giddens' structuration theory that it is 'of all current frameworks for social theory, the closest to the requirements for a theory of gender' (Connell 1987, p. 94).

[87]

There are a number of conclusions to be drawn from this discussion for transformative equal opportunities strategy. In our practice we should not simply substitute the concept of a male power system for that of a class power system, but should be ready to deal with power as faceted and complex. It is clear that to take on its transformative task EO needs to link, conceptually and practically, sex, race, homosexuality, and disability with each other and with class concerns, and thus with trade unionism. It needs to devote energy to encouraging self-identification and organization among disadvantaged groups within the organization and to forming alliances between them on a broad agenda for change. It needs a sense of interaction with the outside world, through the lives of organization members (home and work), through social movements (feminism, anti-racism), and through the organization's dealings with its clients (not just EO for employees but responsibilities inherent in its services, marketing policies etc.).

One particular thought, however, emerges from the discussion of agency and structure. It has become a working rule of thumb in most EO practice that it is 'changing procedures and practices that counts'. Changed attitudes, ideas, feelings may follow – if not *tant pis*. This conventional wisdom has resulted from many bad experiences with 'awareness training' that has been easily trashed and has alienated more people than it has won over. It is widely understood that the reason for the slow pace and the many reverses of EO is that individual resistance, subterranean though it may be, lives on and blocks change. If gender and race oppression have their being as much outside as inside the organization, and if individual agency is effective on and in organizations, surely we cannot avoid in the long run addressing the problem of changing consciousness, which essentially means winning defectors from power systems.

Notes

1 The project 'Men's responses to positive action for sex equality' is currently funded by the Economic and Social Research Council and located at the City University, London, where the author is a Senior Research Fellow in Sociology. The research involves case studies in a private-sector retail firm, a government department, a local authority, and a trade union.

[88]

2 I put forward this idea in an article, 'Equal opportunities: the short and long agenda', *Industrial Relations Journal*, Autumn 1989. The article threw doubt on the popular categorization of EO strategies as either 'liberal' or 'radical'.

3 The socialist-feminist debate on the relationship of the mode of production and patriarchy, or the male-dominated sex/gender system, was well-represented in the two collections, Eisenstein 1979 and Sargent 1981. Two significant subsequent contributions focusing on class and sex relations in the workplace are Walby 1986 and Hearn 1987.

4 Jenson *et al.* (1988) contains several discussions of trends in employment practice and their significance for women.

5 Karen Legge (1987) in her study of personnel management found that when women gain power within an occupation it is because the occupation itself has yet to become significant, or because it is losing significance.

6 It is important to remember how much the 'public profile of men is shaped by their relation to the private' as pointed out by Siltanen & Stanworth (1984, p. 196).

7 Hearn & Parkin (1987, p. 107) suggest that dress and appearance at work 'are both obvious and subtle, such that the categories of "women" and "men" are to a large extent made visible and sustained through them'.

8 On male bonding and the taboo against unbonding see Hey 1986. Rogers (1988, p. vii) in her study of male social organization says of pubs, social drinking, and the world of sport: 'It is important to understand just how well organized they are as men's areas in an ostensibly integrated culture ... they are the visible end of a largely invisible men-only subculture.'

9 Hearn & Parkin (1987) explore this theme in detail.

10 'The problems arise when men and women cannot put sexuality aside in an inappropriate context and when sex is used as a proxy for power' (Epstein 1983, p. 296).

11 See this phenomenon among skilled male print workers in Cockburn 1983.

Part 2

SEXUALITIES

CHAPTER 6

After fifteen years: the impact of the sociology of masculinity on the masculinity of sociology[1]

MICHAEL KIMMEL

It's been thirty-five years since Simone de Beauvoir's *The Second Sex*, and twenty-five years since Betty Friedan's *The Feminine Mystique*, announced the rebirth of modern feminism, transforming the 'woman problem' into a problem of the systematic denial to women of equal rights in the public sphere and consignment to a devalued private sphere. These and other texts noted how women-as-other not only marked women as gendered beings, but made gender invisible to men. That which privileges us is rendered invisible by the very process that constructs that privilege.

It's been fifteen years since male Anglophones became aware that we have a gender also. For those of us trained in the social sciences, the appearance of Pleck and Sawyer's *Men and Masculinity* (1974) and Brannon and David's *49% Majority* (1976) signalled the problematization of masculinity. In literary circles, contemporaneous popular books by Marc Fasteau, Warren Farrell (the *early* Warren Farrell), and Herb Goldberg all saw, with varying degrees of political sensitivity to feminism, the dilemmas, hazards, or problems of growing up male in a society based on male domination.

My own clue that feminist thinking about gender and sexuality had anything to do with me came ten years ago, when I was teaching at the University of California at Santa Cruz. I sat in on a seminar in feminist theory taught by Donna Haraway, an extraordinary historian of science, in the History of Consciousness Program. In one session, I witnessed a confrontation between a white woman and a black woman. Their argument centred around the question of whether their similarities as women were greater than their racial differences. The white woman asserted that the fact that they were both women bonded them, despite racial differences. They shared a common oppression as women, and were both 'sisters under the skin'. The black woman disagreed.

'When you wake up in the morning and look in a mirror, what do you see?' she asked.

'I see a woman', replied the white woman hopefully.

'That's precisely the problem', replied the black woman. 'I see a black woman. For me race is visible every minute of every day, because it is how I am *not* privileged in this culture. Race is invisible to you which is why our alliance will always feel false and strained to me.'

When I heard this, I was startled. For when I looked in the mirror, I thought I saw a 'human being', a generic person, universally generalizable. What had been concealed – race, and gender, and class – was suddenly visible. As a middle-class white man, I was able to not think about the ways in which class and race and gender had shaped my existence. Marginality is visible, and painfully visceral. Privilege is invisible, and painlessly pleasant.

As a sociologist, I soon became aware of the ways in which our discipline was, in part, responsible for the reproduction of gender relations, a set of relations that kept masculinity invisible and rendered femininity problematic. Many social scientists still rely on biological models of sex, as if hormonal balances, reproductive biological organization, or physical maturation contained a kind of theological immanence, an inherent and inevitable will to manifest itself in the world. Biological arguments maintain a privileged status in academic research about both gender and sexuality but, like all science, they help us understand cross-cultural regularities in behaviour and attitudes, but cannot take us very far in understanding cultural variations.

And much social science research has been mired in tired formulations of 'sex roles,' those fixed, ahistorical containers of attributes and behaviours that are said to refer to masculinity and femininity. Biological males and biological females are sorted into these containers, where they are *socialized* into adopting the behaviours and attitudes appropriate to their gender.

The sex role model departs from biological models in its emphasis on the *acquisition* of gender characteristics rather than their *emergence* from a biological imperative. But both assume a functionalist teleology that suggests that what exists is supposed to exist as a result of biological or cultural evolution. Thus relationships based on power – i.e., the power of men over women, or the power of heterosexuals over homosexuals – are seen as inevitable and 'natural', subject to neither challenge nor change. That which is *normative* – constructed and enforced through social sanctions and socialization – begins to appear as *normal*, designed by nature acting through culture. But this is a sleight of hand: the normative is not normal, but the result of a long and complex set of social conflicts among groups. 'It is precisely through the process of making a power situation appear as a fact in the nature of the world that traditional authority works', writes anthropologist Maurice Bloch. By minimizing the historical variability of masculinity and femininity, both models minimize the capacity to change.

As social science researchers, so too as graduate instructors or administrators. As researchers, we often have acted as if our own gender had nothing to do with our work, and treated male scientists as if their being men had nothing to do with the organization of their experiments, the logic of scientific inquiry, or the questions posed by science itself. And yet when blacks, or women, or gays and lesbians do research on blacks, on women, on gays and lesbians we wonder how come they can't think about anything else. We assume that their areas of interest in sociology will centre on these topics; so that for years sex roles and marriage and the family were the 'ladies' auxiliary' of sociology. Only straight white men get to do abstract, universally generalizable science. But it's no more 'objective' and no less 'political' that what marginalized groups do; only that the politics and subjectivity are invisible, embedded in the structure of the work itself.

There's another reason why gender is invisible to men: it serves

[95]

us. Men benefit from the inherited biological or sex-role definitions of masculinity, which implies activity, mastery, rationality, competence. If gender relations are encoded in our genes or culturally mandated, then the extent to which these definitions are based on men's power over women is obscured. Feminism enabled us to see the sleight of hand that substitutes 'normal' for normative. And if we understand today the centrality of gender as an organizing principle of social life, it is because feminist-inspired research and politics has demanded that we do so. In fact, I will argue that the extent to which we are aware of the centrality of gender is directly proportional to the efforts of feminist researchers to politicize the debates.

Fifteen years ago, male social scientists finally realized that we had a gender, and that masculinity could be constructed as a problematic from within a feminist framework. In those early works, however, the other dimensions of division, the other mechanisms of oppression, were conveniently obscured or ignored. Those early works generalized from a white, middle-class, heterosexual masculinity so that *that* masculinity was cast as normative and individual experiences were measured against that construction. Masculinities constructed by non-whites, working-class, gay, or ethnic men were problematized as non-traditional and non-conforming. In a sense, we reproduced the hegemonic construction of 'woman' that had been embraced by white, middle-class women in the late 1970s.

Happily, in the past few years, we've gone beyond that. We've begun to understand that the construction of masculinity contains a political dynamic, a dynamic of power, by which 'the other' is created and subordinated. And we've expanded our understanding of gender relations as a power dynamic to include non-normative masculinities. The constitution of men's power over women is simultaneously the power of one version of masculinity over multiple masculinities. Women are subordinated by men in different but parallel mechanisms by which non-normative men are marginalized from the hegemonic construction. The recent theoretical works by Bob Connell (1987) and Jeff Hearn (1987a) underscore this variability in the construction of masculinities and their constitution into hierarchy, and the anthologies by Harry Brod (1987) and myself (Kimmel and Messner 1989; Kimmel 1987 and 1990) bring together empirical studies of constitution of what we might call, after Freud, 'hegemonic masculinity and its discontents'.

What we know about masculinity, after fifteen years, is that masculinity is a social construction and that it is constructed within a field of power. What I would like to do is take a look at how the social constructionist position on gender has informed social science research in one other field, how our work has begun to filter into the discipline of sociology as a whole. What I will do is examine how the sociology of gender has come to inform the sociology of sexuality.

The social construction of sexuality

Studies of sexuality have always been marked by the uncritical embrace of a biological model or a facile rendering of sex-role imperatives about adequate functioning, thus obscuring precisely what they were intended to demonstrate. Thus they were notable for their *inattention* to gender. Sex researchers routinely use categories of 'male' and 'female' as the independent variables against which various behaviours or attitudes are measured. But what is being analysed is not the behaviour or attitudes of males or females but the behaviours and attitudes of *women* and *men*, social, and gendered, beings. We think of categories of sex, but they are really about gender, which is why our findings are often so difficult to explain. Kinsey's classic studies would have been more accurately titled *Sexual Behavior among American Men* and *Sexual Behavior among American Women*. But even he thought he was dealing with behaviour that was physiological, even if it had been shaped by social opportunities, of 'outlet'.

Like gender, sexuality is socially constructed. By this I mean our sexuality is a fluid assemblage of meanings and behaviours that we construct from the images, values, and prescriptions in the world around us. Such constructions are as much coerced as they are voluntary. As a social construction, sexuality is variable, changing (a) from culture to culture; (b) within any one culture over time (historically); (c) within any one society at any one time in different contexts in which the sexual may or may not be appropriate; and (d) over the course of an individual's life.

Anthropological evidence suggests enormous variability in

sexual behaviours and attitudes. In other cultures, what people do sexually differs significantly from what we do, and this dramatic variation in sexual behaviours indicates how cultures define the erotic and shape the ways in which the erotic is enacted. For example, Kinsey and his colleagues (1948) found that 85% of American men had never had sex with women in any way other than the 'missionary position'. By contrast, anthropologist Clyde Kluckhorn (1948) found that position to be preferred in only 10% of the Native American cultures he surveyed.

The ways in which people are sexual and the meanings we attach to our behaviours change dramatically over time. Think, for example, about the progressive dissociation between sex and reproduction in the United States. Since the 19th century, sexuality has been cut loose from its yoking to reproduction and the family, so that today the pursuit of sexual pleasure, independent of marriage, is both possible and, for many people, desirable. The disentangling of sex and reproduction has been propelled by social changes such as urbanization, which provides the first historical possibility of sexual encounters with relative strangers; by medical advances such as reliable birth control, and technological changes like the automobile, which provides an opportunity to get away from the family as well as a place to engage in sex itself. Secularization of values has loosened the hold of religion, long the chief buttress of the sex–reproduction complex. Although academic research continues to discuss sexuality in relation to marriage – categories in surveys are often coded as 'premarital,' 'marital', and 'extra-marital', with a special category for homo-sexual sex as 'non-marital' – Americans continue to have sex in ways that may, or may not, have anything to do with the institution.

Sexuality also varies through any individual's lifetime. What turns us on when we are adolescents may not turn us on when we are in our mid-50s. As men age, for example, they may become open to more sensual behaviours, such as cuddling and extended foreplay; women often report that their explicitly sexual sensations increase in their late 30s and early 40s. It may be convenient to explain such developments as simple biological maturation of different anatomical creatures, but men and women in other cultures do not 'mature' sexually in this way, nor have they always 'matured' in this way in the United States.

The reliance on biological maturation processes ignores the ways in which men's and women's sexuality are related to one another. That 'his' sexuality shifts toward the sensual just when 'her' sexuality takes a sharp turn toward the steamingly sexual indicates more than simple divergence of biological patterns. In part, this may have to do with the institution of marriage. Marriage domesticates sex, which means that sexuality is increasingly brought into the domain reserved to women: the home. When men feel that sex is no longer dangerous and risky (i.e. exciting), their sexual repertoire softens to include a wider range of sensual pleasures. By contrast, when women feel that sex is no longer dangerous and risky (i.e. threatening), they are free to explore more explicitly sexual pleasures.

Finally, our experience of the erotic depends on its social context. Anatomy textbooks and soft-core pornography may show the reader the same body part, but they usually don't result in the same outcome.

I doubt that clinical explanations of how to put on a condom to practise safer sex will arouse the reader in the same way as a pornographic film loop might. Sexual arousal is ordinarily frowned upon and is actually quite rare at nudist colonies and in art classes. And neither physician nor patient ordinarily experience much sexual arousal during gynaecological or prostrate examinations.

If sexuality is socially constructed, it both changes and it can be changed. The repertoire of sexual behaviours available to women and men can be expanded, and the associations of the erotic with various forms of domination can be re-evaluated. Of course, such a process takes time, but the social constructionist position opens us to the possibilities of transformation and the responsibility to account for our own sexuality. What we do and what we think about do not simply bubble up into consciousness or behaviour because of our genetic programming: we can be held accountable for them.

The male sexual script[2]

I have claimed that sexuality is socially constructed and historically variable, and that the central organizing principle of sexuality is gender. Let me try and outline the content of the contemporary male sexual script, those normative blueprints that determine the shape of the erotic, by specifying some dimensions of masculinity and observing how these are enacted in sexual behaviour. I have found psychologist Robert Brannon's specification of the rules of masculinity (1976) to be helpful here. The rules of masculinity? (a) No sissy stuff: avoid all behaviours that even remotely suggest the feminine. (b) Be a big wheel: success and status confer masculinity. (c) Be a sturdy oak: reliability and dependability are defined as emotional distance and affective distance. (d) Give 'em hell: exude an aura of manly aggression, go for it, take risks.

These four rules do not define a masculinity that is biologically determined, nor do they even capture all masculinities in the United States today. But they do specify a normative masculinity, that version – white, middle-class, heterosexual – that is often used as the standard against which other masculinities are compared and other social groups suppressed. It is a masculinity that is always willing to take risks, able to experience pain and not submit to it, driven constantly to accumulate (power, money, sexual partners). Masculinity is unresolved – never able to be fully demonstrated, subject to eternal doubt. Masculinity needs constant validation; its pursuit is relentless. It is not too difficult to see how masculinity may be a hidden factor in the disproportionate rate of stress-related diseases among men, for incidences of violent accidents of all types, traffic-related deaths and injuries, drunk-driving-related accidents, or even mental illness. As one 19th-century Alabama physician described the etiology of mental illness:

The causes of general paresis are found to prevail most among men, and at the most active time of life, from 35–40 in the majority of cases. Habitual intemperance, sexual excesses, overstrain in business, in fact, all those habits which tend to keep up too rapid cerebral action, are supposed to induce this form of disease. It is especially a disease of *fast life* and fast business in large cities (cited in Hughes 1988, p. 15).

These elements translate into a specific sexual script that is reinforced through adolescent sexual socialization and early masturbatory experience. It is a sexuality that is privatized, detached, phallocentric, driven by fantasy. It is a sexual script that emphasizes scoring (accumulating many partners) instead of caretaking, sexuality without sensuality – it is normative to take risks, engage in

[100]

anonymous sex, have difficulty sustaining emotional intimacy, and validating promiscuity.

Much of peer sexual socialization consists of the conveying of strategic actions that the male can perform to make himself a more adequate sexual partner. Men are often told to think of sports, work, or some other non-sexual event, or to repeat multiplication tables or mathematical formulae in order to keep themselves from premature ejaculation. It's as if sexual adequacy could be measured by time elapsed between penetration and orgasm, and the sexual experience itself is transformed into an endurance test in which pleasure, if present at all, is almost accidental.

The contemporary male sexual script – the normative construction of sexuality – provides a continuum along which men array themselves for the script's enactment. The script contains dicta for sexual distancing, objectification, phallocentrism, a pressure to become and remain erect without ejaculation for as long as possible, all of which serve as indicators of masculinity as well as sexual potency. Adequate sexual functioning is seen as the proof of masculinity.

We can illustrate the ways in which a perspective that stresses the social construction of gender can shed new light on the field of sociology of sexuality by briefly looking at three areas of current research. One of these areas, pornography, has had its research agenda entirely transformed by a gender perspective, while two others – sexual dysfunction and research on AIDS – are only now incorporating such a perspective.

Pornography[3]

Earlier research on pornography measured rates of arousal, types of fantasy, speed of arousal, intensity of masturbatory orgasm. Some research explored the therapeutic value of pornography in alleviating sexual problems. Earlier political debate about pornography centred around an assault by the erotophobic right-wing on all sexual material, and the liberal efforts to block censorship.

What's interesting about the research and political debate is that few researchers were actually looking at the pornography: few actually examined the content of the pornography with an eye towards what those images say about men's sexuality, women's sexuality, and the relationship between women and men. Like other men, sex researchers could look at pornography to gauge reactions, could, in their own ways 'use it', but we could not see it.

The feminist debate about pornography shifted the terms of the political debate. Anti-pornography feminists insisted that we look at what pornographic images actually depict. What one sees are not only images of sex, but images of sexism. Pornographic images are about the subordination of women, these feminists argue and, what's worse, these images make that subordination the basis of sexual pleasure. Pornography, in the words of one writer, 'makes sexism sexy' (Stoltenberg 1985). And its effect on women is to gag the expression of their real sexuality, and to accommodate them to silence. Its effect on men is to reinforce male domination, to make it a turn on.

Anti-pornography feminists level a three-part attack on pornography, and its relationship to male–female relations. First, they argue that pornography *is* violence against women, that the actual depictions of rapes and tortures involve real women often being filmed or photographed against their will. For example, Linda Marciano, star of *Deep Throat*, claims that she was forced at gunpoint to perform the sex acts that made her film the most successful pornographic film of all time. 'Every time someone watches that film', Marciano says in her public testimony to Minneapolis City Council (1983), 'they are watching me being raped.'

Not only do anti-pornography feminists argue that pornography *is* violence, they also argue that it *causes* violence against women, providing a how-to manual for woman-hating. It is said to cause rape and battery, and convince men that when women say no they mean yes and that they secretly want to be raped. And pornography is said to numb men to the violent reality of women's lives. Repeated exposure to pornographic images 'desensitizes people to the abuse of women', noted feminist lawyer Catharine MacKinnon (1986) in an interview, so that we 'become numb to abuse when it is done through sex'.

The anti-pornography feminist position has been challenged politically by another group of feminists which argue that censoring pornography is more like killing the bearer of bad news:

ineffective and ultimately politically dangerous. Many of these feminist women argue that the claiming of a vital, active, and engaging sexuality is part of their feminism, and that they can find some validating messages within the contradictory information presented to them by pornography.

This debate has reframed the entire agenda for social science research on pornography. Where once we measured arousal rates, now researchers are measuring the changes in men's attitudes and behaviours as a result of pornography. And what does the research say? Does it confirm the claims made by the anti-pornography feminists that porn causes violence or inures us to it? Research by social scientists found that there may be short-term increases in callousness to the victimization of women, increases in belief in rape myths (that women secretly want it or like it), but that these effects are not long-lasting. Research by Malamuth, Donnerstein, and Zillman has demonstrated that, as Donnerstein *et al.* (1987) say, 'exposure to degrading pornography did result in more calloused beliefs abour rape' (p. 177) and 'may have negative effects on attitudes about women' (p. 107).

However, when the aggressive pornographic images were dis-aggregated into images of sex alone, sexual violence, and violence alone, the results give one pause. Donnerstein and his colleagues found that non-violent sexual images had no noticeable impact on men's attitudes and behaviours, while images of violence and sexualized violence obtained nearly identical results. From this they conclude that 'depictions of violence against women, whether or not in a sexually explicit context, should be the focus of concern' (p. 175).

Anti-pornography feminists are not convinced by the social science research. 'Does one need scientific methodology in order to conclude that the anti-female propaganda that permeates our nation's cultural output promotes a climate in which acts of sexual hostility directed against women are not only tolerated but ideologically encouraged? asks Susan Brownmiller (cited in Donnerstein *et al.* 1987, pp. 50–1). Well, yes. And despite the fact that the research has not confirmed all of the claims made for pornography, sex researchers can no longer look at pornography as simply sexual representation. *Pornography is gendered speech.* It is by men, for men, and ultimately about men: about our fantasies of our own sexualities: omnipresent, enormous, ever-ready, perpetually erect, hard, rough, and eternally desired and desiring. After the feminist debate, sex researchers can never look at pornography in quite the same way again.

Sexual dysfunction[4]

Nor should we be able to do research on sexual dysfunctions in the same way. But we do. Often, research on sexual problems focuses on issues of functional adequacy (capacity for arousal, ejaculation, etc.) or on pleasure as distinct from arousal (such as research on premature ejaculation and anorgasmia in women). If psychological models are employed, they are based on individual self-concept, almost never on considerations of gender.

For example, Kinsey maintained a physiological understanding of human sexual performance based entirely on a biological model. As with other species, then, Kinsey believed that a rapid ejaculation after brief but ardent thrusting was the superior biological male sexual response, 'however inconvenient and unfortunate his qualities may be from the standpoint of his wife' (Kinsey 1948, p. 508). And sex therapists often treat sexual problems as if they were genderless. For example, Albert Ellis makes the issue entirely 'human' when he writes that the patient finds himself in the following cycle: 'I must perform well sexually; it is awful when I don't; I can't stand my sexual inadequacy, and I am an incompetent person for having it' (Ellis 1980, p. 241). Ellis's preferred method of treatment, therefore, is to encourage the male patient to concentrate more fully on the sexual, since 'sexual arousal depends on the male's concentrating on exciting stimuli and is easily blocked when he focuses on something non-sexual or anti-sexual' (Ellis 1980, p. 238).

To listen to the voices of men who have these sexual problems, or even normally functional men, one would come to the exact opposite conclusion. Sexual functioning is so intimately tied up with one's experience of self as a man that it's often more the surprise that sexual pleasure occurs at all. Take, for example, the ways in which male patients present their problems to sex therapists for the three most common sexual problems: inhibited sexual desire, erectile dysfunction, and premature ejaculation (see Kimmel and Fracher 1987). A premature ejaculator reported that he felt as if he 'wasn't a real man because he can't satisfy a woman'. A man with low sexual interest had only male role models who were strong, competent, utterly devoid of emotion, and he was so terrified that he would fail to please his partner that he hadn't had sex with his wife in over two years. And finally a man whose erectile problems had caused him tremendous anguish told his therapist that 'a real man never has to ask his wife for anything sexually' and that he should be able to please his wife whenever he wants.

Where's the discussion of sexual pleasure? Notice how each refers to sexual problems in *gender* terms. Each fears that his sexual problem damages his sense of masculinity, makes him less of a real man. In a sense, we might say that each of them suffers from masculinity. Notice how the equation of sexual adequacy is about achieving and maintaining erection in almost a hydraulic sense. Sexuality is not about mutual pleasuring, but the confirmation of masculinity, which is based on physical capacities. And these, in turn, require emotional detachment, a phallocentric world view of sexual pleasure, and self-objectification. Is it any wonder that men can transform sexuality into a work role? Listen to our language: we 'get the job done', 'achieve' orgasm, the penis is a 'tool' which, if it fails to live up to unrealistic expectations, will result in 'performance anxiety'.

Given this, men with sexual problems may not be deviants but overconformists to an unrealizable definition of masculinity. And doesn't a gender perspective transform our understanding of that strange new AIDS-era 'disease' known as sexual compulsion or sex addiction? For what is a sex addict but an ardent subscriber to male sexual scripts – always seeking sex and ready for it? Aren't all men who *don't* want sex all the time the true deviants?

There are some indications of movement in this area of research. Leiblum and Pervin's *Principles and Practice of Sex Therapy* (1980) stands at the watershed of a gender perspective, including Ellis's disengendered notions about the psychology of the erection as well as a comment by the book's editors that erection 'is not synonymous with the ability to have or enjoy sex but almost all men regard the loss of erection not only as signalling the end of their sex life, but also as an emasculating slur on their manhood' (Ellis 1980, p. 238). More recent collections, such as Leiblum and Rosen's

[105]

Sexual Desire Disorders (1988), go even further in underscoring the centrality of gender in understanding sexuality.

AIDS[5]

Let me now turn my last area in which a gender perspective on sexuality can have real policy implications: AIDS. I find it startling that although almost 94% of all AIDS patients are men, and AIDS is now the leading cause of death among men aged 33–44 in New York and other major cities, virtually no one is talking about AIDS as a men's disease. No one talks about why men are so overwhelmingly at risk for AIDS. No one talks about the relationship between AIDS and masculinity. (As a public, we continue to talk about AIDS as a disease of gays and IV drug users, missing the fact that both groups are overwhelmingly male.)

One is put at risk of AIDS by engaging in specific high-risk behaviours: activities that ignore potential health risks for more immediate pleasures. For example, sharing needles is both a defiant flaunting of health risks and an expression of community among IV drug users. And the capacity for high-risk sexual behaviours, especially unprotected anal intercourse with a large number of partners, is a confirmation of masculinity.

As sociologists have long understood, stigmatized gender often leads to exaggerated forms of gender specific behaviour. Thus, those whose masculine identity is least secure are precisely those most likely to enact hypermasculine behavioural codes as well as hold most fast to traditional definitions of masculinity. In social science research, hypermasculinity as a cover-up for impaired gender identity has been used to explain a propensity for authoritarianism and racism, homophobia, anti-Semitism, and childhood bully behaviour.

Gay men and IV drug users can also be seen in this light, although for different reasons. Gay men are, in the popular mind, not 'real' men, since masculinity is defined as avoidance of the feminine, and gay men have sex with men, i.e. behave like women. Gay men's gender identity was for centuries a damaged masculinity; gay men were defined precisely by the fact that they were 'failed men'. However, after the Stonewall riots in 1969, and the subsequent Gay Liberation Movement, a new gay masculinity emerged in the gay communities in major cities. The clone dressed 'butch,' always in typically masculine clothes (flannel shirts, jeans) with short hair (not androgynous) and a moustache, was athletic and highly muscular. In short, the clone looked more like a real man than straight men.

These men enacted a hypermasculine sexuality – steamy backrooms and bars where sex was plentiful, anonymous, and very, very sexual. No unnecessary foreplay, romance, or post-coital awkwardness. Sex without attachment. For a time, gay men were the only men in our culture who could legitimately say they were getting as much sex as they want. And I would bet that most straight men felt a little twinge of jealousy underneath our homophobic shells. Of course, it is precisely the clone, who composed between 20% and 35% of all gay men in the 1970s, who are the men most at risk of AIDS.

(Among IV drug users, we see a different pattern, but with some similar outcomes when seen from a gender perspective. IV drug users are overwhelmingly black and Latino, two groups of men for whom the traditional avenues of demonstrating successful gender identity are blocked by poverty and racism. Drug culture offers avenues of demonstrating masculinity beyond the traditional breadwinner role: dealing drugs can provide an income to support a family as well as providing manly risk and adventure. The community of drug users can confirm gender identity – and here the sharing of needles is a demonstration of that community solidarity. Since there is always risk involved in injecting drugs – death by overdose – sharing needles is but another way that hypermasculine bravado may lead to extraordinary risk taking.)

I argued that gay men enacted a hypermasculine sexual script, exaggerating the behaviours most associated with masculinity: detached, phallaocentric, orgasm-focused, often anonymous, sexually adventurous. Now what is the best way to reduce one's risk for contracting AIDS? Not abstinence, mandatory testing, or education campaigns that are vague about sexual practices – these are fuelled as much by homophobic reaction to gay male sexuality as by concern for public health. The way to reduce risk is to encourage men to practise 'safer sex' – to reduce the number of sex partners, preferably to one, to avoid casual encounters, to avoid certain particularly dangerous sexual pratices, and to use condoms and exchange no bodily fluids. In short, safer-sex programmes encourage men to stop having sex like men. In a sense, the term 'safe sex' is an oxymoron: that which is sexy is not safe; that which is safe is not sexy. Sex is about danger, risk, excitement; safety is about softness, security, comfort. Is it any wonder that many men feel the way one gay man reported: 'I find so-called safe sex comparable to putting my nose up against a window in a candy store when I'm on a diet. I'd rather not go near the window at all, because seeing the candy makes me want to eat at least three or four pieces.'

Thus, it is not surprising that a quarter of all gay men report that they have not changed their unsafe sexual behaviour. What is surprising is that about three-quarters of all gay men *have* changed their behaviour. Some gay organizations have produced safer-sex pornographic videos. One writer argued that 'we need to organize huge regular Safe Sex parties in our clubs and gay centres . . . with workshops and expert counseling available. We need to produce hot, sexy, visual materials to take home, telephone sex-talk facilities, and safe sex porno cinemas' (Watney 1987, p. 133). Our surveys also indicate that virtually no heterosexual men have changed their sexual practices. To educate men about safer sex means to confront the issue of masculinity.

If we are to make safer sex into sexy sex we must confront this issue of masculinity, just as we will need to confront the issue of masculinity to help men with sexual problems and to facilitate the disentangling of sex and sexism in pornography. And as sex researchers, understanding gender will help understand sexuality, to help the process of enlarging the definition of what it means to be a man in our culture, so that sexuality will embrace a wider range of behaviours and experiences. We need, as one writer put it, 'to develop a culture which will support the transition to safer sex by establishing the model of an erotics of protection, succor and support within the framework of our pre-AIDS sex lives'.

The process of transforming masculinity is long and hard, and AIDS can spread so rapidly. Sometimes it feels as if there isn't enough time. And there isn't. While we are eroticizing safer sex practices and enlarging the range of erotic behaviours available to men, we must also, as a concerned public, increase our compassion and support for AIDS patients. We must stand with them because they are our brothers. We are linked to them not through sexual orientation (although we may be) or by drug-related behaviour (although we may be), but by gender, by our masculinity. They are not 'perverts' or 'deviants' who have strayed from the norms of masculinity, and therefore brought this terrible retribution upon themselves. They are, if anything, over-conformists to destructive norms of male behaviour. They are men who, like all real men, have taken risks. And risk-taking has always implied danger. Men have always known this and have always chosen to take risks. Until daring has been eliminated from the rhetoric of masculinity, men will die as a result of their risk-taking. In war. In sex. In driving fast and drunk. In shooting drugs and sharing needles. Men with AIDS are real men, and when one dies a bit of all men dies as well. Until we change what it means to be a real man, every man will die a little bit every day.

Notes

1 An earlier version of this chapter was presented as a keynote speech at the conference on Masculinity and social theory sponsored by the Theory Section of the British Sociological Association in Bradford, 16 September 1988. A different version was also presented as an invited lecture to the International Academy of Sex Research annual meetings in Minneapolis, Minnesota, 17 August 1988. I am grateful to both organizations for inviting my participation. I also thank John Gagnon, Jeff Hearn, Martin Levine, David Morgan, and Jean O'Keeffe for helpful comments and criticisms.
2 On the concept of 'sexual script' see Gagnon & Simon 1973.
3 This section on pornography is adapted from 'Guilty pleasures: pornography in men's lives', the introductory essay to Kimmel 1990.
4 This section on sexual dysfunction is adapted from Kimmel & Fracher 1987.
5 This section on AIDS is adapted from Kimmel & Levine 1989.

CHAPTER 7

Beyond sex and gender: masculinity, homosexuality and social theory

TIM EDWARDS

Introduction: historical construction

None of the 1970s Books-About-Men made a serious attempt to get to grips with gay liberation arguments, or to reckon with the fact that mainstream masculinity is heterosexual masculinity. Nor did the 'men's movement' publicists ever write about the fact that beside them was another group of men active in sexual politics; or discuss their methods, concerns or problems. (Carrigan *et al.* 1985, p. 584).

Sex and gender, sexuality and gendered identity, are still largely seen as separate entities.[1] Consequently, sexuality (heterosexuality–homosexuality) and gendered identity (femininity–masculinity) are often totally divorced. As a result, we have a vast literature on sexuality which more or less ignores the construction of gendered identity and an equally vast literature on gendered identity which omits the study of sexuality. In addition, there is a further problem concerning the study of masculinity in particular as the one attempt to remarry the two discourses properly has come from woman-centred and identified feminism which consciously does not include or consider men, masculinity, or male sexuality other than in relation to women, femininity, and female sexuality. Men's studies

[110]

in the 1970s have done little to alter this situation, often focusing unquestioningly on male heterosexuality. However, the gay movement has made even fewer attempts to address this issue, as I shall illustrate later. As a consequence, sexuality and gendered identity continue to be considered as totally separate entities.

This conceptual split is no accident and has developed through a series of historical, theoretical, and political developments starting with Marx's, Weber's, and Durkheim's attempts to demonstrate the importance of the economic, political, and social spheres in influencing human life. This developed in direct opposition to the genetically reductionist Social Darwinism popularizd and promoted in the 19th century. Consequently, a conjunction of the study of society with the now well-known dualism between nature and culture was created. This was, in itself, a reflection of the rise of science in the 19th century sharply contrasting with the previously adopted modes of metaphysical thinking used to understand 'the nature of things'. In addition, this dualism was also a demonstration of the need to understand a world which was rapidly changing under the impact of industrialization and urbanization. These developments help to explain the division of sex and gender in parallel with the separation of nature and culture respectively. Consequently, sexuality and gendered identity also became separated through the same conceptual split.

However, the problem was, and what is more still is, that the one approach could not and cannot answer the questions of the other within the limits of its own conceptual framework. This has therefore tended to lead towards endless attempts to re-amalgamate them. The most infamous of these is psychoanalysis, in itself a follow-on development from the same rise of science in the 19th century that required the understanding of human life and now sought scientific inquiry into the workings of the human mind (Freud [1905] 1977). This attempt to understand human motivations led to the formation of set-pattern models of individual development leading, in turn, to a problem of imposing interpretations of 'correct' outcomes, a form of pro-conformity conservatism. Conversely, the parallel development of social anthropology tried to prove the opposite point of the variation in, rather than universality of, individuals and society (Mead 1935, Oakley 1972). Consequently, the nature–culture dualism was deepening academically as early psychoanalysis was centred on a scientific notion of innate instinct or drive whilst, conversely, social anthropology sought to illustrate the importance of cultural socialization. The political implications of this rapidly developing dualism were also already becoming apparent. In particular, early psychoanalysis was opposed by the expanding homosexual and women's movements which sought to prove that they were neither deviant nor neurotic nor naturally inferior, a necessary precursor to political action.

It is important to point out, though, that none of these developments were without their share of apparent paradoxes or contradictions. The early women's purity campaigns were based on a notion of controlling an essentialist 'natural' male lust, whilst some early legitimation for homosexuality was achieved through Magnus Hirschfeld's and Havelock Ellis's attempts to prove its innateness and set up a Scientific Humanitarian Committee for Sexual Reform.[2] However, these theories often had the adverse effect of imposing a stereotype of effeminacy upon homosexuals. For example, a contemporary, Karl Heinrich Ulrichs, himself homosexual, postulated the theory that homosexuality was the result of faulty differentiation in the brain, coining the term 'urning' as a name for those suffering from having 'a feminine soul in a male body', whilst Hirschfeld proposed the idea of the homosexual as being man and woman in one as a 'third sex', similar to Edward Carpenter's 'intermediate sex'. The turning point, however, was the development of a homosexual community, increasingly politically motivated and opposed to its medicalization. In addition, the enforced gender divisions of the two world wars, in developing opportunities for forming relationships, led to a slowly increasing awareness of the normality rather than the pathology of homosexuality.

Moreover, with the ever-increasing diversity of modern society came many more groups simultaneously attempting to comprehend and improve their position: the rise of racial minorities, sects, ethnic groups, and Marxist, socialist, and political affiliations. In relation to this discussion, two of these are of particular interest: first, the women's movement, concerned with women's emancipation and an understanding of their oppression; and, second, the development of minority groups, following increased immigration, seeking to take control of their socio-structural position. Most importantly in this process, it became deeply politically necessary for the women's and the minority movements, including the homosexual movement, to separate their social, economic, and political position from their natural inheritance if they were to gain momentum and oppose their oppression. Women's liberation crucially depended upon the assertion that marriage and motherhood were not inevitable determinants of being female and that their lack of status in the male world was due to the construction of femininity and male oppression, not natural inferiority. The various minorities were equally concerned to prove that their oppressed position was the result of their lowly status in society and not the outcome of a self-deserving destiny. In addition, the development of these minority movements was facilitated by urbanization and social change. Large cities created collectivities within their more economically and socially oppressed parts and inadvertently provided opportunities for positive political development. In sum, political motivations as well as conceptual separations led to a division of sexuality and gendered identity.

Moreover, the relative affluence of the 1950s and 1960s and the rise of education and universities further facilitated the development of the study of social problems and minority-oriented deviancy theory.[3] This developed in parallel with the second wave of feminism and renewed political activity centred on minorities and groups of the oppressed: women, homosexuals, blacks, and the youth of the 1960s. None of these movements achieved all of their goals in isolation though they did manage to make some significant progress into public consciousness and into alleviating their oppression in combination.

However, the overwhelming problem, as was seen so soon in the 1970s, was the fragmentation of these movements into less powerful sects and groups. In particular, this confirmed the separation of the women's movement from the other minorities who in turn fragmented into the concerns of their various constituents. This meant that sexuality became the interest solely of the sexually deviant: the new positively self-identified, gay community.

Consequently, in conjunction with the application of constructionist, and in particular symbolic interactionist, perspectives developed primarily in opposition to structural approaches and set-pattern psychoanalytic theory, the attempt to reintegrate issues of gendered identity and sexuality was challenged theoretically and attacked politically as supportive of oppressive conservative structures. However, as new social, economic, and political changes were presented, new problems arose, particularly in relation to developing a more powerful opposition to a parallel reassertion of right-wing moralism and religious fundamentalism. The problem has become one of trying to recombine these sets of studies in order to develop their positive assets and provide a stronger political opposition to the conservatism that threatens them. This is, I feel, the way forward, and I propose to illustrate this through demonstrating the relationship between homosexuality and masculinity, via a study of the male gay movement over the past twenty years, as one example of the overall interrelationship of sexuality and gendered identity.

The new (gay) man

> The paradox of the 1970s was that gay and lesbian liberation did not produce the gender-free communitarian world it envisioned, but faced an unprecedented growth of gay capitalism . . . and a new masculinity. (Adam 1987, p. 97).

Homosexuality undermines masculinity. In recent centuries the male homosexual has been perceived as being a queen, a queer, a pansy, limp-wristed, a faggot: in short, effeminate (Ariès and Bejin 1985, Bray 1982). This socially, economically, and politically enforced stigma led initially to a counter-reaction of camp: a deliberate and dramatic exaggeration of effeminacy that acted as a defence against its attack on masculine identity. However, in the 1970s following on from Stonewall gay liberation, a second counter-reaction was created in relation to the previous action, this time trying to prove that gay men were 'real men' too and a process of what I shall call 'machoization' ensued (Blachford 1981).

Machoization is defined as a reification of the masculine exemplified through a series of identities, dress codes and psycho-sexual meanings epitomized in the practice of promiscuous public sex, cruising, and, in particular, clone culture. Clone culture refers to the construction of an identity of apparently complete uniformity: individual differences are erased through the adoption of a specific identity, even including physical appearance through the use of body building and toning into one particular, mesomorphic shape. Clone culture is also a deeply masculine construction. The various

[114]

identities are related to occupations traditionally defined as 'masculine' or 'real man's work': the western cowboy (button-fly jeans, plaid shirts, boots), the construction worker (helmet, heavy denims, overalls), the military (soldiers), athletes (vests, shorts), police (uniforms), 'piss elegance' (executive culture, suits), and 'leather' (biker culture, sadomasochism). These costumes or uniforms reinforced the overall 1970s machoization of male homosexual culture as a counter-reaction to previous stereotypes of effeminacy: gay men were now 'real men' too who related to other men as men. Consequently, intimacy, and in particular emotional commitment, were kept to a minimum.

The gay community was also actively asserting the positivity of its alternative sexuality. Consequently, this process of machoization developed into sexual practice itself: anonymous, promiscuous, and genitally focused. The question was raised as to what extent this construction of masculine identity was, most importantly, one of unconscious conformism or self-conscious nonconformism, acceptance or ridicule (Gough 1989). For example, the 1970s disco pop group The Village People, where each person in the group represented one particular clone, were clearly laughing all the way from their satirical lyrics (the YMCA and the Navy were particular targets) to ludicrous dress sense. It was clearly often the case that this was a self-conscious exaggeration of traditional male identities: its seriousness was questioned. Equally, though, it was a semi-conscious acceptance or even a downright celebration of traditionally conceived male sexuality. Sex and sexuality themselves remained necessarily serious.

More importantly, it should not be assumed that this process was simply a sudden development. It was also part of a wider series of social, economic, and political changes concerning the family, work, education, and the capitalist processes of production and consumption. The homosexual subculture had been steadily developing over the previous century, growing in numbers and activity according to patterns of industrialization and urbanization as we have seen.[4] The effect of gay liberation was to set light to an increasingly incandescent situation whilst it asserted and reconstructed an identity as part of a developing political process.

Whilst this had the positive effect of creating a stronger community, increasing individual validity and decreasing internalized stigmatization, it also had the added negative effect of creating a

[115]

reification of the masculine and an over-emphasis on sex, itself a reflection of the problematic position of self-definition solely through sexual orientation. In terms of individual identity this led to rigidity and problems of over-conformism, often covering up a multitude of difficulties in making emotional contacts and developing lasting relationships. Thus, underpinning all of this was the infamous male fear of intimacy.

Attempts to explain this process were only fully explored through functionalist sex-role theory, criticized as circular or teleological; and set-pattern psychoanalytic theory, equally criticized as conservative and astructural, as stated earlier. A partly politically necessary rejection of this whole set of issues ensued and the tendency to support politically and academically the separation of the study of sexuality and gendered identity continued.

In sum, this meant that whilst the institutions of heterosexism were challenged through a rejection of the ideology of the monogamous family, male dominance and capitalism remained unchanged and unchallenged. The male gay community, in fact, was effectively co-opted into the already exploding development of capitalist consumerism through the expansion of a profitable subculture which in turn exploited the disposable incomes, psycho-sexual concerns with physical appearance and sense of inadequacy of many gay men (Altman 1982; D'Emilio 1983). This was demonstrated through the increased numbers and profitability of bars, clubs, bath-houses and other social-sexual facilities, including the already exploding fashion industry now turning its attention to men as well as women. In addition, the male gay community's unwillingness or difficulties in addressing issues of power and inequality became blatantly obvious, particularly under the influence of Second Wave feminism. This highlighted the further deleterious effects of reinforcing sexism, racism, and ageism, initially illustrated in the conflicts between lesbians and gay men, and further by some gay men's extreme *laissez-faire* attitudes towards sadomasochism and profoundly paternalist practice of pederasty. The male gay movement's resistance to these issues, when apparent, was one of self-protection and not one of active political conviction.

Public sex successfully formed the ultimate expression of this masculine value system as the eroticization of an oppressed position through co-opting pleasure into danger: risky became sexy.[5] The

[116]

masculinity expressed in this process was illustrated through the use of hard bodies, hard stares, and even harder constraints on intimacy, communication, and emotional commitment. Moreover, the gay movement equally successfully failed to develop and support an alternative: private love. Consequently, a series of SOS networks were set up such as: Switchboard, the London-based Friend, and counselling services.

However, with these developments of the gay movement came the simultaneously increasing regulation and control of sexuality (Weeks 1985). Consequently, far from being 'wild abandon in the bushes', public sexual behaviour in bars, clubs, saunas, parks, or public toilets was stringently controlled. Hence, as the numbers of bars, clubs, and bath-houses increased so did the numbers of police used, raids, and *agents provocateurs*.[6] Moreover, homosexual relationships were never socially validated in relation to the law, state, or attitudes. In addition, as gay men climbed the socially acceptable ladder of developing a private, monogamous, long-term relationship more restrictions were heaped upon them. In sum, homosexual men were trapped in an oppressive Catch 22 situation as their promiscuous public sex lives felt the full force of sexual regulation and moral condemnation and their long-term relationships faced countless structural impositions placed upon their existence, particularly concerning commercial services such as mortgage arrangements or life insurance policies. In short, these structural considerations provided some of the answers to some of the questions concerning male homosexuality.

The rest of the answers centre on the problem of masculinity's relationship with sexuality: gay men remain men despite attempts to undermine this through the stigmatization of effeminacy as well as their homosexuality. The male gay movement remains responsible for at least some of its own actions, although in no way are gay men to become simply part of a blame game in relation to the outcome. The problem with some Second Wave feminism has been lesbian separatism's obsession with the issues of 'promiscuity' and 'pro-capitalist consumerism' (Stanley 1982) practised by some, probably a minority of, gay men who, although personally responsible, remain too socially, economically, and politically oppressed to be 'blamed' or forced to conform to feminist demands. Their attempts to assert an otherwise deeply stigmatized sexuality and gendered identity positively remain commendable

[117]

and ultimately understandable as products of their oppression. The construction and maintenance of masculine identity, particularly concerning its reinforcement of often oppressive positions, however, often raises further problems of defensiveness. Moreover, even constructive criticism has, again understandably, never been welcomed by people in oppressed positions including the gay male community. Curiously strong reactions are aroused at the mere mention of the word 'promiscuous' and much emphasis has been placed on gay men's capacity to form lasting relationships or on the importance of identities in maintaining personal and political strength (Weeks 1985). There is truth in all of these statements.

The problem is that these statements still seem to miss the point and do not answer the important questions of why gay men choose one specific identity as opposed to another, or why they adopt one set of attitudes, behaviours, or lifestyles as opposed to another. All this illustrates the fact that neither historical deconstruction nor psychological analysis alone can resolve these issues. Purely historical or political deconstruction of history or representations cannot answer significant questions concerning social-psychological interactions or address the issue of gendered identity's maintenance of sexuality, or vice versa; whilst psychoanalysis overemphasizes the importance and power of the individual. In addition, sexuality and gendered identity need studying in interaction not as separate entities. This is a complex relationship which raises important questions of individual and social interaction, in a process of biographical-historical construction and academic deconstruction. In conclusion to this section, the study and practice of sexuality and gendered identity in relation to male homosexuality were separated as part of a political opposition to stereotypes of effeminacy. However, they have remained related at a different level and need reintegrating in handling current academic difficulties and contemporary political problems. The implications of this process are, of course, far reaching ...

Problems and implications

Without some attention to the social, historical change cannot be explained. Yet the consideration of psychological processes does not preclude an analysis of the social context in which they occur. Psychology and sociology are not mutually exclusive; rather, they complement one another. (Greenberg 1988, p. 495).

Sex and gender, and consequently sexuality and gendered identity, need reintegrating into a study of their interaction and not into a process of separate analysis. This requires a reconsideration of psychological as well as historical construction. Historical constructionism, for all its advantages in understanding continuity and change, still cannot account for individual motivations and actions or explain why one person is attracted to another and for what reasons.[7] Psychoanalysis has traditionally tried to answer these questions but at the considerable expense of imposing set patterns of development which are simply, at most, a matter of interpretation. In addition, psychoanalysis suffers from almost completely missing the importance of the social, economic, and political context in constructing individual personality. The significance of this process in shaping the outcomes of events is also, I hope, illustrated in the earlier sections of this paper.

The development of personality is social as well as individual and this creates a difficulty in studying it due to the need to consider socialization and interaction, structure and action. One solution to this stituation is to see the development of family relationships in themselves as forming innumerable individual outcomes but limited within the framework of the social, economic, and political context that surrounds the family network itself. For example, the primacy of mothering is, in itself, an historical contextual fact as well as of very significant psychological importance in the formation of sexual and gendered identity (Chodorow 1978). Consequently, what is needed academically is a psychological deconstruction of behaviour combined with an awareness of the historical social, economic, and political context in constructing and interacting with this development.

However, there are still considerable inadequacies involved in using purely deconstructive techniques. Academically, the inadequacies of deconstructionism are, I think, threefold. First, it is unable to account for the persistence of events and behaviours across temporal and spatial lines. It overemphasizes the variations across time and space derived from social anthropology and deconstructed history, and underestimates persistence, resistance, and continuity. Second, it fails to account for the full range of feelings and meanings attached to individual acts: in short, the emotional motivation of the act is removed through cerebralized distance and rationalization. For example, it therefore cannot account for the fear and loathing attached to homosexuality across centuries and continents, seemingly implying that the stigmatization of same-sex relations is unique or particular to modern capitalism. Neither can it explain why a particular man should batter or rape a particular woman, or man, as no amount of historical or material deconstruction can account for these reactions. Third, social constructionism constantly confuses the deconstruction of history with the destruction of ideology. As if holding up a gauze over the event, it effectively defuses the issue and creates an implicit political conservatism as pragmatism becomes intellectualism, and it constantly deviates action into thinking. Consequently, deconstructionism is also problematic politically. It is no coincidence that major political achievements – the women's movement and Stonewall gay and lesbian liberation – have been based on an essentialist notion of freeing the 'real self' rather than through the assertion of deconstruction. In addition, Section 28 is centred on a precise concern that homosexuality is not necessarily inherited biologically but is constructed and therefore may be 'promoted'. The simple assumption of the positive virtues of social constructionism has become problematic and politically suspect.

The solution to some of these problems lies in the amalgamation of the social with the psychological. There is no inevitable reason why they cannot be combined. The problem, as sociologists have often pointed out, is political. Traditional psychology and psychoanalysis have often had too great a concern with a reliance on conservative notions of set-patterns of development which are not actually necessary to proving the relevance of unconscious motivations or drives in everyday life, or even the fundamental formation of the personality through the internalization of the interrelations of the family. Psychoanalysis, in particular, also fails to relate this to processes of historical or social change. Deconstructionist or interactionist sociology fails, however, to address fully questions of individual motivations and the development of the personality, due to its primarily political opposition to the tendency towards notions of normal development and determinist unconscious instincts, drives, or needs. The development of the personality of the baby is, in effect, thrown out of the bathwater with the theory, and this is a prime example of politics preceding analysis.

There is no need to prove above all else the importance of drives or set patterns of development for all time. There is no need to prove at all costs that there are no instincts, no needs, and no determining drives whatever. There is no need to go to either extreme and every requirement to find an alternative. What has developed over the past century is a dualistic discourse that has lead to ever-increasing extremities of reaction on either side, derived from an overenforced separation of nature and culture first presented in the 19th century. What is needed is an ability to combine elements of both and to develop an understanding of the interaction of the conscious and the unconscious through the development of psychological as well as social deconstruction. However, to prove nurture valiant over nature is an unwitting and unnecessary internalization of scientific ideology that can have the adverse effect of reinforcing the already well-developed 19th-century dualism between nature and culture. It is not necessary to prove that there are no innate drives or instincts, it is merely necessary to deconstruct how they work and interact with the importance of the economic, social, and political construction in this process. Consequently, deconstructionism's ability to clarify ambivalence can be maintained whilst accounting for the emotional reactions and motivations: sex and gender may be recombined and, consequently, so may the study of sexuality and gendered identity.

Lastly, as a result of this process, there are three important implications for social theory. First, the relationship between sex and gender, sexuality and gendered identity, as it is traditionally conceived, is called into question as it is clearly incorrect to see these simply as two distinct categories. They should, instead, be seen as interactively related through a process of social-psychological construction. Second, this then calls for investigation into the interdependence of this process upon the historical context and in particular the influences of social, economic, and political changes at any given moment. This requires reconsideration of the historical construction of masculinity, and this includes its relation to changes in sexualities and gendered identities as well as the general social, economic, and political context or climate. Third, this leads to a reconsideration of sociological and psychological methodology in the light of personal–political interaction and the relationship between researcher and researched. The whole of this process is personally and politically, theoretically and ethically, threatening, as social researchers are forced into sometimes uncomfortable consideration of their own motivations and subjectivities involved in their research. Furthermore, it threatens the theoretical and scientific tradition still all too strong within sociology which regards subjectivity as subordinate to objectivity and asserts rational control at all-too-expensive costs of insensitivity to sexual political issues. Objectivity is one level of historically constructed, masculine subjectivity. The enforced maintenance of these standards can be seen as a defensive reaction on the part of often male social researchers in maintaining often powerful oppressive positions. This process is also ultimately challenging politically as those in powerful positions as researchers, defined as middle class and frequently of influence, are forced to reconsider their present and future work. Thus, this represents a challenge for change within the whole of social science:

> It also means breaking open masculinity's best kept secret, forcing men to look at themselves self-consciously *as men*, rather than the norm which defines everything else. (Mort 1988, p. 195).

Postscript: the AIDS epidemic

On originally writing this article in August 1988, I rigidly decided that AIDS would not enter into it. AIDS was everywhere and was not justified theoretically here. However, on rewriting it nearly a year later and following on from my comments at the Bradford conference and a year in the field of interviewing gay men, I feel that AIDS *forces* the issue of sexuality and gendered identity. Definitions of sex and sexuality are deeply interrelated to gender and gendered identity. This relationship is, of course, complex and not within the scope of this postscript or chapter. The point, put simply, is that if one is to open a discussion or raise questions concerning definitions of 'real men' then one must also address the issue of 'real sex', often defined as 'high-risk' anal or coital intercourse. Consequently, 'sex' means something different to men and to women, heterosexuals and homosexuals, and this leads to a consideration of the definitions of 'feminine' and 'masculine', 'heterosexual' and 'homosexual' sex. The implications, for men and women, heterosexual and homosexual, are I think limitless. Whilst the male-defined missionary position is successfully questioned, concern is raised for women who, in relation to men, lack control over the sexual act. This could, I think correctly, lead to an added feminist attack on straight male sexuality. The difficulty is that whilst AIDS offers the opportunity for challenging notions of 'real sex' and heterosexuality it can also lead to an added damnation of 'deviant' sexuality, particularly 'promiscuity', and an undermining of the positivity of sexuality *per se*. This particularly affects gay male sexuality which has felt the full force of a restigmatization process of defining gay men as 'at risk' and also 'putting at risk'.[8] This makes the feminist perspective more problematic: it simply is not permissible to 'put the blame on gay men' for sexism (misplaced on a minority anyway), and criticize their attempts to maintain a positive sexualized identity under the impact of AIDS. The problem remains that feminism is probably incompatible with a positive gay male sexual identity, and particularly within the present parameters of the feminist perspective and under the impact of the contemporary AIDS epidemic.

Notes

1 Sex is defined as the act and not the characteristic in the context of this discussion, although there is of course a relation.
2 For a full discussion of these developments and sexology generally, see Weeks 1985.
3 I refer here to Becker 1963; and the earlier work of the Chicago School.
4 And see Weeks 1981.
5 For a fascinating ethnography of this, see Delph 1978.
6 *Agents provocateurs:* police arrest of homosexuals using dupes and disguise.
7 Foucault 1976 is an excellent example.
8 The literature here is vast; however, see Altman 1985, Shilts 1987, Watney 1987.

CHAPTER 8

Pornography and the alienation of male sexuality

HARRY BROD

Introduction

This chapter aims to augment, not refute or replace, what numerous commentators have said about pornography's role in the social
construction of sexuality. My primary focus is to examine pornography's model of male sexuality. Furthermore, in the discussion of pornography's role in the social construction of sexuality,
I wish to place more emphasis than is common on the social
construction of pornography. As I hope to show, these are related
questions. One reason I focus on the image of male sexuality in
pornography is that I believe this aspect of the topic has been
relatively neglected. In making this my topic, I do not suggest that
this is the most essential part of the picture. Indeed, I am clear it is
not. The main focus of discussion about the effects of pornography
is and should be its harmful effects on women, its principal victims.
Yet, there is much of significance which needs to be said about
pornography's representation, or perhaps I should more accurately
say misrepresentation, of male sexuality. My focus shall be on what
is popularly conceived of as 'normal' male sexuality, that is,
consensual, non-violent heterosexuality, as these terms are conventionally understood. I agree with arguments that this understanding assumes distinctions which are at least highly problematic, if
not outright false, which argue that this 'normal' sexuality is itself
coercive, both as compulsory heterosexuality and as containing
implicit or explicit coercion and violence. My aim is to present an

analysis of neglected aspects of the links between mainstream male sexuality and pornography, between men's taking pleasure in and taking profit from women's bodies. I would argue that the aspect of the relation between male sexuality and pornography usually discussed, pornography's incitement to greater extremes of violence against women, presupposes a connection with the more accepted mainstream. Without such a link, pornography's messages would be rejected by rather than assimilated into the institutions, attitudes, and perceptions which form and misinform male behaviour. My intention is to supply this usually missing link. Because I wish to analyse the formation of dominant forms of male sexuality, I focus on heterosexuality and heterosexual pornography.

My analysis proceeds from both feminist and Marxist theory. Just as Marxism understands class *as power*, rather than simply understanding class differences as differences of income, lifestyle, or opportunities, so a distinctive contribution of feminism is its understanding of gender *as power*, rather than simply as sex role differentiation. Neither class nor gender should be reified into being understood as fixed entities, which then differentially distribute power and its rewards. Rather, they are categories continually constituted in ongoing contestations over power. The violence endemic to both systems cannot be understood as externalized manifestations of some natural inner biological or psychological drives existing prior to the social order, but must be seen as emerging in and from the relations of power which constitute social structures. Just as capitalist exploitation is not caused by capitalists' excess greed but rather by the structural imperatives under which capitalism functions, so men's violence is not the manifestation of some inner male essence, but rather evidence of the breadth and depth of the political struggles through which genders are forged.[1]

For my purposes here, to identify this as a socialist-feminist analysis is to articulate a methodological commitment to make questions of power central to questions of gender, and to understand gendered power in relation to economic power, and as historically, materially structured.[2] If the most intimate aspects of the lives of the dominant group can be understood in these terms, areas usually taken to be the furthest afield from where one might expect these categories to be applicable, then this reinforces claims of socialist-feminist theory to comprehend the totality of our social

[125]

world. I consider this analysis of male sexuality as part of a wider socialist-feminist analysis of patriarchal capitalist masculinity, an analysis I have begun to develop elsewhere.[3]

As will be abundantly clear, I do not take a 'sexual liberationist' perspective on pornography. I am aware that many individuals, particularly various sexual minorities, make this claim on pornography's behalf. I do not minimize nor negate their personal experiences. In the context of our society's severe sexual repressiveness, pornography may indeed have a liberating function for certain individuals. But I do not believe an attitude of approval for pornography follows from this. Numerous drugs and devices which have greatly helped individuals have also been medical and social catastrophes – the one does not negate the other.

I shall be claiming that pornography has a negative impact on men's sexuality. This is a claim that an aspect of an oppressive system, patriarchy, operates, at least in part, to the disadvantage of all those it privileges, men. This claim does not deny that the overall effect of the system is to operate to men's advantage, nor does it deny that the same aspect of the system under consideration – that is, male sexuality and pornography under patriarchy – might not also contribute to the expansion and maintenance of male power even as it also works to men's disadvantage. Indeed, I shall be arguing precisely for such complementarity. I am simply highlighting one of the 'contradictions' in the system. My reasons for doing so are partly analytic: to bring to the fore relatively neglected aspects of the issue. Further, I also have political motivations for emphasizing this perspective. Raising consciousness of the prices of male power is part of a strategy through which men might mobilize against pornography's destructive effects on women and men.

The structure of my argument follows that of a segment of Marx's 'Economic and philosophic manuscripts' of 1844 in which he argued that a system of domination also damages the dominant group, preventing them from realizing their full humanity. Just as capitalists as well as workers are alienated under capitalism according to Marxist theory (in a certain restricted sense, even more so), so men, I shall argue, and in particular male sexuality, are also alienated under patriarchy. Given the need for brevity, I shall assume a working familiarity with Marx's concept of alienation, the process whereby one becomes a stranger to oneself and one's own powers come to be powers over and against one. Since later in the paper I make use of some of Marx's more economistic concepts, I should however note that I see more continuity than rupture between Marx's earlier, more philosophical writings and his later, more economic ones.[4] Much of this paper presents an analysis of men's consciousness. While alienation may indeed register in one's consciousness, I follow Marx in veiwing alienation not primarily as a pscyological state dependent on the individual's sensibilies or consciousness but as a social condition caused by a system of alienation.

Alienated pornographic male sexuality can be understood as having two dimensions: objectification of the body, and loss of subjectivity. I shall describe various aspects of pornographic male sexuality under each heading in a way intended to bring out how they may be conceptualized in Marx's terms.

(1) Objectification of the body
In terms of both its manifest image of and its effects on male sexuality, pornography restricts male sensuality in favour of a genital, performance-oriented male sexuality. Men become sexual acrobats endowed with oversized and overused organs which are, as the chapter title of a fine book on male sexuality describes what it calls 'the fantasy model of sex', 'two feet long, hard as steel, and can go all night' (Zilbergeld 1978). To speak non-euphemistically, using penile performance as an index of male strength and potency directly contradicts biological facts. There is no muscle tissue in the penis. Its erection when aroused results simply from increased blood flow to the area. Social mythology aside, the male erection is physiologically nothing more than localized high blood pressure. Yet this particular form of hypertension has attained mythic significance. Not only does this focusing of sexual attention on one organ increase male performance anxieties, but it also desensitizes other areas of the body from becoming what might otherwise be sources of pleasure.

The predominant image of women in pornography presents women as always sexually ready, willing, able, and eager. The necessary corollary to pornography's myth of female perpetual availability is its myth of male perpetual readiness. Just as the former fuels male misogyny when real-life women fail to perform to pornographic standards, so do men's failures to perform similarly fuel male insecurities. Relating to one's body as a performance machine produces a split consciousness wherein part of one's attention is watching the machine, looking for flaws in its performance, even while another is supposedly immersed in the midst of sensual pleasure. This produces a self-distancing self-consciousness which mechanizes sex and reduces pleasure.

(2) Loss of subjectivity

In the terms of discourse of what it understands to be 'free' sex, pornographic sex comes 'free' of the demands of emotional intimacy or commitment. It is commonly said as a generalization that women tend to connect sex with emotional intimacy more than men do. Without romantically blurring female sexuality into soft focus, if what is meant is how each gender consciously thinks or speaks of sex, I think this view is fair enough. But I find it takes what men say about sex too much at face value. I would argue that men do feel similar needs for intimacy, but are trained to deny them, and are encouraged further to see physical affection and intimacy primarily if not exclusively in sexual terms. This leads to the familiar syndrome wherein, as one man put it; 'Although what most men want is physical affection, what they end up thinking they want is to be laid by a Playboy bunny' (Betzold 1977, p. 46).

Looking to sex to fulfil what are really non-sexual needs, men end up disappointed and frustrated. Sometimes they feel an unfilled void, and blame it on their or their partner's inadequate sexual performance. At other times they feel a discomforting urgency or neediness to their sexuality, leading in some cases to what are increasingly recognized as sexual-addiction disorders. Therapists are here not talking about the traditional 'perversions', but behaviours such as what is coming to be called a 'Don Juan syndrome', an obsessive pursuit of sexual 'conquests'. A confession that sex is vastly overrated often lies beneath male sexual bravado. I would argue that sex seems overrated because men look to sex for the fulfilment of non-sexual emotional needs, a quest doomed to failure. Part of the reason for this failure is the priority of quantity over quality of sex which comes with sexuality's commodification. As human needs become subservient to market desires, the ground is laid for an increasing multiplication of desires to be exploited and filled by marketable commodities.[5]

For the most part the female in pornography is not one the man has yet to 'conquer', but one already presented to him for the 'taking'. The female is primarily there as sex object, not sexual subject. Or, if she is not completely objectified, since men do want to be desired themselves, hers is at least a subjugated subjectivity. But one needs another independent subject, not an object or a captured subjectivity, if one either wants one's own capacities validated, or if one simply desires human interaction. Men functioning in the pornographic mode of male sexuality, in which men dominate women, are denied satisfaction of these human desires.[6] Denied recognition in the sexual interaction itself, they look to gain this recognition in wider social recognition of their 'conquest'.

For women to serve as social validation for men's prowess, a woman 'conquered' by one and awarded as a trophy to the victor must be a woman deemed desirable by others. Hence pornography both produces and reproduces uniform standards of female beauty. Male desires and tastes must be channelled into a single mode, with allowance for minor variations which obscure its fundamentally monolithic nature. Men's own subjectivity becomes masked to them, as historically and culturally specific and varying standards of beauty are made to appear natural and given. The ease with which men reach quick agreement on what makes a woman 'attractive', evidenced in such things as the '1–10' rating scale of male banter and the reports of a computer program's success in predicting which of the contestants would be crowned 'Miss America', demonstrates how deeply such standards have been internalized, and consequently the extent to which men are dominated by desires not authentically their own.

Lest anyone think that the analysis above is simply a philosopher's ruminations, too far removed from the actual experiences of most men, let me offer just one recent example, from the *New York Times Magazine*'s 'About men' weekly column. In an article entitled 'Couch dancing', the author describes his reactions to a sort of cocktail bar, where women 'clad only in the skimpiest of bikini underpants' 'dance' for a small group of men for a few minutes for about 25 or 30 dollars, men who 'sat immobile, drinks in hand, glassy-eyed, tapping their feet to the disco music that throbbed through the room' (McWalter 1987, p. 138).

Men are supposed to like this kind of thing, and there is a quite natural part of each of us that does. But there is another part of

[129]

us – of me, at least – that is not grateful for the traditional male sexual programming, not proud of the results. By a certain age, most modern men have been so surfeited with images of unattainably beautiful women in preposterous contexts that we risk losing the capacity to respond to the ordinarily beautiful women we love in our bedrooms. There have been too many times when I have guiltily resorted to impersonal fantasy because the genuine love I felt for a woman wasn't enough to convert feeling into performance. And in those sorry, secret moments, I have resented deeply my lifelong indoctrination into the esthetic of the centerfold.

Alienation and crisis

I believe that all of the above can be translated without great difficulty into a conceptual framework paralleling Marx's analysis of the alienation experienced by capitalists. The essential points are captured in two sentences from Marx's manuscripts:

> *All* the physical and intellectual senses have been replaced by the simple alienation of *all* these senses; the sense of *having*. (Marx 1964, pp. 159–60).

> The wealthy man is at the same time one who *needs* a complex of human manifestations of life, and whose own self-realization exists as an inner necessity, a need. (Marx 1964, pp. 164–5).

Both sentences speak to a loss of human interaction and self-realization. The first articulates how desires for conquest and control prevent input from the world. The second presents an alternative conception wherein wealth is measured by abilities for self-expression, rather than possession. Here Marx expresses his conceptualization of the state of alienation as a loss of sensuous fulfilment, poorly replaced by a pride of possession, and a lack of self-consciousness and hence actualization of one's own real desires and abilities. One could recast the preceding analysis of pornographic male sexuality through these categories. In Marx's own analysis, these are more properly conceived of as the results rather

[130]

than the process of alienation. This process is at its basis one of in-version, a reversal of the subject–object relationship, whereby one's active powers become estranged and return to dominate one as an external force. This conception is most useful in understanding how men's power turns against them. How is it that pornography, in and by which men dominate women, comes to dominate men themselves?

To answer this question I shall find it useful to turn to two other concepts central to Marxism, the concept of 'crisis' in the system and the concept of 'imperialism'.[7] Marx's conception of the economic crisis of capitalism is often misunderstood as a prophecy of a cataclysmic doomsday scenario for its death. Under this interpretation, some look for a single event, perhaps like a stock-market crash, to precipitate capitalism's demise. But such events are for Marx, at most triggering events, particular crises which can shake the system, if at all, only because of the far more important underlying structural general crisis of capitalism. This general crisis is increasingly capitalism's ordinary state, not an extraordinary occurrence. It is manifest in the ongoing fiscal crisis of the state as well as recurring crises of legitimacy, and results from basic contradictory tensions within capitalism. One way of expressing these tensions is to see them as a conflict between the classic *laissez-faire* capitalist market mode, wherein capitalists are free to run their own affairs as individuals, and the growing inability of the capitalist class to run an increasingly complex system without centralized management. The result of this tension is that the state increasingly becomes a managerial committee for the capitalist class, and is more and more called upon to perform functions previously left to individuals. As entrepreneurial and *laissez-faire* capitalism give way to corporate capitalism and the welfare state, the power of capitalism becomes increasingly depersonalized and wrested from the hands of individual capitalists and collectivized, so that capitalists themselves come more and more under the domination of impersonal market forces no longer under their direct control.

To move now to the relevance of the above, there is currently a good deal of talk about a perceived crisis of masculinity, in which men are said to be confused by contradictory imperatives given to them in the wake of the women's movement. Though the male ego may feel uniquely beleaguered today, in fact such talk regularly surfaces. The 1890s in the United States, for example, was another period in which the air was full of a 'crisis of masculinity' caused by the rise of the 'new woman' and other factors.[8] I wish to put forward the hypothesis that these particular 'crises' of masculinity are but surface manifestations of a much deeper and broader phenomenon which I call the 'general crisis of patriarchy', paralleling Marx's general crisis of capitalism. Taking a broad view, this crisis results from the increasing depersonalization of partriarchal power which occurs with the development of patriarchy from its pre-capitalist phase, where power really was often directly exercised by individual patriarchs, to its late capitalist phase where men collectively exercise power over women, but are themselves as individuals increasingly under the domination of those collective patriarchal powers.[9] The sense of there being a 'crisis' of masculinity arises not from the decrease or increase in patriarchal power as such. Patriarchal imperatives for men to retain power over women remain in force throughout. But there is a shift in the *modes* of that power's exercise. The sense of crisis results from the simultaneous promulgation of two conflicting modes of patriarchal power, the earlier more personal and the later more institutional form. The crisis results from the incompatibility of the two conflicting ideals of masculinity embraced by the different forms of patriarchy, the increasing conflicts between behavioural and attitudinal norms in the political/economic and the personal/familial spheres.

From patriarchy to fratriarchy

To engage for a moment in even broader speculation, I believe that much of the culture, law, and philosophy of the 19th century can be reinterpreted as marking a decisive turn in this transition. I believe the passing of personal patriarchal power and its transformation into institutional patriarchal power in this period of the interrelated consolidation of corporate capitalism is evidenced in such phenomena as the rise of what one scholar has termed 'judicial patriarchy', the new social regulation of masculinity through the courts and social welfare agencies, which through new support laws, poor laws, desertion laws, and other changes transformed what were previously personal obligations into legal duties, as well as in the 'death of God' phenomenon and its aftermath.[10] That is, the loss of the personal exercise of patriarchal power and its diffusion through the institutions of society is strongly implicated in the death of God the Father and the secularization of culture in the 19th century, as well as the modern and postmodern problem of grounding authority and values.

I would like tentatively and preliminarily to propose a concept to reflect this shift in the nature of patriarchy caused by the deindividualization and collectivization of male power. Rather than speak simply of advanced capitalist patriarchy, the rule of the *fathers*, I suggest we speak of fratriarchy, the rule of the *brothers*. For the moment, I propose this concept more as a metaphor than as a sharply defined analytical tool, much as the concept of patriarchy was used when first popularized. I believe this concept better captures what I would argue is one of the key issues in conceptualizing contemporary masculinities, the disjunction between the facts of public male power and the feelings of individual male powerlessness. As opposed to the patriarch, who embodied many levels and kinds of authority in his single person, the brothers stand in uneasy relationships with each other, engaged in sibling rivalry while trying to keep the power of the family of man as a whole intact. I note that one of the consequences of the shift from patriarchy to fratriarchy is that some people become nostalgic for the authority of the benevolent patriarch, who if he was doing his job right at least prevented one of the great dangers of fratriarchy, fratricide, the brothers killing each other. Furthermore, fratriarchy is an intragenerational concept, whereas patriarchy is intergenerational. Patriarchy, as a father-to-son transmission of authority, more directly inculcates traditional historically grounded authority, whereas the dimension of temporal continuity is rendered more problematic in fratriarchy's brother-to-brother relationships. I believe this helps to capture the problematic nature of modern historical consciousness as it emerged from the 19th century, what I would argue is the most significant single philosophical theme of that century. If taken in Freudian directions, the concept of fratriarchy also speaks to the brothers' collusion to repress awareness of the violence which lies at the foundations of society.

To return to the present discussion, the debate over whether pornography reflects men's power or powerlessness, as taken up, for example, by Alan Soble in his book *Pornography: Marxism, Feminism, and the Future of Sexuality* (1986), can be resolved through such a distinction between personal and institutional male power. Soble cites men's use of pornographic fantasy as compensation for their powerlessness in the real world to argue that 'pornography is therefore not so much an expression of male power as it is an expression of their lack of power' (Soble 1986, p. 52).[11] In contrast, I would argue that by differentiating levels of power one should more accurately say that pornography is *both* an expression of men's public power *and* an expression of their lack of authentic personal power. Pornography's image of male sexuality works to the detriment of men personally even as its image of female sexuality enhances the powers of patriarchy. It expresses the power of alienated sexuality, or, as one could equally well say, the alienated power of sexuality.

Through this approach, one can reconcile the two dominant but otherwise irreconcilable images of the straight male consumer of pornography: on the one hand the powerful rapist, using pornography to consummate his sexual violence, and on the other hand the shy recluse, using it to consummate his masturbatory fantasies. Both images have their degree of validity. Through the analysis presented here one can understand not only each depiction, but their interconnection.

Embodiment and erotica

In the more reductionist and determinist strains of Marxism, pornography as ideology would be relegated to the superstructure of capitalism. I would like to suggest another conceptualization: that pornography is not part of patriarchal capitalism's superstructure, but part of its infrastructure. Society's increasing use of pornography's commodification of the body and interpersonal relationships paves the way for the escalating ingression of capitalist market relations into the deepest reaches of the individual's psychological makeup. The feminist slogan that 'the personal is political' emerges at a particular historical moment, and should be understood not simply as an imperative declaration that what has previously been seen solely as personal should now be viewed politically, but also as a response to the real increasing politicization of personal life.

This can be illuminated through the Marxist concept of imperialism. The classical Marxist analysis of imperialism argues that it is primarily motivated by two factors: exploitation of natural resources and extension of the market. In this vein, pornography should be understood as imperialism of the body. The greater public proliferation of pornography, from the 'soft-core' pornography of much commercial advertising to the greater availability of 'hard-core' pornography, proclaims the greater colonization of the body by the market and by men's power.[12] The increasing use of the male body as a sex symbol in contemporary culture is evidence of advanced capitalism's increasing use of new styles of masculinity to promote images of men as consumers as well as producers.[13] Today's debates over the 'real' meaning of masculinity can be understood in large part as a struggle between those espousing the 'new man' style of masculinity more suited to advanced corporate, consumerist-patriarchal capitalism and those who wish to return to an idealized version of 'traditional' masculinity suited to a more production-oriented, entrepreneurial-patriarchal capitalism.[14]

In a more theoretical context, one can see that part of the reason the pornography debate has been so heated, dividing people usually allied, is that debate between civil libertarians and feminists has often been at cross-purposes. Here one can begin to relate political theory not just to political practice but to metaphysical theory. The classical civil-liberties perspective on the issue remains deeply embedded in male theoretical discourse on the meaning of sexuality. The connection between the domination of nature and the domination of women has been argued from many Marxist and feminist points of view.[15] The pivot of this connection is the masculine overlay of the mind–body dualism onto the male–female dichotomy. Within this framework, morality *par excellence* consists in the masculinized mind restraining the feminized body, with sexual desires seen as the crucial test for these powers of restraint. From this point of view, the question of the morality of pornography is primarily the quantitative question of how much sexual display is allowed, with full civil libertarians opting to uphold the extreme end of this continuum, arguing that no sexual expression should be repressed. But the crucial question, for at least the very important strain of feminist theory which rejects these dualisms that frame the debate for the malestream mainstream, is not *how much* sexuality is displayed but *how* sexuality is displayed. These theories speak not of mind–body dualism, but of mind/body

[135]

holism: the body is seen not as a limitation or barrier for expression of the free moral self, but as the most immediate and intimate vehicle for expression of that self. The question of sexual morality here is not that of restraining or releasing sexual desires as they are forced on the spiritual self by the temptations of the body, but that of constructing liberating sexual relationships with and through one's own and others' bodies. Here sexual freedom is not the classical liberal freedom *from* external restraint, but the more radical freedom *to* construct authentically expressive sexualities.

In contrasting imposed and authentic sexualities I am not endorsing a sexual essentialism, but simply carving out a space for a more personal freedom. Any distinction between pornography and erotica remains problematic, and cannot be drawn with absolute precision. Yet I believe some such distinction can and must be made. I would place the terms not in absolute opposition, but at ends of a continuum. Gradations along the continuum are marked not by the explicitness of the portrayal of sexuality or the body, nor by the assertiveness vs. passivity of persons, nor by any categorization of sexual acts or activities, but by the extent to which autonomous personhood is attributed to the person or persons portrayed. Erotica portrays sexual subjects, manifesting their personhood in and through their bodies. Pornography depicts sex objects, persons reduced to their bodies. While the erotic nude presents the more pristine sexual body *before* the social persona is adopted through donning one's clothing, the pornographic nude portrays a body whose clothing has been *more or less forcibly removed*, where the absence of that clothing remains the most forceful presence in the image. Objectification remains present, indeed emphasized, in pornography, in a way in which it does not in erotica. Erotica, as sexual art, expresses a self, whereas pornography, as sexual commodity, markets one. The latter 'works' because the operation it performs on women's bodies resonates with the male gaze's 'pornographizing' of women in other areas of society.[16] These distinctions remain problematic, to say the least, in their application, and disagreement in particular cases will no doubt remain. Much more work needs to be done before one could with any reasonable confidence distinguish authentic from imposed, personal from commercial, sexuality. Yet I believe these concepts correctly indicate the proper categories of analysis. Assuming a full definition of freedom as including autonomy and self-determination, pornography is therefore incompatible with real freedom.

Conclusions

It has often been noted that while socialist feminism is currently a major component of the array of feminisms one finds in academic feminism and women's studies, it is far less influential on the playing fields of practical politics.[23] While an analysis of male sexuality may seem an unlikely source to further socialist feminism's practical political agenda, I hope this chapter's demonstration of the interconnections between intimate personal experiences and large-scale historical and social structures, especially in what may have initially seemed unlikely places, may serve as a useful methodological model for other investigations.

In one sense, this chapter hopes to further the development of socialist–feminist theory via a return to Hegel, especially the Hegel of the *Phenomenology*. Not only is Hegel's master–servant dialectic the *sine qua non* for my use of the concept of alienation, but the inspiration for a mode of analysis which is true to the experiential consciousness of social actors while at the same time delimiting that consciousness by showing its partiality and placing it in a broader context is rooted in Hegel's *Phenomenology*. It is not a coincidence that the major wave of socialist–feminist theory and practice in the late 1960s and early 1970s coincided with a wave of Marxist interest in Hegel, and that current signs of a new feminist interest in Hegel coincide with signs of the resurgence of radical politics in the United States.[17] Analogous to the conception of socialist feminism I articulated in the introduction, my conception of Hegelianism defines Hegelianism as method rather than doctrine. In some sense, contemporary Marxism and feminism can already be said to be rooted in Hegel, in the case of Marxism through Marx himself, and in the case of feminism through de Beauvoir's *The Second Sex*. A more explicitly Hegelian-influenced socialist feminism would embody a theory and practice emphasizing the following themes: the dialectic between individual consciousness and social structure, a thoroughly historical epistemology, a non-dualistic metaphysics, an understanding of gender, class, and other differences as being constituted through interaction rather than consisting of isolated 'roles', the priority of political over moralistic or economistic theory, a probing of the relations between state power and cultural hegemony, a programme for reaching unity through difference rather than through sameness, a tolerance of if not preference for ambiguity and contradiction, and an orientation towards process over end-product.

I would like to conclude with some remarks on the practical import of this analysis. First of all, if the analysis of the relationship between pornography and consumerism and the argument about pornography leading to violence are correct, then a different conceptualization of the debate over the ethics of the feminist anti-pornography movement emerges. If one accepts, as I do, the idea that this movement is not against sex, but against sexual abuse, then the campaign against pornography is essentially not a call for censorship but a consumer campaign for product safety. Or, rather, this is the conclusion I reach remaining focused on pornography and *male* sexuality. But in the broader context of pornography's effects on *women* I alluded to at the beginning, women are not the consumers of pornography, but the consumed. Rather than invoking the consumer movement, perhaps we should then look to environmental protection as a model.[18] On this line of reasoning, one could in principle then perhaps produce through tort law of product liability much of the regulation of sexually explicit material some are now trying to legislate, perhaps developing a new definition of 'safe' sexual material.

Finally, for most of us most of our daily practice as academics consists of teaching rather than writing or reading in our fields. If one accepts the analysis I have presented, a central if not primary concern for us should therefore be integrating this analysis into our classrooms. I close by suggesting that we use this analysis and others like it emerging from men's studies or the critique of men to demonstrate to the men in our classes the direct relevance of feminist analysis to their own lives, at the most intimate and personal levels, and that we look for ways to demonstrate to men that feminism can be personally empowering and liberating for them while simultaneously emphasizing the corresponding truth that this will also require the dismantling of male privilege.

[138]

Notes

An earlier version of this paper was presented at the Philosophers for Social Responsibility national workshop on Pornography, Eastern Division Meetings of the American Philosophical Association, New York, December 1987. I am grateful to members of the audience, and to Roger Gottlieb, Jeff Hearn, Lenore Langsdorf, Maria Papacostaki, and Ricky Sherover-Marcuse for helpful comments.

1   I am indebted for this formulation to Carrigan *et al.* 1987.
2   For the *locus classicus* of the redefinition of Marxism as method rather than doctrine, see Lukács 1972.
3   See my introduction to Brod 1987. For other recent books by men I consider to be engaged in essentially the same or a kindred project, see Hearn 1987, and Connell 1987, particularly the concept of 'hegemonic masculinity', also used in Carrigan *et al.* 1987. Needless to say, none of this work would be conceivable without the pioneering work of many women in women's studies.
4   For book-length treatments of Marx's concept of alienation, see Mészáros 1972, and Ollman 1971.
5   I am grateful to Lenore Langsdorf and Paula Rothenberg for independently suggesting to me how this point would fit into my analysis.
6   Cf. Benjamin 1980.
7   An earlier version of portions of the following argument appears in Brod 1989b.
8   See the essays by Brod and Kimmel in Brod 1987.
9   Compare Brown 1981 on the shift from private to public patriarchy.
10   According to May 1987, from whom I learned of these changes, the term 'judicial patriarchy' is taken from Grossberg 1985.
11   I agree with much of Soble's analysis of male sexuality in capitalism (1986), and note the similarities between much of what he says about 'dismemberment' and consumerism and my analysis here.
12   See D'Emilio & Freedman 1988.
13   See Ehrenreich 1983, and Haug 1986.
14   See Brod 1989a.
15   This features prominently in the work of the Frankfurt school as well as contemporary ecofeminist theorists.
16   I learned to use 'pornographize' as a verb in this way from the introduction to Beneke 1982. See also Tong 1982 on etymology.
17   For the most recent feminist re-examination of Hegel see Raven 1988, Mills 1987, Easton 1987. Hegel enters contemporary radical legal thought primarily through the critical legal studies movement. Especially relevant here is the work of Drucille Cornell (e.g. Cornell 1985). See also papers from the conference on 'Hegel and legal theory', March 1988, at the Cardozo Law School of Yeshive University, New York City, published in the special issue of *Cardozo Law Review* (1989).
18   I am indebted to John Stoltenberg for this point.

Part 3

IDENTITY AND PERCEPTION

CHAPTER 9

The significance of gender politics in men's accounts of their 'gender identity'

ALISON THOMAS

The rather glib use of the label 'post-feminist', frequently employed by the media to characterize contemporary society, might appear to suggest that the feminist struggle against women's oppression is now over and done with, and women's equality finally achieved. Yet, reviewing women's position today, it is clear that there has been little, if any, real change with regard to the established divisions between the 'public' and the 'private' spheres and the identification of men with the former and women with the latter.

For while increasing numbers of women – single and married – are now in paid employment, recent research (e.g. Lewis 1986) suggests that there has not been a reciprocal increase in men's involvement in housework and childcare, and that it is still women who typically retain primary responsibility for both these in addition to their work outside the home. What we have so far seen thus indicates not the overturning of traditional gender roles in any 'androgynous revolution' (as heralded in the 1970s by social psychologists such as Bem 1975), but the assimilation of women into 'male' social roles (cf. Rossi 1976) – a 'masculinization' of women without any corresponding 'feminization' on the part of men (cf. Jones *et al.* 1978).

The underlying reasons for this state of affairs are not hard to identify, and involve both economic factors and the influence of social attitudes. While men's average earnings remain higher than those of women (Department of Employment's New Earnings Survey annually) – and therefore in the majority of cases a man earns more than his female partner – there are at present no obvious economic incentives for them to consider reversing traditional parenting roles. The poor provision of childcare facilities and limited parental leave in this country likewise conspire against those parents who might otherwise choose to share parenting more equally. Our society is thus structured in such a way as to obstruct possibilities for change with regard to gender roles.

However, I am here concerned with the other important obstacle to progress, namely the dominance of traditional attitudes, especially the widespread belief that it is both 'natural' and desirable for women to 'mother' and for fathers to be breadwinners. For even when the state initiates moves towards greater equality between the sexes, the evidence is that public attitudes may often lag behind. In Sweden, in spite of enlightened legislation which enables either or both parents to take parental leave to care for their children when young, at present only a minority of fathers take advantage of their rights to such leave (Moss & Fonda 1980; Sandqvist 1987). One explanation for this has been the basic conservatism of both fathers and employers alike (Lamb & Levine 1983) which, as Pleck (1978) points out, 'pragmatically benefit[s] men by justifying a social order in which males have relative advantage and privileges', and thereby prevents change.

Indeed, as noted earlier, where progress has so far been achieved, it has tended to involve change on the part of women, and only minimal accommodation on the part of men; yet as Jaggar (1983) points out, 'women cannot transform reality alone', and can only go so far in advancing a new society without male co-operation. Until men themselves, both as workers and employers, are prepared to re-evaluate the male role in the family and actively share (rather than simply help with) housework and childcare, it seems that there is likely to be no effective progress towards loosening the straitjacket of traditional gender roles. It is important, therefore, to understand both how far men's attitudes to gender roles may in fact be shifting and how responsive they are to the possibility of change in their own lives.

In this chapter I propose to report on some of the findings of my own recent work on the significance of gender politics in men's accounts of their 'gender identity', focusing in particular on the extent to which their accounts reflect any familiarity with or support for feminist ideas. The study as a whole involved both sexes, and sought to explore the ways in which we construct accounts of our personal identities as women and men in relation to the wider discourses of gender politics current in society (Thomas 1987).

In tackling this complex subject I chose to employ a research methodology which combines many of the virtues of both quantitative and qualitative approaches. Q-sort methodology (Stephenson 1953, Brown 1980) basically involves participants ranking a set of propositions or attitudinal items (the Q set) to fit a quasi-normal distribution (see Fig. 9.1) according, typically, to the extent of their agreement or disagreement with them, and in such a way as to 'map' out their construction of the topic in question. In doing this, participants are in effect both ranking and rating each item (here, from −5 to +5) in relation to the others in the Q set, and this technique thus offers an almost infinite variety of configurations of items.

Factor analysis of the resultant Q-sorted data clusters together those Q sorts which show high positive intercorrelations, and the factors so derived therefore represent the shared perspectives of those Q-sort participants on that particular topic and can be treated as a collective 'account' (e.g., a specific discourse of gender). The 'account' represented by each such factor can be reconstructed by

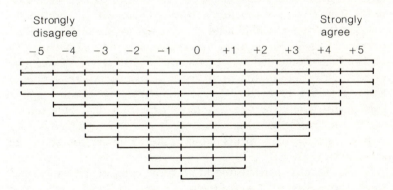

Figure 9.1 Q sort distribution for seventy-seven-item Q sort.

the researcher for interpretation by forming a single composite Q sort (or 'factor representation') from the appropriately weighted individual Q sorts that best define it; from this, the values (−5 to +5) associated with each Q-set item can then be compared with those from other factor representations and their 'accounts'.

For this study three Q sets, each comprising seventy-seven items, were constructed to tap the three facets of 'gender identity' that I wished to examine. The first Q set, on self-representation, consisted of descriptions of 'personality' traits and behaviours commonly associated with 'masculinity' or 'femininity', e.g. 'Is warm and gentle'; 'Is confident and self-assertive'. The second Q set, on gender salience, tapped self-perception in terms of masculinity and the consciousness of one's identity as a man, e.g. 'I don't think of myself as particularly masculine'; 'Being a man is not the most important thing about me.' The third, on gender ideology, concerned the network of basic attitudes and beliefs about men and women utilized in accounting for gender roles, e.g. 'The "psychological" differences between the sexes cannot be denied or wished away – they are part of our biological make-up'; 'There's nothing to stop a talented woman from "getting to the top" in our society today, if she has the ambition and drive to do it.'

For each Q set, items were drawn from a variety of sources and were designed to cover as wide a range of potential perspectives as possible – from extreme radical positions to extreme conservatism, for example, in the case of the ideology Q set. This involved collecting and modifying ideas from the various media, as well as from informal interviews and other measures of gender-role attitudes. The seventy-seven items in each Q set which were finally selected (following a pilot study) offered a reasonable 'balance' of items in each case, such that participants could be expected to find sufficient statements in the set to represent their own feelings or perspective on the topic in question. However, there were no *a priori* meanings attached to any of the items, the idea being that participants should be free to interpret them in their own terms, and that the pattern of meanings associated with particular items by different sets of participants would emerge in the course of the subsequent analysis.

Forty-five men participated in all three parts of the study, and were recruited on the basis of their diversity, the intention being to involve as wide a range of people and potential views as possible.

To this end I sought to include participants with known views on gender politics and representing different sexual orientations, as well as paying attention to those basic demographic characteristics thought likely to affect people's perspectives (e.g., age, class). Participants' ages ranged from 15 to 81, and they included unemployed, retired, and working men (across a whole range of occupations from manual to professional), as well as both higher education and school students.

One of the most striking features of the Q-sort accounts obtained from both men and women participants in this study was their sheer diversity: amongst the men, the three Q sorts generated 13, 11, and 10 interpretable factors respectively. However, here I shall confine myself to discussing the accounts derived from just four factors for the second and third Q sorts only (gender salience and gender ideology), picking out key differences between them in the ways in which they give priority to different Q sort propositions.

Gender identities

The gender-salience Q sort was intended to tap participants' subjective experience of their gender role. Although women's experience of their identity has been widely studied by social psychologists in recent years, male identity has remained relatively under-researched by comparison. In so far as male gender identity has been theorized, it has yielded two somewhat contrasting approaches. The first of these presumes that male identity is essentially unproblematic – at least by comparison with that of women, who are seen as experiencing problems in maintaining a positive sense of self-esteem, either as a consequence of their theoretically unsatisfactory social identity as women (Hacker 1951) or through 'penis-envy' (Freud 1925). Men, by contrast, are the favoured sex, in so far as they collectively enjoy a higher social status, and the individual is therefore presumed to derive positive self-esteem from his gender (Williams & Giles 1978).

However, a number of psychological theories have also postulated the reverse, suggesting that males experience the greater difficulties developing a positive gender identification. This approach may also be traced back in part to Freudian theory, and the need for a boy to move from his primary identification with his

[147]

mother to a more permanent identification with the father, via the trauma of the 'Oedipus complex'. Other analyses (e.g. Hartley 1959, Chodorow 1971) emphasize the difficulties of forming a male identity when male role models may not be readily available and the child may end up learning how to be masculine by learning how not to be feminine (or 'sissy'). According to this 'male sex role identity paradigm' (Pleck 1981), this particular developmental sequence is therefore hypothesized to lead to a potentially insecure masculine identity.

There are thus various theoretical grounds for expecting men's experience of their gender to be ambivalent, and just as complex as women's engagement with theirs, but to be characterized more by uncertainty with respect to the male role than by any lack of satisfaction with it (as is presumed to be the equivalent case for women). The influence of feminism has in both cases been assumed to have exacerbated such gender role difficulties, leading to a renewed preoccupation with questions of gender and identity amongst not only women, but men also (Tolson 1977), and this has sometimes been perceived as a crisis point for men and masculinity (e.g. Hodson 1984).

In my own study of men's experience of their gender I was therefore particularly interested in seeing how feminism might have influenced participants' identifications with male gender roles. The four identity accounts I here wish to focus upon in discussing the data from the gender salience Q sort can be identified as: 'liberal' and pro-feminist (F I); 'liberal individualist' (F V); old-fashioned masculinity (F X); and a self-consciously 'macho' identity (F II). (The different values given by each account to various of the Q sort items can be found in Table 9.1, in which selected items and their associated scores are presented in numerical order.)

Factor I's account stands out from the others as being the only one to reject conventional ideas of gender (note responses to items 49 and 12) and to express a positive commitment towards progressive change (item 28). In this account gender issues are highly salient (item 23) and the influence of feminism is clearly acknowledged (item 70); indeed, there is a sense of discomfort with being a man in a patriarchal society (item 17). As with several of the identity accounts, there is a sense of being an individual, first and foremost, and identifying as a person rather than as a man (items 71, 72). Yet here these feelings seem to go further, backed by an

Table 9.1 Selected items from gender salience Q sort.

Item		I	II	III	IV	V	VI	VII	VIII	IX	X	XI
						Factor						
(12)	I am aware that my ideas about gender and sexuality have changed quite a lot.											
(12)		+3	−2	+1	−1	+2	−3	0	−1	−1	+1	+3
(17)	I feel proud to be a man.											
(17)		−4	+1	−5	−2	+3	−4	0	+3	−3	+1	+5
(18)	I find it annoying the way people prejudge others on the basis of sexual stereotypes.											
(18)		+4	−3	+2	0	+1	+4	+2	+2	+1	0	+2
(23)	Ordinarily I don't think about gender and sexuality very much.											
(23)		−5	+3	0	−3	+4	−5	+1	−1	−3	−4	−5
(28)	I dislike attempts to change our language with words and expressions like 'Ms', 's/he' or 'chairperson'.											
(28)		−4	0	+1	−1	+1	+5	+5	+5	+5	+5	+1
(34)	I generally understand sexual jokes and stories.											
(34)		+2	+5	+3	+1	+5	+2	+4	0	+5	+4	0
(35)	I don't think that the masculine and feminine stereotypes that we hear so much about actually bear much relation to what men and women are really like.											
(35)		+4	−2	0	−1	+3	−5	+4	−2	0	−1	+4
(36)	I enjoy doing things that other people would regard as unconventional for a man.											
(36)		+3	−4	−4	−1	−3	+4	+3	+2	+1	0	−3
(38)	I dislike effeminacy in men.											
(38)		−2	+4	−3	+3	+2	−1	0	−3	−1	+4	+4
(45)	I would rather have been born female.											
(45)		+1	−5	−2	−1	−5	+5	−4	−4	−4	0	−5
(49)	I have fairly conventional ideas about sexuality and relations between the sexes.											
(49)		−5	+2	+3	+1	+1	+1	+3	+3	−1	+4	+3
(55)	How masculine or feminine I am doesn't worry me.											
(55)		+5	−5	+1	−2	0	−1	−3	−3	−5	+2	−4
(62)	I find masculinity in women very unattractive.											
(62)		−2	+3	+4	−4	+5	+3	+1	+1	+2	+5	−1
(66)	My fantasies tend to be erotic rather than romantic.											
(66)		+1	+5	+1	+2	+4	0	+2	−4	−3	0	+1
(69)	I don't think of myself as particularly masculine.											
(69)		+4	+1	+2	+2	+4	+3	+1	−2	+3	0	0
(70)	I don't really feel that the women's movement has had much influence on my life.											
(70)		−4	+2	+2	−3	−4	−4	+3	+4	+1	+3	+1
(71)	Being a man is not the most important thing about me.											
(71)		+5	−4	+2	+4	+3	0	+4	+4	−3	−1	−2
(72)	Generally, when I am aware of myself it is not as a person, but specifically as a man.											
(72)		−5	−2	−2	−4	−2	−2	−2	−3	−2	+1	+4

explicit rejection of 'masculinity', both at the personal level (items 55, 69) and in relation to sex-role stereotypes more generally (items 18, 35). As one of the participants representing this account reported:

> As I frequently found my feelings, actions, interests at odds with . . . society's expectations I soon became one who did not see myself as a 'real man' and began to reject masculinity . . . my individuality, selfdom is much more important. (070)

Several other accounts share this general emphasis on individuality (cf. items 71, 72) – e.g. Factors IV, V, VII, VIII. For Factor V especially this is again backed up by self-perception as non-masculine (item 69), though this may be because being male is simply taken for granted (cf. item 23). There is certainly a strong assertion of being glad (and, indeed, proud) to be male rather than female (items 17, 45). Here, as in several other accounts, the influence of feminism is given clear recognition (item 70), albeit in the context of an otherwise fairly conventional awareness of gender (item 49), manifested here in a disapproval of masculinity in women (item 62) and the assertion of conventionally 'masculine' sexual interests (items 34, 66). This account, while generally liberal in tone, suggests an approval of gradual change, but without any real commitment to it (items 18, 28). The justification for such inertia seems to be found here in the argument that it is ultimately our biology which prevents the wholesale dismantling of traditional gender roles: 'The fact that women have babies and therefore the maternal instinct is with the female, means, to me, that men will continue to remain predominant as the business leaders and therefore continue to make it a man's world' (088).

However, other accounts do not even bother to pay lip-service to feminism and cling resolutely to 'old-fashioned' values. Factor X's account provides one such example, expressing a general mistrust of masculine women and effeminate men (items 38, 62). Traditional attitudes towards gender roles (items 49, 70) are further reflected in a denunciation of attempts to introduce anti-sexist language (item 28) – considered 'pretentious' by one of the participants concerned.

Whereas Factor X's account is based to a large extent on the Q sort of the oldest participant in the study, Factor II's, which provides another example of resistance to feminism, is drawn from the Q sorts of the youngest – three teenagers. This account is one of the few in which being a man is experienced as central to personal identity (items 71, 45), even though responses to items 69 and 55 indicate an uncertainty and lack of confidence in one's own masculinity, especially *vis-à-vis* the peer group. (As one participant complained, 'I don't like it if I'm called a puff [*sic*], like when I miss a shot in football' (096).) Such insecurities (which according to Levinson (1978) are a common feature of male adolescence) appear to be compensated for by a close adherence to conventional masculine behavioural norms (item 36) and by a form of 'conspicuous consumption' in asserting one's maleness (items 34, 66). This corresponds with the observations of other researchers, e.g. Willis (1977), and Kagan & Moss (1962), who noted that:

> one of the concomitants of maintaining a traditional masculine identification is a preoccupation with and an ostentatious display of sexual ideas. The individual gains support for his masculinity by announcing his concern with sexuality.

Not surprisingly, there is generally strong support for conventional gender-role behaviour here (items 38, 62) and little apparent concern about the prevalence of sex-stereotypes in society (items 18, 35).

Although I am here concerned only with the identity accounts of the men who participated in this study, it is instructive to compare these with those of the women participants. One of the principal differences concerns the degree of preoccupation with personal masculinity or femininity: many of the women's accounts professed not to care about this, and in those cases where there was any concern, it was to maintain an already positive image of personal femininity. In the men's accounts, by contrast, there was a far more widespread concern regarding the level of personal masculinity (item 55), often combined with the feeling of not being particularly masculine (item 69). From the treatment of these two items, it can be seen that only Factor I seems totally unconcerned in relation to self-perceived masculinity: amongst the remainder there seems ample evidence of the sort of insecurity that has been hypothesized (cf. Pleck 1981). This is also borne out in responses to various other items, where there are, for example, strong denials of acting

[151]

unconventionally for one's gender (especially among the accounts of Factors II, III, V and XI). There is thus some support for various of the general theoretical assumptions concerning the insecurities supposedly inherent in the male gender identity.

With regard to the impact of feminism, although several accounts acknowledge its influence to some degree (item 70), only Factor I's account suggests any substantial shift away from conventional ideas about gender issues (items 12 and 49). None the less, several of those accounts which manifest some dissatisfaction with prevailing sex stereotypes (cf. items 18, 35) appear to experience some ambivalence concerning their gender, in so far as they are uncomfortable with the idea of feeling proud to be male (Factors I, III, IV, VI, and IX). A number of the accounts also claim to experience their maleness as secondary to their sense of individuality as a person (especially Factors I, IV, V, VII, and VIII). However, whereas the women's accounts, which claimed to experience the self as a 'person', rather than primarily as a woman, also tended to be those which showed broadly unconventional views regarding gender issues, the same is not true of the men's accounts seen here, again with the exception of Factor I. This seems to be the only account in which the personal rejection of a close gender identification, along with conventional gender-typing, is integrated with an explicit gender politics.

The whole tone of these accounts of the subjective salience of gender thus tends to be rather different from that found in the accounts provided by women participants, in which a basic dissatisfaction with traditional 'femininity' appears for many to be the starting point for a feminist analysis of gender roles. Judging from the men's accounts, such a baseline has not yet been reached by many men, and a preoccupation with (rather than resistance to) conventional standards of 'masculinity' remains the norm. I shall return to this point in a more general discussion of these research findings, following consideration of the results of the gender ideology Q sort.

Gender ideologies

Research on attitudes towards changing gender roles in contemporary society has again been concerned primarily with women's

[152]

rather than men's responses to such change. Where men's attitudes have been considered, attention has often focused on the 'male chauvinists' opposed to such change, in spite of findings that men are frequently no less liberal in their attitudes to gender issues than women (Erskine 1971). In this way, men's sexism and traditionalism have commonly been contrasted with women's enthusiasm for change in the light of their newly discovered feminism (cf. Pleck 1978).

A second focus of research on men's gender attitudes has been to question the sincerity of some men's apparent support for liberal pro-feminist values, suggesting that there is frequently a considerable gulf between commitment in principle and in practice to egalitarianism. As Williams and Giles (1978) put it: 'Some men are undoubtedly sympathetic, though the relationship between ideological and practical egalitarianism is often somewhat strained.'

Tavris (1973), in a detailed analysis of both sexes' gender ideologies, further noted that men's views on gender issues tended to be in line with their general political beliefs (broadly 'liberal' or 'conservative'), and were a matter of principle, while women's views seemed more obviously related to their personal experience of sexism, discrimination, or role conflict, and were less obviously part of a more general political stance. This suggests the possibility that women expressing liberal/pro-feminist views are articulating a practical commitment, born out of their own personal experience, while men have often not engaged personally with the implications of their liberal views and therefore do not translate their beliefs into practical behaviour. Hence, Tavris referred to the tendency for men to inhabit 'the easy middle ground, where attitudes are liberal and behaviour is traditional'. With the men's gender ideology Q sorts I was therefore especially interested in the extent and depth of any apparent engagement with feminist thinking in their accounts.

In evaluating the results of this part of the study I am again focusing on just four factor representations, illustrative of the overall diversity of the accounts elicited here. One (Factor I) gives clear support for a liberal feminist ideology of gender, while another (Factor IX) is outlined as typical of a number of 'middle-of-the-road', more or less egalitarian accounts. Here again we also find several decidedly reactionary accounts, especially those of Factor II (talking 'macho') and Factor X (expressing a traditional conservatism).

[153]

Table 9.2 Selected items from gender ideology Q sort.

Item		FI	FII	FIII	FIV	FV	FVI	FVII	FVIII	FIX	FX
(2)	Women are born with a definite maternal instinct.										
(2)		−4	−1	+1	+2	+4	−1	+4	+2	+2	+4
(3)	Sexual discrimination is no longer really a serious problem in our society.										
(3)		−5	−1	−1	−5	−2	+1	−2	−1	−5	0
(5)	Seeing men and women as equal is central to my beliefs.										
(5)		+5	−5	+3	+3	−1	−1	+1	−5	+4	−2
(8)	The 'psychological' differences between the sexes cannot be denied or wished away – they are part of our biological make-up.										
(8)		−4	+5	+4	+3	+3	0	+3	+4	+2	+3
(10)	The assumption that women are mainly interested in clothes, cooking, and 'getting a man' has more than a grain of truth to it.										
(10)		−3	+5	0	0	−1	−1	+1	−1	0	−3
(13)	Too much emphasis is placed on the differences between the sexes, and not enough on all that they have in common.										
(13)		+2	−3	−1	+2	+1	−2	+5	−2	0	−2
(17)	It is pointless to claim that one sex is superior to the other – basically they are simply 'equal but different'.										
(17)		+3	−1	+3	+4	+2	+1	+5	−2	+4	−1
(20)	Much of our sexuality is inborn, not made.										
(20)		−4	+4	+4	−1	+1	0	+5	+3	0	
(22)	There's still a lot to be said in favour of the institution of marriage.										
(22)		−1	+1	0	+3	+1	+3	+5	−1	+4	+5
(24)	I feel that the demands of conforming to what society expects of men and women are a serious limitation upon personal growth and freedom.										
(24)		+5	0	+5	+3	−1	−4	−1	0	−1	0
(30)	Much of the sexual harassment women experience they bring on themselves.										
(30)		−3	+2	−3	−3	−5	+1	−3	−1	+1	+3
(33)	Men whistling at women is a form of sexual harassment.										
(33)		+2	−5	+2	−4	−2	−3	−3	+1	+2	−1
(34)	Children learn how to behave appropriately for their sex in much the same way as they learn anything else – it doesn't just 'come naturally'.										
(34)		+4	−5	−1	−1	+1	−2	+3	−1	−1	+3
(48)	The women's movement has done women more harm than good.										
(48)		−5	0	−4	+5	+1	+1	0	0	−2	0
(66)	When it comes to a conflict between work and home, a woman should put her family first.										
(66)		0	+4	−1	−1	+5	+2	0	+1	+4	+5
(68)	If two people really love each other, then it shouldn't matter whether they are a man and a woman, two women, or two men.										
(68)		+4	−2	+1	+3	−4	+1	+1	+3	−5	−4
(73)	The ideal of remaining a virgin – or 'saving oneself' – for the right person is still a worthwhile one.										
(73)		−2	−4	+1	−4	0	+3	+4	−4	+3	+2

From the responses to various items in Table 9.2 (e.g. items 17 and 5) it is possible to distinguish those accounts which are broadly egalitarian (I, III, IV, VII, and IX) and those which are not (II, V, VI, VIII, and X). Looking further, we can see that the liberal, pro-feminist account already referred to (Factor I) also expresses concern about sexual discrimination (item 3) and gives strong support to the women's movement (item 48), echoing many of the sentiments expressed in the liberal-feminist account which I obtained from the women participants in the study. There is concern regarding the constraints of normative gender roles (items 24 and 68), which are held to be socially constructed (items 2, 8, 20, and 34) and to exaggerate sex differences unnecessarily (item 13). There is also the recognition that whistling may be experienced by women as sexual harassment, and a rejection of the idea that women bring this upon themselves (items 33 and 30). From such responses it is clear that this is basically a pro-feminist discourse which is being advanced here.

Factor IX is one of several which support many of the basically 'middle-of-the-road' liberal values (e.g. items 3, 5, and 17), but in other respects this account appears relatively conservative, both with regard to issues concerning sexuality (item 68) and women's responsibility for childcare (item 66). It endorses the notion of basic gender differences (items 2, 8, 20, and 34) and also supports traditional ideas concerning the value of marriage (item 22) and premarital virginity (item 73). It thus displays a 'gloss' of liberalism over what is otherwise a basically conservative ideology, based to a large extent on religious beliefs, as became clear from the participants' later comments.

In both of these accounts (Factor I and Factor IX) there is support for Tavris' assertion that men's gender attitudes are tied to their wider political beliefs, since the participants providing these accounts made explicit reference to the sense in which the beliefs they expressed represented part of a wider philosophy. Both participants exemplifying Factor IX prefaced many of their comments on specific Q sort items with a reference to the influence of their religious faith, for example: 'As a practising Christian, I believe in the sanctity of marriage' (051). What is particularly interesting here is that this religious influence was not straightforwardly conservative (as suggested in other studies, for example Tavris 1973), but supported a number of fundamentally egalitarian

[155]

values. Thus, in spite of expressing support for traditional social institutions and conservative moral values, overall this account stood out from some of the more reactionary conservative accounts because of its clear commitment to the principle of the equality of the sexes (items 3, 5, and 17, in particular). Those exemplifying Factor I similarly stressed that their support for the women's movement and commitment to the equality of the sexes was part of a general opposition to social divisions and minority-group oppression.

In contrast to the basic egalitarianism of several of these accounts there are also some rather more reactionary ideologies of gender evident here. Factor X, for example, echoes all the conservative moral values expressed in Factor IX's account, but supports none of the egalitarian principles affirmed there. Instead, women's inferior status in society (in itself felt to be no real cause for concern – item 3) is justified by reference to the essential, innate biological differences between the sexes (items 2 and 8).

Another highly reactionary account is that provided by the trio of teenage participants (Factor II), again with very conventional views about 'a woman's place' (item 66). Sex differences, human sexuality, and sex-role identity are all thought to be naturally preprogrammed (items 8, 20, and 34), and homosexuality is accordingly viewed as fundamentally unnatural (item 68). There is indifference to the women's movement as such, but a clear rejection of its values: indeed, it is maintained that if women suffer harassment, they bring it upon themselves (item 30), while whistling at them is (as their comments make clear) 'just a bit of fun' (item 33). This account thereby forms part of a 'macho' and generally misogynist gender discourse (cf. item 10), which, like Factor X, makes an explicit rejection of the principle of the equality of the sexes (item 5).

Overall, these findings provide evidence of the wide range of contrasting discourses of gender which coexist in contemporary society, as well as showing how the accounts people give of their 'personal' gender ideology tend frequently to combine elements from several different discourses. Thus, while there is considerable evidence of exposure to feminist ideas here, in many instances this proves only to be a liberal 'gloss' on a generally more conventional outlook. For example, liberal sentiments concerning the equality of the sexes are often juxtaposed with beliefs in a biological basis for our gender roles (items 2, 6, etc.), which inevitably implies a rejection of the desirability (or even the possibility) of significant change. (It should also be borne in mind that the principle of equality in difference (cf. item 17), here given widespread support, can itself serve as a justification for existing gender roles, on the grounds that each sex should be valued for its specific contribution to society.)

In general, it thus appears that feminist discourse has so far had only a limited impact upon men's thinking about gender: only one account (Factor I) gave explicit support to feminist principles, while the remainder of those identifiable as broadly 'egalitarian' appear more half-hearted about it. Hence, while there is general approval of the gradual improvements to women's status in society, there is only very limited enthusiasm for any radical change (and only Factors III and IV agreed with Factor I in expressing any real dissatisfaction with existing sex roles): progress is welcomed, it appears, only in so far as it takes place on terms acceptable to men. Many of these accounts therefore appear to correspond to what Gackenbach and Auerbach (1975) identified as the voice of the 'well-meaning liberal male' who, they observed, 'talks a current liberal stereotype but does not believe or behave as he talks'.

This returns us to the issue of how far men have engaged with feminist thinking and its implications for them, and whether their gender attitudes reflect any integration of the 'personal' and the 'political' (cf. Tavris 1973). In this study, certainly, only one of the men's accounts (Factor I for both gender salience and gender ideology) showed signs of having made such a connection between the personal experience of dissatisfaction with traditional male roles and a political analysis (informed by feminism) of the social construction of gender. In general, it seems that gender politics have yet to make a significant impact on men's understanding of their gender identity. I shall accordingly conclude by considering some of the possible reasons for men's apparent failure to make the necessary connections between the 'personal and the political' in their own lives.

For many women, feminism has provided a focus for their dissatisfactions with the female role in contemporary society by alerting them to their common cause as an oppressed group, rather than as isolated individuals, and by offering them a theoretical tool for analysing and duly challenging the gender-role system. Not all

[157]

women seek an explicitly political analysis of their lives in this way, yet feminism's wider influence upon society has forced the majority to in some way confront certain fundamental questions about their gender-role identity. As an example, most women will have experienced the need to explain (or justify) their reasons for wanting a job – thereby addressing the issue of the relative importance of work and home/family in their lives. Similar issues are also debated in women's magazines and women regularly rehearse them in discussion with each other. As a consequence, many have been able to apply a 'political' analysis (at however minimal a level) to their personal conflicts in this domain – something which was apparent in the identity accounts I obtained from the women who participated in my research.

However, the situation is clearly different for men. To start with, at present relatively few are likely to experience serious dissatisfactions with their gender role on the same scale that women have done – gay men here being the possible exception. Moreover, as was noted in the discussion of the gender salience accounts presented earlier, even where there is a feeling of not matching up to normative standards of masculinity, this often appears to remain suppressed, as a private dissatisfaction, rather than leading on to a questioning of the gender role expectations themselves, as more often appeared to be the case amongst the women participants in this study. Thus, even those male accounts which here emphasized personal identity as an individual, rather than primarily as a man (i.e. to some extent dissociating themselves from a traditional male identity), nevertheless often expressed a preoccupation with the need to maintain a masculine image (e.g. Factor IV for the gender-salience Q sort), by contrast with the corresponding women's accounts. Rather than drawing upon a political analysis of gender as socially constructed in order to question the need to conform to some masculine standard, most men instead continue to bolster the cult of masculinity that makes them feel insecure in the first place (something that was particularly apparent in the accounts provided by the adolescent participants).

Secondly, men seldom face the same sort of conflict of interests between work and home that women do, and though they might like to be able to spend more time with their children they are not made to feel guilty about this in the way that the working woman is. Men can still 'have their cake and eat it', as far as career and children are concerned: practical fathering for most consists of 'helping' with the children after work or at weekends and is often treated as a leisure activity or 'a bit of a luxury' (Lewis 1986); it does not alter the definition of a man's 'proper' job.

For these various reasons, then, men have not on the whole been driven to question their identification with their gender role as women have done, and have instead continued to take the male gender role for granted. As a consequence, they are less likely to have applied a political analysis of gender to their own lives in the way that many women have done. However, there is a further specific obstacle to men developing a political awareness of their identity: that is, that in analysing their position as members of a particular gender 'class' in a patriarchal society (as women have done through feminism), they would be obliged to recognize the part they thereby play in oppressing women. While some men have accepted this responsibility (as seen in this study), they are still clearly in a minority. Men's reluctance to confront this issue is perhaps understandable, yet until they do so, there can surely only be limited progress for both sexes towards a society in which gender no longer constrains us.

Notes

1 The work reported here was carried out as part of a doctoral research study, funded for three years by the Economic and Social Research Council.
2 I would like to thank the various friends and colleagues who provided helpful comments on an earlier version of this chapter, especially Peter Baehr and Rex Stainton Rogers.

CHAPTER 10

Masculinity, identification, and political culture

BARRY RICHARDS

In this chapter I want to use psychoanalytic theory to consider the significance of gender identification in political culture, specifically in the present political cultures of the United States and Britain. Part of my argument is that the predominant approaches to gender which have emerged from social theory in recent years have not helped us to understand the psychological dimensions of the political climates of the 1980s. In partisan terms, this is to say that they have not helped in the political task of nurturing a constructive and realistic opposition to neo-liberalism and its populist strategies.

The theoretical conceptions of gender identification which have most influenced political debate and practice in recent years are, in very general terms, these. Of femininity, there are two conceptions: femininity as interiorized oppression, and femininity as revealed essence. In the first, femininity is bad: it is the damaging imprint in the female psyche of patriarchal society. Its characteristics are passivity, self-effacement, irrationality, impulsiveness, sentimentality, and so on. In the second conception, femininity is good: it is the spontaneous, essential nature of women. The feminist movement may be seen as concerned with discovering and releasing this essence, so that it may take the space vacated by patriarchal femininity as the latter is subverted. Of masculinity, there is but one predominant conception, and it is a negative one: it is of masculinity as domineering and defensive, as the installation in the male psyche of the presumptions of patriarchal power.

Two features of this conceptual scheme stand out, and they are

[160]

related. One is the absence of a positive conception of masculinity, and the other is the basically asocial nature of the positive characterization of femininity – it may need a social movement to aid its release, but it is not intrinsically a social, relational quality. The connection between the two features is that in this scheme there is an absence of a conception of gender identities as simultaneously relational and positive. The two *bad* images are complementarily relational: the oppressing masculinity and the oppressed femininity help to sustain each other. Gender difference and its reproduction is here located firmly in the field of social relations.

There are, however, no correspondingly relational images of a benign femininity and masculinity, of gender difference as an interactive, intersubjective, and also positive phenomenon. We can immediately suggest two reasons for this. One is that theoretical work has been so overwhelmed by the experience of fundamentally destructive relationships between men and women, and by what it takes to be the experience of patriarchal oppression, that it has not been possible for it to give much effort, or much credence, to the conceptualization of benign interchange between gender-differentiated persons. The second is that for a long time much psychological theory held out to us an image of benignly differentiated genders which we have since concluded to be a lie. The wave of feminist criticism in the 1970s established that large tracts of theory in developmental and social psychology and in psychoanalysis, particularly their visions of male–female complementarity, were rationalizations for the oppression of women. In this context it was understandable to suspect *any* positive presentation of gender differences to be a resurgence of sexist ideology.

However, these are explanations of a lacuna in social theory, not justifications of it. There have been many recent attempts to move towards more complex theorizations of gender, to which I am not doing justice. I have been talking not so much about the subtleties of current thinking but about the cruder notions of gender identity deposited in the wider intellectual culture as a result of the last fifteen or twenty years of social and psychological theory.

It is at this more popular level of thinking and debate about gender that conceptions of gender identity are likely to have an impact on understandings of the political process. But before moving on to look directly at contemporary politics, and to

[161]

prepare for doing so, I want to consider the contributions of psychoanalysis to the theorizations of gender.

There are several different psychoanalytic accounts of masculinity, found in or derived from different parts of the psychoanalytic tradition. For some time now this tradition has been a complex and variegated creature, much of it far removed from its beginnings in the early works of Freud and his circle. I will distinguish between three psychoanalytically-based models of masculinity. There are probably more, and there are certainly many qualifications and elaborations that could be added to the outlines I shall give, but I think that these three are worth focusing on in their fundamentals, as they are important reference points for debate. We can discuss them all in terms of how they conceptualize identification with the father – why this identification occurs, and what aspects of the paternal image or 'object' are being identified with, and how. I use the term 'object' as it is used in psychoanalytic theory, to refer to a person or image of a person much more often than to an impersonal thing. The point of this questionable usage is not to equate persons with impersonal objects but to convey that people are being considered in the context of the mental life of one particular individual, a *subject* for whom others are the *objects* of relationships.

Psychoanalytic models of masculinity

The first model is probably still the most familiar. It is often the centrepiece of popular accounts of Freud (I discuss some of these in Richards 1989), and it informs some early feminist thinking about masculinity as a problem. In this model the identification with the father is defensive, and arises out of the need to defend against castration anxiety. The identification is made in fear; it is what Anna Freud (1936) was to term 'identification with the aggressor'. The son is averting castration by renouncing his Oedipal desire for his mother, and by converting his rivalrous hostility towards his father into an angry emulation of him. Thus the emotional basis of male domination is reproduced; the son takes on the father's punitive possessiveness, and joins in the fearful, competitive rites of masculinity in which he hopes to lose forever his fear of castration.

This is a powerful tale, and it remains so despite the number of times it has now been told and the various banal reductions to which it has been subject in popularizations of Freud. It is worth noting that in Freud's account, and more so in that of later psychoanalytic theories, much of the hatred and rage that are seen as thus condensed in the masculine identity are not simple imitations of the father's wrath, but are the boy's own psychic productions and projections, issuing from the helplessness and frustration of early experience. So although this model does portray masculinity as bad, it does not in itself support the notion that boys are bullied into masculinity by the tyrannical behaviour of fathers.

The second model provides another negative image of masculinity. It is to be found in some very influential feminist writing from the mid-1970s on, especially that initiated by the work of Dinnerstein (1976) and Chodorow (1978). I would say that this is now the most influential derivative of psychoanalysis in the intellectual culture of feminism and the Left. Here again the masculine identification with the father is seen as defensive, but in a different way. The threat being awarded off is not fundamentally that of castration but of engulfment by the mother. It is the boy's way of struggling free of his primary bond with his mother and the state of total dependency which that entails. Identification with the father is a desperate escape from fusion and from the threat of ego-loss in symbiotic closeness with the mother. Because of the gendered division of labour in child care, women and femininity are equated with this early state and its terrors, while masculinity offers differentiation and freedom. The escape is at a crippling cost, however, in that it is into a rigid selfhood premissed on an aggressive rejection and denial of the realm of intimacy, nurture, and sensuousness represented by woman.

This is another compelling tale, one which has helped to bring psychological depth to a lot of current thinking about gender identity. Again, though, it is worth noting that it tends to draw selectively upon psychoanalytic theory, which has another much more favourable way of discussing the role of the father in assisting differentiation from the primary identification with the mother. The father can be seen as playing a positive role for both boys and girls. In his being available as a love-object and as an object of identification he can bring a *legitimate* support to the child's ego in its struggle to separate from the mother.

The third model is not intrinsically incompatible with either or both of the first two, since all formulate real and important aspects of the development of masculinity. The third model is, however, radically different from the first two in that it posits the identification with the father as being a loving one. It is not a defensive manoeuvre but a major element in the development of integrated selfhood. An image of the father as a protective and facilitating other, as a loving and beloved parent, is here the object of identification. Whatever frustrations the father has caused the son (either in reality or in the son's phantasy) are outweighed by the son's gratitude. The identification is not a contingent defence, but a crucial instance of the core developmental process whereby good images of others are internalized to form the substance of a good sense of self. When this process is the dominant one in the boy's relationship to his father, then the aggression and Oedipal anxiety which will also inevitably be present can be contained.

Here in this third model we have an image of masculinity as a benign, indeed necessary, quality of psychic life in men. It is also rooted in social relations in that it is a product of identification, which is one of the most powerfully social and relational concepts in psychoanalytic theory. What I wish to draw attention to is the absence or marginality of this kind of image in much social theory, and consequently in much contemporary thinking about the significance of gender identity in political culture.

Masculinity in crisis: a case study

Against this general theoretical background I will consider some recent psycho-political analyses of the Reagan presidency. These analyses point towards an approach in which through the use of a positive vision of masculine identity a deeper understanding may be obtained of more pathological forms of identification with the father.

Michael Rogin, in *Ronald Reagan: The Movie* (1987), identifies the Oedipal anxieties that Reagan struggled with in the 1940s after the death of his father. Shortly after his father died, Reagan had to play a scene in which he wakes up to find that his legs have been amputated. He later described this as for him the most difficult task he had ever faced as an actor. Psychoanalytic theory could have predicted this difficulty, seeing this scene as mobilizing in Reagan

[164]

his castration anxiety and Oedipal guilt. In his phantasy the amputation was the punishment for having killed his father.

Lloyd DeMause, in his startling book *Reagan's America* (1984), extends this line of analysis and suggests that for several years, from his father's death in 1941 until his conversion to anti-Communism in 1947(?6), Reagan was anxiously depressed. The Hollywood crusade against Communism gave him an opportunity to arrive at an organization of his emotional life that freed him from guilt. The aggression towards authority, the hatred of the father – which Reagan feared and loathed in himself – he could now project onto 'Commies'. He could devote his life to fighting this threat since he now located it in others, in what he was later to call the 'evil empire'.

Thus after years of being crippled by Oedipal guilt, Reagan left behind his early Democrat New Deal leanings and began his real political career. This Oedipal resolution is in the manner of the first model of masculinity which I described. Reagan saw an alternative to guilt and amputation by renouncing his Oedipal desires and identifying himself with the punitive father.

In his recent book *Taken In: American Gullibility and the Reagan Mythos* (1988), Stephen Ducat adds to this analysis the hypothesis that this stabilization of Reagan's psyche also contained elements of the second model I have outlined, of masculinity as the repudiation of woman and of dependency. Reagan apparently has very little of emotional substance to say about his own mother in his auto-biography and in interviews, but from what is known about her Ducat concludes that Reagan's flight into hyper-masculine Holly-wood heroism (and later into neo-liberal brutalism) was also a defence against annihilation in the embrace of an effusive, smother-ing mother, who could love people only if they were weak and dependent. Hence Reagan's occasional claustrophobia, and his enduring contempt of what for him is the engulfing, emasculating mother of Welfare.

Why, though, did these negative crystallizations of masculinity occur in Reagan's case to the exclusion of any significant element of a more benign development along the lines of my third model? Why did his masculine identification with authority take such a pathological and projective form? One answer to this question is offered by Ducat through a consideration of what is known of Reagan's actual father, Jack. He was an unsuccessful shoe salesman, a chronic alcoholic who was violent with his son but was also a weak and ineffectual parent. Having to some extent to look after his father, Ronald developed a precocious maturity and pseudo-autonomy. In the terms of psychoanalytic theory, we would expect this kind of family situation to have damaging effects, at a number of levels.

To understand these effects we may consider that a major task of emotional development is the giving up of the illusion of omnipotence. Many schools of contemporary psychoanalysis now agree broadly on the idea that the mental life of the infant is characterized by a state of narcissistic illusion in which the existence of other people as fundamentally separate agents is omnipotently denied, as a defence against recognizing the helpless dependence on others which is the infant's real condition. This illusion is relinquished as the distinction between self and others is slowly and imperfectly established. The establishment of a firm distinction between self and other is never final, and infantile phantasy remains an active force in the unconscious.

Thus the son's Oedipal phantasy of possessing his mother is basically a revival and variation of the early infantile illusion of omnipotence. If it is unchallenged by a paternal assertion of the parents' marital togetherness, then the overcoming of this illusion is made that much more difficult, and the boy is more likely to become a man whose grasp of reality is seriously impaired by grandiose phantasy.

As a corollary of this, the son gets no help from his father in coping with his Oedipal guilt – he finds that he is in effect triumphing over his father. In the course of development outlined in my third model, the father survives the son's rivalrous attacks on him, and neither his love for his son nor his strength are diminished. Thus the son can feel less anxious and guilty about the consequences of his aggression. This was clearly not the case for Ronald Reagan. In the third model, another aspect of the father's failure to be present as a good and potent person is that the son's developing self will not be able to gather into itself images of a strong and forgiving father. Accordingly, in the absence of a realistic basis for identification with a good father, the son will instead identify with an omnipotent, idealized father, an image created by the projection of his own omnipotence.

Reagan's personality then is not distinguished by an excess of strong masculinity. Rather it consists, at least in part, of the absence in his mind of a realistic, adequate father, and his retreat instead into omnipotence and into massive projections of his destructiveness, thus setting the psychic stage for Star Wars. It is important not only for sexual politics but also for our understanding of the role of gender identity in national leadership that the nature of Reagan's pathology be understood in this way, as a *failure* in the development of healthy masculinity rather than as some sort of inevitable extension of the masculine identity.

The importance of this point can be emphasized if we consider another aspect of Reagan's persona observed by Ducat. This is that he frequently deploys in his speeches a language of maternal plenitude and strength; Ducat contends (1980, p. 92) that Reagan's fatherly presence is actually less important to his appeal than 'the ease with which he can link himself to seductive images of maternal fusion'. One major way he has of doing this is with the ancient imagery of the motherland. He speaks of 'her' as if he and his audience are in a state of total identification with 'her'. This might seem surprising in view of some of what I have said: is this sub-mergence in the great mother not something which the hyper-masculine defence is intended to prevent?

This is only an apparent paradox. The masculine self which Reagan and the many men like him construct is at root a matter of *pseudo*-differentiation. While at one level in flight from the mother, at another level it remains embedded in the realm of narcissistic fusion. It rests upon the omnipotent projection of badness and guilt, and the omnipotent self is not a really differentiated one, however ruggedly independent its inhabitant may appear to be. Psychic differentiation is a state of disenchantment to which we can struggle through only by giving up infantile illusions of omnipotence and by accepting that we are dependent on and limited by others. In the overcoming of illusion a key element is the recognition of *difference*, which is the sign of the other. In the world of omnipotent phantasy, there is no fundamental difference between things; the narcissistic self is everything. Differences mark limits. In the experience of the infant, structured by those who care for it and by its own corporeality, gender difference is sensually and socially the most powerful of differences. Internalizing this fact of gender difference, and locating ourselves (men and women) in relation to it, is therefore a crucial step in psychic development, in

[167]

the movement from omnipotence in phantasy to potency in reality. The establishment of gender identity is basic to the differentiation between self and other.

Where the opportunity for identification with a good-enough paternal figure is lacking, combined with a mother who in her own relationship with her son does not sufficiently facilitate his masculine otherness, then a masculine identity based in love and in reality *may* be impossible to achieve. These seem to have been the conditions in which Ronald Reagan grew up. The imperfectly differentiated self which does develop in such conditions is grounded in narcissism, and must be all things to itself since it cannot tolerate the reality of others and so cannot have complementary relationships with others. It must be mother and father, masculine and feminine. Hence the fusion in Reagan's addresses of images both of the vengeful father and the encompassing mother. Here may lie the basis of his appeal, in the *completeness* of his presence rather than in either its paternal or maternal evocations.

To move on from a discussion of Reagan's own psyche into an analysis of his popularity, and the links between his popularity and the content of his psyche, raises a host of questions which there is not time here to explore fully. I will just refer to one point, made forcefully by DeMause and Ducat, and with which I agree, which is that Reagan somehow mirrored a state of mind which is widespread in the American people. His success was based on his emotional suitability to express their needs and their illusions. It then follows from this analysis that difficulties in the path of self-differentiation linked to failures in gender identification are also widespread in the United States, and are the psycho-historical dimension of the belligerent neo-liberalism and its paranoid world view which the Reagan administration embodied.

Champions of the individual?

I will conclude with the suggestion that a similar line of analysis may be a fruitful approach to the study of British political culture in the 1980s. Margaret Thatcher's family background seems to have been less disturbed than Reagan's, and more importantly of course the whole national context is very different. However, we have a striking instance here of a national leader who is both resoundingly feminine in some respects yet is also an aggressive, punitive, and stereotypically masculine figure, and whose popularity rests on just this combination. Moreover, this combination is inextricably linked with her contribution to the transformation of British politics, injecting new life into some of its most paranoid and regressive traditions. So again an ambiguously gendered quality of leadership is linked to an omnipotent style and to fascinated and at times rapturous support from a significant proportion of the electorate. Thatcher is for us a realization of the phantasy of a combined parental figure with whom, if we are her supporters, we may also merge.

We are thus spared the task of distinguishing and separating masculine and feminine, self and other. We can project our omnipotence into her and be reassured by the confidence with which she assumes it, so confirming our belief in it, just as Reagan confirms Americans in their illusions of omnipotence. From a psychoanalytic point of view, it would not be at all paradoxical if these two strident champions of the 'individual' were found to be the political expression of a widespread *failure* in the psychological processes of individuation and gender-differentiation. Efforts to develop a political culture which is not so dominated by regressive phantasy need to address themselves to this possibility.

CHAPTER 11

Male perception as social construct

LEONARD DUROCHE

In this chapter I would like to raise some questions about three separate but interrelated problems, which if not queried thoroughly – which is impossible in a brief presentation – are at least hovering ominously about on the edges or in the background as I go about other things. The first, of course, is the matter of perception and the question whether its foundations are exclusively located in structures of the mind and the body or whether cultural factors also play a role. There is, I believe, considerable evidence for the latter position. The second question inserts the gender issue into the discussion and asks to what extent perception, so understood, is not gender-neutral, but gender-specific. The third issue, which will have to be dealt with largely by implication, has to do with the consequences for hermeneutics – for example, to use my own field, literary study, what does that mean for readers and writers and for the act of interpretation? What I am currently trying to explore in my own research is the kind of literary connections made between feeling and knowing and the extent to which there are in literary texts gender differences in the way the senses are cultivated, particularly as metaphors for knowing. I will not get that far in what I try to unfold here, but that is at least the direction in which I am headed.[1]

What I am about to undertake then is the attempt to frame a question: what are the issues that need be raised, how might one go about investigating the extent to which the perceptions have a history? And if they do and if gender position is a factor in that history, how much of it can be recovered and where might one look? Perception is seen then as a part of 'body language', a semiology of the senses that is at various times cultivated or ignored. Accepting the phenomenological evidence that there is such a thing as bodily/embodied knowing as well abstract knowing, the connection I wish to make here is between the body and knowing, *how* the body knows, how that knowing has been moulded by social and political forces at different times and in different places, and what part the gender of the knower – or more accurately, the social control and regulation of the gender role – has played in historical forms of perception.

My query is stimulated by and based on the recent discovery that the human body has a history, that how the body has been viewed has changed enormously over time, that the changes in how the body has been viewed have had less to do with new developments and discoveries in science than with changes within the social order, that in fact social change has often seemed to have had the effect of encouraging science to produce empirical and phylogenetic evidence that will support social policy (Weeks 1985, p. 177). One of the best entries into the newly emerging history of the body is the excellent collection of essays from a wide range of fields edited by Catherine Gallagher and Thomas Laqueur under the title of *The Making of the Modern Body*. The combined effect of individual efforts in a number of disciplines, partly historical, partly anthropological, partly psychological and medical, has worked together with 'social historians' deepening interest in culture', with 'the thematization of the body in modern philosophy (especially phenomenology)', and with a new awareness of the significance of gender in literary and cultural analysis, to produce a quite different picture of how we live and breathe and do all those other bodily things (Gallagher & Laqueur 1987, p. vii).

Beginning somewhere in the 18th century a major reinterpretation of sexual difference began to take place. As Gallagher and Laqueur state it, 'the reinterpretation of women's reproductive biology solved ideological problems inherent in eighteenth- and nineteenth-century social and political practices' (Gallagher & Laqueur 1987, p. viii). A part of that history that still has not been written is how the reinterpretation and reformulation of perception and the senses played a part in this reinscription of the body and whether the transformation of perceptual emphases, practices, and patterns served, or at least reinforced, the same kinds of essentially ideological purposes.

[171]

There are strange and contradictory developments in this revolutionary rewriting of sexual difference that I can only point to in the present context, but which pose questions for further investigation. There is the paradox, for example, of the feeling-unfeeling woman. At the same time that the modern notion of woman was beginning to assign to her an increased responsibility for emotional life in the psychological division of labour that takes place within emerging bourgeois capitalism, a view of the female body developed that saw it/her, if not as a machine, at least as driven by mechanisms of a more or less automatic and cyclical nature that would take care of the important business of providing progeny[2] with little or no need for gratifying any sexual feelings she might have, though it was doubted she had any (Laqueur 1987, pp. 1, 30, 35).[3] Alongside this there also occurred a narrowing and reduction of male sensibilities. The more uninhibited expression of male emotions characteristic of the age of sentimentality, of *Sturm und Drang* and early Romanticism, with their emphases on strong and close, often deeply intimate, male friendships, is replaced in the 19th century by a muting of the emotions, a transforming and often dulling of male perceptual awareness, and an increasing homophobia.

What I find particularly interesting in all of this is that in a period in which almost obsessive attention has been paid to the female body, the male body has often seemed invisible, in fact, unimportant. As Rosalind Coward, (1984, p. 227; quoted in Lehman 1988, p. 91) has said in writing about contemporary cinematic use of this heritage:

> Under this sheer weight of attention to women's bodies we seem to have become blind to something. Nobody seems to have noticed that men's bodies have quietly absented themselves. Somewhere along the line, men have managed to keep out of the glare, escaping from the relentless activity of sexual definitions.

As Peter Lehman (1988, p. 105) has argued, also talking about film: 'Traditional patriarchal constructions of masculinity benefit enormously by keeping the male body in the dark, out of the critical spotlight. Indeed, the mystique of the phallus is, in part, dependent on it.' But has the male body escaped definition? I want to take issue here with Stephen Heath who contends that there can be no male equivalent to the lived, embodied discourse of women, 'telling the truth about one's body' (Heath 1987, p. 25), though up until now most of the evidence has been on his side. A lot has been written about the changing spaces of men and of women from the 18th century to the present; I mention Donald M. Lowe's *History of Bourgeois Perception* as just one example. I propose that we begin to take a look not just at social space in the way that is usually understood, but at perceptual space as well, at visual space, auditory and olfactory space, and how the perceiving gendered subject at the heart of that space is transformed as the space is transformed. But before getting into those issues, let me turn to why the body, at least the female body, suddenly became so very important towards the end of the 18th century.

As Thomas Laqueur has indicated (1987, p. 2 and *passim*), the human body was, for all practical purposes, until well into the 18th century, taken to be an ungendered, generic body. The male body was indisputably the norm. But the female body had all the parts of the male; they were simply rearranged, outside-in, deformed. Woman was an inferior man (Laqueur 1987, p. 2 and *passim*). The revolutionary shift that took place somewhere in the 18th century was that a model of hierarchical difference, based on homologies between male and female reproductive systems, began to crumble and an 'anatomy and physiology of incommensurability replaced a metaphysics of hierarchy' (Laqueur 1987, pp. viii, 3). Londa Schiebinger's fascinating historical study of the first medical illustrations of the female skeleton in the 18th century lends further credence to Laqueur's contention that no one cared about 'anatomical and concrete physiological differences between the sexes until such differences became politically important' (Laqueur 1987, pp. 3f.). And the reason why they became important had to do with one of the great dilemmas of Enlightenment egalitarianism. As Laqueur indicates, the human body inherited from antiquity presented the body politic of liberalism with a nasty conundrum, namely, how – given Enlightenment beliefs in universal, inalienable, and equal rights –

> to derive the real world of male dominion [over] women ... from an original state of genderless bodies. The dilemma, at least for theorists interested in the subordination of women, is resolved by grounding the social and cultural differentiation of

the sexes in a biology of incommensurability that liberal theory itself helped bring into being. A novel construal of nature comes to serve as the foundation of otherwise indefensible social practices. (Laqueur 1987, p. 19).

Thus it is perhaps not surprising that the 'new biology' appears 'at precisely the time when the foundations of the old social order were irremediably shaken' (Laqueur 1987, p. 16). That the body, especially the female body, has come to occupy a crucial position for us in political discourse is clear (Laqueur 1987, p. 1). But what about the male body?

To answer this question we need to consider some other issues. Though they cannot be examined in detail here, the following issues need to be kept in mind in thinking about the deadening of the male body and the transformations of male perception: the transformation of the sense of space (including gendered space); the process of privatization (thus shifting from an emphasis on public/anonymous space to private/personal space); the growth of the bourgeois concept of the individual; and the requirements of the new emerging bourgeois-capitalist industrial order. Sensual perception is implicated in each of these categories and strikes me as a particularly suitable avenue to the examination of the redefinition of masculinity that has taken place since the Enlightenment.

Given what I believe is the importance of socio-historical factors in perceptual experience, there is an incredibly small scholarly literature devoted to the subject. It is as if there had been a plot *not* to call attention to the connection between perception and its socio-historical contexts, at least for adult males. There is not even any clarity on what the term means. Or perhaps there is. Electronic data searches of the sociological and psychological literature indicate what is most likely a patriarchal bias: get out of the body, get into the head! Most entries under the rubric *perception* have to do with attitude (for example, *self-perception, social perception*).[4] Perception does not mean 'What do I sense? What do I feel?', but 'What do I think? What do others think?' This undoubtedly reflects bourgeois embarrassment with the body. Almost from the moment when Baumgarten first invented the word 'aesthetics', which has to do with feeling, with sensory perception, western (mostly male) thinkers have been trying to negate, to transcend the body. Fortunately, from Rabelais and Voltaire to the present, the French, at least, have not allowed us to forget it. There is a very fascinating literature, almost exclusively French, on the cultural history of perception. Much of it is based on the work of Sartre and Merleau-Ponty, combining existentialist-phenomenological perspective with Marxist and/or Freudian cultural analysis. Although it poses only randomly and often only implicitly the question of gender, in so far as it critiques dominant western social practice, which is to say the practices of patriarchy, it is worth further examination. The major works, at least for our purposes, are the very early phenomenogical study of Jean-Pierre Richard, *Littérature et Sensation* (1954), *Noise: The Political Economy of Music* by Jacques Attali (1985), and *The Foul and the Fragrant* by Alain Corbin (1986). In what follows I need to order the senses. I am going to reverse the usual order and bypass the sense of sight, so often associated with the male and on which there is already a sizable literature, some of the best of which is in the area of film theory (for example, Kaplan 1983; see also Fox-Genovese 1987, p. 21, Benjamin 1983, p. 294, and Buci-Glucksmann 1987, p. 222).

It was particularly in considering the way in which vision fails in Kafka's *Metamorphosis (Verwandlung)* and the way in which Kafka calls attention to all the other senses that I began to attend to the portrayal of perception in male narratives. In a piece I have written on *Verwandlung* (Duroche 1987a) I have argued that attending to the senses other than sight enhances our chances of *hearing* multiple voices in the male text. It has become a cliché that men are unfeeling, that the male of western industrial society, certainly the middle-class American or West European male, no longer 'senses' a full range of choices for living a complete life, partly because he has narrowed his sensual contact with the world. As Richard Palmer has asserted, in the place of an openness towards the world and others the western male has privileged one or two senses and has withdrawn into a narrowly confined perceptual shell where correctness of perception is defined as correct *seeing* (Palmer 1969, pp. 142f.). The world eludes *man's* 'grasp' because *he* has cultivated only limited ways of connecting with or grasping it.[5] There is in linguistic usage a hierarchy of the senses in which seeing and feeling (touching) rank at the top as the most assertive, and smelling, hearing, tasting are considered more passive/receptive. Feel and smell are ambiguous in that they are more likely to represent acts or emanations of a subject, though all the senses can be construed as either active or passive experiences. Traditionally, sight has been thought of as the 'male' sense. It is associated with distance, with cognition, with abstraction (cf. *vision*, German *wissen*, English *witness*). The ability to distinguish subtler sensual differences (for example, flavours and fragrances) has often been thought of as 'typically feminine'. Except for a few comments on sound/listening, I want to concentrate on what has often been thought of as the most primitive of the senses, the most animalistic, namely the sense of smell. Taste and touch I will have to ignore altogether as well as the question whether there is any correlation between the different cultivation of the perceptions among men and women and the patterns of dominance and submission that exist and/or are cultivated by each gender.

'Sound', as Jacques Attali tells us, 'is a way of perceiving the world. A tool of understanding.' He speaks of our refusal to draw conclusions from our senses, how the knowledge that is there is effectively censored. He thus emphasizes the urgency, the necessity of imagining 'radically new theoretical forms, in order to speak to new realities' (Attali 1985, p. 4). Listening is what men supposedly do least well. Our training has taught us to hear the sound of machines, the ping in the engine which our wives can never hear, but to block out the sound of people, children squabbling in the other room while we read the paper. Attali opens his book on noise with the marvellous phrase: 'For twenty-five centuries, Western knowledge has tried to look upon the world. It has failed to understand that the world is not for the beholding. It is for hearing. It is not legible, but audible' (Attali 1985, p. 3). His examination of the politics of noise, controlled and organized noise, disruptive noise, and the institutionalization of silence, illustrates perhaps most forcefully that to regulate patterns of perception is to control probably the most crucial aspect of semiosis. Obedient conformist subjects hear what they are trained to hear, see what they learn to see, and so on through the other senses. Apprenticed to attend only to certain ranges of perceptual signals, a large part of experience remains quite literally 'meaningless' for me, in a sense does not exist for me.

Though Attali focuses on issues of social control, his emphasis is on class, rather than gender, race, or some other context of antagonism and domination. Yet the implications of his argument for gender studies are clear, and if he does not insert the gender issue, Susan McClary, in her afterword to the English translation makes sure of doing so in her short discussion of the phenomenon of marginalization of discourse and her brief listing of contemporary composers who have refused 'to be silenced by the institutional framework, [and] who are dedicated to injecting back into music the noise of the body, of the visual, of emotions, and of gender' (Attali 1985, p. 157). A colleague of mine has used Attali's book in a seminar on the position of gays in current socio-political discourse to provide a theoretical model for understanding how the politics of gay liberation are defined by much of the mainstream heterosexual community as noise.

Attali underlines the connections of sound and knowledge, sound and power. He, too, deals with the process of privatization and the ways in which our modes of consuming electronic signals have cut us off from one another and increased our isolation. In moving from music as ritual, through music as representation, to music as repetition we have moved from collective communal consumption to the privatizing of listening, the best symbol of which is the Walkman, intensifying one more stage of our monadization.[6] Most important, he documents changes in the nature of listening. Combining his insights into the control of sound and silence, the power to legislate what noise is, with some implications of Bakhtin as mediated by recent feminist scholarship on attending to different voices in social discourse would seem to offer provocative and fruitful possibilities for gender studies. Dale Bauer shares the view of Patrocinio Schweickart 'that "*certain*" (not all) male texts merit a dual hermeneutic: a negative hermeneutic that discloses their complicity with patriarchal ideology, and a positive hermeneutic that recuperates the utopian moment' (Schweickart 1986, pp. 43–4); cited by Bauer 1988, p. 19. See also Duroche 1987a, 1987b). She demonstrates how '[w]ith Bakhtin's dialogics, critics can theorize the process by which alien or rival social languages are excluded and silenced' (Bauer 1988, p. 6). Though the methodologies differ, curiously enough the impulses and the epistemological optimism behind writers otherwise as diverse as Bakhtin and Heidegger and his pupils are remarkably similar in that both camps hold out the possibility of going 'behind the text to ask what the author did not and could not say, yet which in the text comes to light as its innermost dynamic' (Palmer 1969, p. 147). Identifying the tension between controlling and letting go,

[177]

seeing and hearing, asserting and accepting, not assuming a finished and final reading as 'the sole object of interpretation', but rather nurturing an attitude that is 'creatively open to the as yet unsaid' (Palmer 1969, p. 147), Heidegger, too, suggests possibilities of recovering muted voices from beneath the dominant chords of conformity.

For the remainder of this paper I want to focus on the history of smell as it has been detailed, at least for 19th-century France, by Alain Corbin (1986), and try to pull together what I believe are some of the implications and conclusions of that very rich study for the developing field of gender studies. I shall begin by providing a map of the ground I intend to cover. At some point around the middle of the 18th century there suddenly appeared a new keenness in the sense of smell, an awareness of being situated in and oriented to the fine articulations of an olfactory space; Corbin speaks of the redefinition and lowering of the thresholds of tolerance. Evidence seems to show that then contemporary science, which was also beginning to change in the part it played in the shaping of public policy, had a great deal to do with this historical phenomenon. Though many of the theories of osphresiology, the scientific study of smell, ultimately proved to be false, the 'new alertness to the olfactory environment within a very specific milieu: that formed by doctors, chemists, and reformist campaigners' (Corbin 1986, p. 56) had a crucial impact on the shaping of public attitudes and beliefs, so much so that even after the sensualist theories of the osphresiologists were discredited and were replaced by those of the more exact sciences of chemistry and the biological sciences, and after Pasteur had disproven the pathogenic nature of smell, many of the attitudes and beliefs remained. Considering the timing of this transformation, one notices that it began just before the major shifts of population distribution, thus is not initially attributable to increasing urban pollution caused by industralization. However, it does overlap with the industrial revolution for much of its history and undoubtedly has a connection with the transformations of public and private space that came about in part because of the process of industrialization. It coincides also with the emergence of the bourgeoisie as the dominant social class and is also reinforced, if not 'caused', by the intensification of privatization in numerous areas of daily personal life, a process that is still with us, seemingly with no end in sight. It obviously has some connection with the growth of the bourgeois concept of the individual and the development of a notion of private personal space, the space of the individual, as clearly distinct from public space, and it coincides with the concern for and redefinition of gender differentiation, which is amply documented in Gallagher and Laqueur (1987).

As far as where the history may be found for what Corbin has called an 'economy of desire and repulsion', 18th-century osphresiologists are probably the best place to begin. They demonstrate the almost official status of sensualist philosophy at the end of the century, the importance of the empirical evidence of the senses in the construction of knowledge, and they were obsessed with finding such evidence to support their hypothesis that the sexes, to name one opposition, could be distinguished by smell. The range of possible markers seemed to be: sex, age, race, class, with sex the most significant and class, at least initially, in the arena of public space, the least: 'no distinction was made between the smell of the poor and that of the rich; it was the crowd as such that was putrid' (Corbin 1986, p. 53). This was a clash of the personal space of the bourgeois (male) citizen, who increasingly thought of himself as an individual, and a public space which violated the boundaries of the Self.

By the eve of the French Revolution there was already a sizable literature, based in part on sympathetic theories, on smell as the 'sense of affinities' and 'the arousal of attraction or repulsion through personal odour' was a frequent literary theme (Corbin 1986, p. 53). The further progression of distinctions seems to have developed in the following manner: starting from an initial separation of public and private space, based in part on the fear of pathogenic qualities of smell, and from a gross distinction between the sexes, there began a long process of deodorizing public and then later private and domestic space, a process that has reached its culmination, if not apotheosis, in the United States. The cultural phenomena that are connected with this development are decorporealization, especially the increasing disembodiment of male experience, the 'abstracting' of the senses, removing them from their link with our bodies. Corbin (1986, p. 229) reminds us that 'Kant excluded the sense of smell altogether from aesthetics. Physiologists later regarded it as a simple residue of evolution. Freud assigned it to anality' – an inheritance perhaps of the 19th-century obsession with sanitation, its fear of human waste and the increas-

[179]

ing privatization of its disposal, and the link between mephitism and infection, resulting in what he calls 'an apprenticeship in smelling directed entirely toward excrement' (Corbin 1986, p. 60).[7] Hand in hand with the rise of the strong state responsible for maintaining and regulating public space was the rise of the concept of the individual, including the perceptual and perceived individual. This was and is an individual with not only more sharply defined political and psychological contours but of sensory contours as well. This explains part of the revulsion to the crowd: 'The fact that the odours of the "I" were better defined, more intensely felt, could only stimulate repugnance to other people's odours' (Corbin 1986, p. 61). The pre-Enlightenment preference for musk, an animal fragrance, over vegetable fragrances, gave way to the notion of the delicacy of smell (Corbin 1986, p. 68), in fact, of the more delicate sensitivity, that is, of evidence of refinement, of the bourgeois male over the proletarian,[8] and there were many instances of the deleterious effects of strong smells on men. There was likewise an increasing suspicion of the male use of perfume generally, in part out of the fear that something dirty was being covered up (Corbin 1986, p. 69), in part because of the importance of intensely experiencing the Self, 'revealing the uniqueness of the "I"' (Corbin 1986, p. 72), in part because 'of the much wider criticism of artifice, affectation, effeminate fashion' – in short, all the tendencies suspected of leading to 'degeneration' of the male – turning him into a woman. To that one can add the notion that 'perfume, linked with softness, disorder, and a taste for pleasure, was the antithesis of work ... What disappeared or became volatile symbolized waste' (Corbin 1986, p. 69). This is but one more example of how transformations in many different areas of experience in the 19th century collaborated, at least in their consequences, to dull male perception, encapsulate men in unfeeling bodies, which they neglected and abused, and increased the sense of isolation, separation that ultimately led to a growing homophobia. Gradually, the ability of men to detect subtle odours, fragrances, and aromas seemed to weaken and was passed on to women as part of woman's work, which was restricted largely to domestic space. The emphasis on private hygiene reinforced both the fear of physical contact and the repulsion caused by smelling another's body. Smell, and the aim not to offend by smell, began to play a not insignificant part in establishing models of behaviour and new codes of etiquette

(Corbin 1986, p. 73). Slowly these attitudes were passed on to the lower classes: 'The masses gradually came to feel the same repulsion. The new sensitivity reached that fringe of workers who spent their nights trying to escape being haunted by their involvement in manual labor' (Corbin 1986, p. 151), the odour of which they tried to scrub away:

> The warm consolation of sleeping more than one to a bed had to be given up. Norbert Truquine, railway navvy, felt his gorge rise when he breathed the odour of brandy and tobacco exhaled by his companions; forced to share his pallet, he confessed that he could no longer without repulsion tolerate contact with another man. (Corbin 1986, p. 115).

Balzac and others (for example, Emile Gaboriau and Guy Thillier) devoted considerable attention to the odours of masculine space, particularly offices, 'corrupted by emanations from the bachelors who people it' (Corbin 1986, p. 168), and college boardinghouses.[9] In a somewhat different context, writing about urban reactions to rural space and the smell of peasants, Corbin admits that almost all authors dealing with this period, including himself,

> have rather naively used the copious discussions by bourgeois observers for their own purposes. It would have been more valuable if they had tried to unravel the tangled systems of images and, above all, shown that the basic historical fact was not the actuality (which had probably changed little) but the new form of perception, the new intolerance of traditional actuality. (Corbin 1986, p. 155f.).

As public space became purified, at least the portion of it reserved for bourgeois activities, and as the lower classes became somewhat less threatening for a more secure bourgeoisie (Corbin 1986, p. 157), certain aspects of proletarian experience were elevated and incorporated into the ideal of 'masculinity', and certain smells and signs signifying smell were revalorized. The ennobling of tobacco, workers, and sailors is such a case. Though the smell of tobacco had ranked earlier among the worst of odours, it was gradually accepted as an appropriate manly fragrance. Corbin argues that its ultimate victory as an acceptable sign of masculinity

[181]

also symbolized the victory of liberalism; it bore witness to increasing male domination of social life before it actually became its instrument. Like proscription, to which its spread was largely due, tobacco was decked with 'patriotic', egalitarian qualities. It was in this context that it earned its title to nobility. 'Smoking [like pissing] creates an equality among its confraternity . . . rich and poor rub shoulders, without being surprised by the fact, in places where tobacco is sold,' *and only there.* (Corbin 1986, p. 150, my emphasis).

As tobacco has been deodorized so, too, have two images of stench, at least for earlier generations, the sailor and, in America, the cowboy. Despite the obvious raunchiness and hints of debauchery there still today remains something exciting in the public mind, or at least in the mind of the advertiser, in these figures. To an urban society no longer required, for the most part, to earn its bread by the sweat of its brow, they, like the construction worker, represent male strength, hardness, and control. The total deodorization, sanitizing, and 'whitening' of these images is a signal of their unreality.

There are other developments in men's olfactory history during the 19th century that one could explore, but I hope I have made my point. There developed at this time a politics of smell.

Deodorization seemed to become a necessity with the emergence of bourgeois capitalism, which is to say, with the rise of the modern western form of the patriarchal state. The transformation of perceptions has attended the transformation of the social order. The bourgeois has so totally deodorized *his* world that *he* can no longer tell the difference between shit and Shinola.[10] An historical phenomenology of male perception is needed to understand *that* and *how* men have been desensitized in the use of the other senses.

Given the persuasive evidence that gender position is indeed a constituent of hermeneutic activity, that a part of my historical reality is belonging to and coming out of a cultural experience that further articulates itself as a woman's culture and a man's culture, that my embodied experience is a precondition of all my acts of understanding, even at the fundamental level of perception, then it makes sense to attend to the senses in literary and cultural analysis. Though some sociologists may question using literary sources as equally valid documentation, in the absence of other kinds of evidence there is little recourse but to consider our literary history, which is still one of the best documents we have, a kind of phenomenological record, not only of how we think, but also of how we feel or do not feel (for a defence of literature in the service of sociology, see Lepenies 1969, pp. 43ff; also Benard & Schlaffer 1987, p. 71).

Because much that I have talked about has to do with gender-specific spatial experience, I believe one of the issues that still needs to be explored is the gradual shift of male space since the end of the 18th century from a homosocial to a homophobic space. One of the best explorations of that issue in a literary context is D. A. Miller's essay on sensation and gender in Wilkie Collins's *The Woman in White*. He contends the west 'has routinely subjected male homosocial desire' to a kind of 'aversion therapy', the aim of which 'is not to redirect men's desire onto women but, through women, onto boys: that is to privatize homosocial desire within the middle-class nuclear family, where it takes the "normal" shape of an Oedipal triangle' (Miller 1987, p. 133). Weeks argues in a similar vein, citing Deleuze and Guattari: 'The Oedipal triangle is the personal and private territoriality that corresponds to all of capitalism's efforts at social reterritorialization. Oedipus was always the displaced limit for every social formation, since it is the displaced representative of desire' (Deleuze and Guattari 1983, p. 33; cited by Weeks 1985, pp. 173f.).

I have pointed to some of the possible causes for the growing sense of separation and isolation among men. But there is much that is still puzzling. Why, for instance, did the sexes have such opposing reactions to the transformation of social space in the 19th century? As Judith Stacey has pointed out (1987, pp. 7, 24, and *passim*), the isolation of women in the home may have been quite ironically an impetus toward the development of a feminist solidarity during the 19th-century reorganization of family, social, and gender relations. Without wanting to indulge in conspiracy theories, I do want to suggest that the consequences have been the same *as if* a collective will had created the kind of personality that capitalist society required (see Weeks 1985, pp. 21f., 74), *as if* the threatening gathering of large numbers of men in the workplace had necessitated or somehow called into play societal mechanisms that led to the development of modes of discourse and interaction and fostered the homophobia that undermined any potential

[183]

collective male consciousness and possibility of male solidarity, a thesis which is strongly supported by many of the essays in Mangan and Walvin (1987), especially those of Stearns and Rotundo. Another way of saying this, suggested at least by implication by Barrett and McIntosh in their book *The Anti-Social Family*, is that the privatizing of homosocial desire within the family has drained all other social relations between men of much of their meaning or at least 'normality' (1982; see Weeks 1985, p. 42). The process of the growth of homophobia is perhaps one of the most important issues to unravel and one avenue is to explore the role of feeling and the perceptions as part (a blocked part?) of a communication system between men, to explore the examples of and the barriers to male intimacy and friendship. To understand that even in our perceptual behaviour we are constituted as historical subjects in a process of instrumentalization is to recognize the possibility of structuring differently our subjectivity and, thus, our society.

Notes

I gratefully acknowledge receipt of a grant from the West European Area Studies programme of the University of Minnesota, which made it possible for me to attend the conference.

1 I have already touched upon the problem in earlier projects. See Duroche 1987a, 1987b.
2 See Londa Schiebinger's comment (1987, p. 53) on the possible influence of '[m]ercantilist interests in population growth ... in the rise of the 18th-century ideal of motherhood'; also Gallagher 1987. Foucault (1980, pp. 36f.) also posits the thesis of a strict utilitarian economy of reproduction under bourgeois capitalism.
3 In actuality the most contradictory arguments were put forward, ranging from those that equated menstruation with rutting and 'animal heat', to those that saw in women a 'superior capacity to transcend the brutish state'. In Laqueur's words, woman could be 'simultaneously a periodically excited bomb of sexuality and a model for the power of civilization to keep it from exploding' (1987, p. 30).
4 The source of searches was the PsycINFO database, which covers the world's literature in psychology and related disciplines, including among others sociology, anthropology, education, and linguistics. Monographs, periodicals, dissertations, and technical and conference reports were searched for English, French, and German.

[184]

5   The differences between *physical seizure/control* and *mental 'catching'/ understanding* are blurred in the English *'grasping'*. German insists on distinguishing between *greifen* ('grabbing'/'seizing'/'apprehending'), emphasizing active, if not aggressive, tactility, and *begreifen* (*'understanding'/'comprehending'*), which is a mental activity.

6   Jessica Benjamin sees among the disastrous consequences of privatization, isolation, and rigid social control the urge to violate the boundaries, those of the Self and the Other, in order to experience 'losing the Self' (Benjamin 1983, p. 296).

7   Much of what Corbin says of the French applies to other western industrial countries as well. The later 19th-century witnessed the rise of sanitary obsession documented recently by the British television special programme 'On the Throne', a cultural history of sanitation and the flush toilet.

8   See Corbin (1986, pp. 140–1) on the unequal development of olfactory sensibilities along economic and class lines. The poor man smelled because he was not fully human: 'he had not crossed the threshold of vitality that defined the species' (Corbin 1986, p. 144). The analogy was extended to other 'sub-human' groups, women, particularly prostitutes, prisoners, and 'half-women' such as Jews and homosexuals (Corbin 1986, p. 145).

9   In note 31 to Chapter 10, 'Domestic atmospheres' (p. 276), Corbin writes: 'The importance of smells of this environment [the college boardinghouse] in the genesis of male sensitivity in the 19th-century cannot be overemphasized. Once again, repulsion was associated with the absence of coeducation. The college boardinghouse was an accumulation of the mephitism of the walls, the social stench of the domestic staff, and the odour of the sperm of the schoolmaster and his masturbating pupils. This stench, perceived as male, sharpened desire for the presence of females.'

10 A popular American slang expression, referring to a well-known brand of shoe polish. Thomas Pynchon uses the expression in *Gravity's Rainbow*, in writing about the obscenity of the bourgeois order and imagining John F. Kennedy possibly visiting the men's room of the Roseland Ballroom where Malcolm X worked as a shoeshine boy (Pynchon 1973, p. 688).

[185]

CHAPTER 12

Doing masculinity/ doing theory

WIL COLEMAN

In this paper I argue that the task of *theorizing* masculinity is misconceived. I argue that not only does the theorist become enmeshed in irresolvable methodological problems, but to the extent that these problems are amenable to being ignored it still leaves the theoretical analysis of masculinity with what I claim to be its central fault; that it misrepresents the very topic of its inquiry, the doings of men.

Central to much current thinking among sociologists concerned to theorize masculinity and sexuality is the suggestion that masculinity is *socially constructed*. The way that the notion is employed in the literature (e.g. Kitzinger 1987, Plummer 1981, Weeks 1985, 1986) can be seen as an answer to the question: What sustains and underpins the production and reproduction of behaviour seeable as 'male' or 'masculine'?, or, in short, What sustains masculinity? There are broadly two possible ways of answering that question sociologically. The first is structural in form. In it, 'masculinity' as regards the individual is treated as the outcome of a developmental process at least in part social. In it, 'masculinity', both in the individual and in the culture is conceived as sustained and under-pinned by processes and structures amenable to both sociological and psychological analysis. The second focuses on the individual as actor. Here 'masculinity' is seeable as sustained by a continual work of 'presentation management' on the actor's part. The model is dramaturgical. Goffman is my example. Only on two occasions do we find Goffman dealing with the topic of the relations of men and women directly (Goffman 1977, 1979). Nevertheless of course, we can find abundant support for attributing to him a dramaturgical model of social behaviour from *The Presentation of Self in Everyday Life* (1959) onwards. We find a similar view of gender expressed in Garfinkel's depiction of the life of the transsexual 'Agnes' (Garfinkel 1967). In these cases we are persuaded to see gender in terms of gender-*display* and in terms of 'bricolage'; a making do with whatever is to hand in order to sustain one's self-presentation as a *properly* gendered person.

I suggest that there are problems with both these answers and that the problems are similar to all those that bedevil the 'structure versus agency' debate in sociology. I suggest that a compromise between the two (even if granted the epithet 'dialectical') fails to offer a satisfactory solution. Instead, I suggest that the problems are endemic and follow from the nature of the questions asked. In the second part of this paper, therefore, I invite the reader to focus her attention on the *questions* and to the *occasions* of their asking.

First, then, we have a sociology of masculinity that treats 'men' as the outcome of a developmental process which is – at least in part – a social process; call it a process of socialization. How is this process conceptualized? Take Plummer and Weeks as our examples. When they argue that masculinity is socially constructed, they are saying this: something is to be seen as invariant (bodies: their anatomy, their morphology), while something else is to be seen as open to variation (the way those bodies are understood; the different 'meanings' that are read into them). Also open to variation are the ways (male) persons are expected to behave: their rights, duties and responsibilities. It is the latter, the variable part, that is to be seen as socially constructed. The distinction, a common one of course in sociology, is the distinction between 'sex' and 'gender'. Now there's nothing in principle wrong with such a view. After all, we can all – as sociologists, and as lay persons – be expected to know that different cultures have different expectations of what 'men' should do. We can all be expected to know that 'masculinity' is culturally and historically relative. We can suggest in fact, then, that the distinction between sex and gender is a thoroughly commonsense one. In the same light, talk of multiple 'masculinities' rather than some single 'masculinity' is relatively straightforward and unproblematic.

I think we can take it as incontestable that, indeed, every parent knows that, while something is, as it were, 'given' (the body and its powers), that still leaves plenty of scope to alter, adapt, change, influence, and so forth, the developmental process. But, again as every parent knows, the bringing up of children is far from an exact science: the child, its body, the person, resists our attempts to mould and adapt her or him as we wish. None the less, experts as diverse as Doctors Spock and Freud agree that the years of childhood are consequential for the person who is their outcome. Sociologists can be expected to agree: adult men can be seen as the end result of a developmental process in significant parts social. We shall also expect to find a broad measure of agreement in this: that should we wish to see changes in the ways men are then – at least in part – we need to consider changing the ways that children are brought up. I say 'at least in part', for we should also allow that men and women are able to respond to changes in attitudes and expectations (let alone material and economic changes) that may intervene on their adult life. And so the sociologist will attempt to map those social forces and the changes to which they give rise. All this is surely uncontroversial.

Yet we should examine what is being claimed more closely. It is postulated that masculinity (M) is sustained by some structure (S) (or some process, discourse, or other candidate or candidates), where the link between masculinity (M) and (S) is a causal one. (The possibility of alternative formulations of the way masculinity is sustained – *viz.* the dramaturgical model – suggests that the link is other than purely a conceptual one.) An empirical claim is being advanced: the analyst is concerned to theorize the link between (M) and (S), and to trace the causal relationship of (S) on (M). In the developmental model, men come to embody or internalize structural determinants (S). Some accounts stress childhood socialization. Typical in this respect are psychoanalytical accounts. Other accounts stress adult socialization. In both, the existence of a mediating link between structure (S) and male behaviours (glossed as (M)) is frequently hypothesized. 'Ideology' often plays this role. Persons either 'respond' to 'ideological influences', or else ideology is equipped with causal powers: in this case it is alleged that ideologies *determine* how men behave.

In the following pages I shall develop my objections to this way of thinking about men and the doings of men. I shall suggest that the alternative version, the dramaturgical, is also flawed, though I go on to claim that it possesses a number of positive features. In the latter part of the paper I shall suggest that the analytical task is rendered problematic through the very election of the term 'masculinity'. But first I shall attend to what I see as the central problem with the approach outlined above. There are objections above and beyond those I raise here. But these are objections that can be mounted against all and any 'structuralist' sociological account. For that reason I shall not develop them here.

What, then, are my objections?[1] Centrally, that there are irresolvable methodological problems that must be ignored if the theoretical task is to get under way at all. The problem is this: how is the theorist to identify instances of 'masculinity'? Or, to put it another way, by what *criteria* are these instances identified? We should note that the theorist must be able in principle to identify (M) as a necessary prolegomenona to asking what sustains it. Now I suggest that this is properly seeable as a problem for the theorist for I think we can agree that a whole diversity of activities, tasks, experiences, beliefs, things, places, and so forth, *can* be seen on some occasions at least as displaying or exemplifying masculinity, or of being 'typically masculine' activities, tasks, experiences, beliefs, things, places, and so forth. I also suggest that it is properly seeable as a *theoretical* issue in that, in order to undertake an analysis of the sort outlined above, the analyst is required to employ a rigorous and clearly specifiable notion of (M); she must do so if *theoretical* analysis is to be distinguished from what she might claim is unrigorous lay thinking in these matters.

One possible solution can be dismissed from the start. That is that the criterion governing identification be simply that the activity, task, or whatever be performed by, avowed by, used by, or owned by some (at least one) adult male person. This answer is unsatisfactory for two reasons. First, that some men on some occasions can be seen as 'more feminine' than other men. To say that these men or these behaviours are to be excluded on principle is to beg the question, for it leaves unresolved what that principle might be. Second, a whole diversity of activities, experiences, tasks, things, and so forth are common to both men and women. How is the theorist to distinguish them? She has need of some independent criterion of masculinity. Suppose, then, that the theorist simply *decides* what is to count as an instance of masculinity. Is this a solution? Well, on what *grounds* is she to substantiate her choice? That the instance in question be findable in at least one adult man? Surely not, for that is to return us to the problems

[189]

already outlined. To decide by theoretical fiat is not to render the theorist thereby immune from the demand to provide grounds for her choice. One possible solution might be to advance the claim that some particular 'masculine' behaviour, say, is linked in some more or less obvious way to some socio-structural feature (S). For example, particular socio-economic conditions of deprivation might be seen to be connected to some particular form of male behaviour – 'male machismo'. Yet once more this is to beg the question of how 'machismo' might be seeable in the first place.

The theorist has a need, then, for some rigorously defensible criterion for what is to count as 'masculinity'. None seems forthcoming. Despite this, however, the theorist, like any other adult person in the society, is perfectly well able to identify typical masculine behaviour, typical male tasks and things, typical male experiences, and so forth. Indeed, the very notion of a *criterion* governing the proper attribution of the label 'masculinity' depends upon an ability to make these identifications, an ability common to the theorist and her readers alike. The idea of the possibility of a 'private criterion' is an incoherent one (Wittgenstein 1958, pp. 250f.). I suggest that the *theoretical* problems arise from the very way in which the analytical task is conceived. They follow from the theorist's commitment to causal analysis. I shall substantiate this claim in two parts. First, we need to understand the analytical preference for causal analysis exemplified by 'theory'. Second, we need to understand the consequences of that choice.

Causal analysis can be contrasted with an analysis in terms of the motivational accounts provided by (in this case) men on the occasion of their being invited to give reasons for the actions they take, the choices they make, the beliefs they hold, and so forth (cf. Louch 1969). A preference for the former follows from principled rejection of (some if not all) actors' accounts on the grounds of their (relative) falsity. For theory is seen as necessarily *critical* theory: it is only *theoretically* that masculinity will be explicable. The springs of action remain hidden until revealed *theoretically*.

One of the consequences of this view we have seen already. In that a theoretical account of masculinity required that a rigorous independent criterion of what is to count as 'masculine' behaviour be identified, the theorist will become enmeshed in methodological problems. Connect this with my point above regarding the theorist's principled rejection (on the basis of a commitment to social critique) of actors' accounts of their reasons and motives for doing what they do: in rejecting actors' accounts in favour of causal analysis, the theorist ignores and must ignore the skilled ways that persons-in-the-society theorize, question, analyse, argue over, and explicate gender identities. In so doing, the theorist is compelled (on grounds of theoretical rigour) to reject *her own* skills as a person-in-the-society to identify, and identify unproblematically, instances of 'masculinity'. It is this that leads to the methodological impasse I have outlined above. *In practice* what we find is that the theorist employs, and *necessarily* employs, the categories 'masculine' and 'masculinity' in methodical yet commonsense ways. In the latter part of this paper I shall attend in more detail to those ways.

I suggest, then, that there are no alternative, *theoretical* grounds upon which to identify instances of masculinity. The only grounds are those of the skills possessed by the analyst in common with other persons in the society. These skills in the attribution and avowal of gender identities can be directly related to Wittgenstein's employment of the term 'grammar' (Wittgenstein 1958, pp. 180ff.), to remind us how competent adult members of a society are skilled in the use, the grammar, of its language. Thus persons in the society can be seen as skilled in the use of words, and things too (skilled in the *grammar* of their use), in the accomplishment of gender identities. At this point I turn to the second of the two ways in which to theorize 'masculinity', namely, the dramaturgical model.

The dramaturgical model has on the face of it a number of advantages over one that stresses the workings of hidden structures. First, it explicitly depends on the fact that persons in the society are skilled at identifying, using and displaying instances of 'masculinity'. Second, it can explicitly allow that the sociologist herself is also so skilled, and that she is dependent on those skills *qua* sociologist. Third (and I suggest that this *is* an advantage) it privileges *description* over theoretical/causal analysis. For in this version, persons are seeable as acting for *reasons* rather than causes. Persons are seeable as 'doing' masculinity, rather than it being something that is done to them or that happens to them. 'Masculinity' from this point of view is something that has to be achieved, worked at. Once again, masculinity is conceived of as socially constructed, yet now we are to see that work of construction not in genetic or historical terms, wherein causal powers are attributed to structures (S), but as contingent and occasioned, wherein the work of construction is accomplished by the individual as agent. And here sociological interest is focused on (the alleged) moment-to-moment accomplishment of masculinity. We are on the familiar ground of a sociological account of social action that stresses 'agency' over 'structural causation'.

Now Goffman has been accused (e.g. Schegloff 1988) of preferring the persuasive use of the vignette over close empirical analysis of naturally occurring social occasions, but there is no reason in principle why such empirical analysis of 'the doing of gender' should be impossible. Indeed, Garfinkel's account of 'Agnes' (Garfinkel 1967) indicates otherwise (albeit that 'Agnes' is concerned above all with displaying 'herself' as a 'proper woman' and hence has a different relationship with the 'masculinity' she seeks to deny than does the average man). None the less, if we take Goffman as our guide here, particularly as regards the 'presentation of self', then we run into problems. A familiar criticism of Goffman is that his dramaturgical model transforms us all into actors and dissemblers self-consciously pursuing strategies of impression management. There is some truth in these criticisms. It is not always clear to what extent we are to take Goffman's terms of art ('impression management', 'front stage'/'back stage', and the like) metaphorically or literally. (For a discussion of this issue see Manning 1980). And the problem is, when it come to 'masculinity', then it just doesn't seem to be something that must be continuously impression-managed. On the contrary, it seems that in this respect men simply *do what they do*. And they do it on most occasions without considering whether or not they are presenting a satisfactory presentation of themselves as 'men'. Hence of course that very sense of the 'spontaneity' and 'naturalness' of masculinity which the theorist is anxious to disabuse us of and have us see as nothing of the sort, but as 'socially constructed' through and through. (It is worth noting that there is clearly a contrast to be made here with Garfinkel's 'Agnes' for whom the 'doing of gender' was far from natural and spontaneous – but this is precisely what makes 'her' unusual and hence unsatisfactory as a representation of what women and men *ordinarily* do.) When compared to the dramaturgical model, the alternative 'structuralist' version has at least this in its favour; it can account for the apparent 'spontaneity' and 'naturalness' of gender, and it does so in terms of a familiar

[192]

appeal to structures and processes imperceptible to quotidian consciousness (though just how persuasive we find such an account is altogether another matter).

On the one hand, then, we have the dramaturgical version wherein masculinity is sustained by a continuous and ongoing performance and display. On the other hand we have a version of masculinity that treats it as sustained by hidden yet discoverable determinants. There are reasons for finding each of them attractive – yet flawed. We are caught between the Scylla of agency and the Charybdis of structure; a familiar dilemma! A dilemma, it must be said, that I have no intention of resolving. I intend instead something different: to show that the sociologist need not adopt a position as between 'structure' and 'agency', and that these dilemmas follow inevitably from the nature of our questioning. It is for this reason that I return at this point to the sociologist engaged in 'doing theory'. I suggest:

(a) That we see the question: What *sustains* masculinity? as a question asked on certain occasions. I suggest we turn our attention to these occasions, one of which (though not the only one) is the occasion of the sociologist 'doing theory'.

(b) That the question itself and the occasion of its asking should be seen as internal to the *theoretical* construction of 'masculinity'. Treating 'masculinity' as a theoretical construction, we observe the *work* of its construction in and as *theory*.

(c) More generally, that we attend to the 'grammar' of the terms 'masculine' and 'masculinity'. I use 'grammar' in the Wittgensteinian sense (Wittgenstein 1958, pp. 180ff.) already alluded to above, such that we attend to the occasions of the *use* of these terms. In so doing we shall see that one of the ways they are used is to render the doings of men visible and analysable as topics of social inquiry – and to render them visible and analysable as *problematic*.

(d) We have seen that the theorist's problems are in good part due to the ways the theoretical task is conceptualized. What is more, however, in so far as the theorist renders the doings of men problematic, she risks traducing the very topic of her inquiries: the *actual* doings of men. The theorist risks doing so in so far as she ignores the specific and occasioned activities of *actual* persons, in favour of speaking *generically* of

[193]

'men'. It is here that the category 'masculinity' plays a central role in the theoretical task, and particularly in the way this task is conceived of as *critique*.

I shall deal with (c) and (d) first. If we attend to the ways that persons use the terms 'masculinity' and its cognates, we can note how they are used as descriptive categories. I refer at this point to Sacks's (1972) employment of the term 'category' and the notion of a 'category-bound activity'. Take the category 'man'. We can treat the category as having certain properly attributable activities (and by extension things, experiences, and so forth) bound or tied to it. These are *normative* ties. There are those activities and so forth that are seeable as *proper* to the category 'man' and, by extension, to the person so categorized. Gender is a normative issue, and arguments concering masculinity involve questions concerning the proper attribution of gendered activities, gendered things, gendered motives, gendered experiences, and so forth. The theorist relies upon and uses the fact that everyone knows that not only are there men and women but that activities, experiences, things, tasks, places, and so on, can also be seen as gendered. These attributions are often contested – as we know. But disagreement over proper attributions requires that parties to a disagreement already possess a notion that activities, things, experiences, places, and so on can be, are, and *should* be seeable in gendered terms. Indeed, it is by means of such ties between the category 'man' and, say, the activity 'fixing the car', that a person is seeable as a proper (or otherwise) incumbent of the category 'man'. The very fact that gendered activities, things, places, and so forth are known to exist (by theorist and reader alike) is what enables the theorist to use the concept 'gender' in the way she does, contrasting it with what is asocial or biological. The use of the concept 'gender' focuses attention on women and men as social beings with social and not just biological differences between them. It focuses our attention in particular ways. It is to those ways that I now turn.

The theorist renders the doings of men problematic. She does so by constructing arguments concerned with what is and what is not proper to the categories 'woman' and 'man'. (This will be found to be true whatever the political persuasion of the theorist-as-critic; whether coming from Left or Right, critics share a common ground in so far as arguments are and should be the *proper* doings of men). The argument, then, is concerned with those activities and so forth that can on some occasion be seeable in gendered terms. The notion that some activities *should* be seen as gendered finds its practical and theoretical warrant in the doings of actually existing men and women. Competent persons-in-the-society can be assumed to be skilled in the attribution of, avowal of, use of, and engagement in gendered activities, things, experiences, beliefs, motives, things, places, and so forth. It is by using their skills in the grammar of gender categories that persons-in-the-society are able to identify others as and to display themselves as proper incumbents of such sorts of men as 'tough guy', 'lady's man', 'father', 'husband', 'feminist', 'wimp', and so on. To be able to do so can be a condition of one's competence as a proper social member. To be unable to do so is to be unable to participate in the practices of the society: it is to court the risk of being an object of others' projects, never the subject of one's own. Analytically, it should be noted that the tie between the activity (or thing, experience, etc.) and the category is a reflexive one. By that I mean that we should think not in terms of *here* gendered persons ('men') and *here* gendered activities and so on ('fixing the car', 'wearing trousers'), with the two sets (persons; activities) quite independent of one another. On the contrary, neither persons nor activities should be seen as gendered independently of the 'gender-producing work' in which they are implicated.

Further, then, to my point, (c), by attending the 'grammar' of the terms 'masculine' and 'masculinity' we note the ways it is used by the theorist to render the doings of men, but not only of men, visible and analysable as topics of social inquiry. The theorist's use of the terms 'masculine' and 'masculinity' serves to collect a diverse set of activities, things, and so forth in so far as each of them can be related to one (at least) actually existing male. Hence all these things can be seen as the doings of 'men'. The problem, however, is this. While any number of things can be seen quite properly as the doings of 'men', they might also on some occasion be seeable as the doings of 'teachers', 'fathers', 'voters', 'police officers', 'someone cooking a meal', and so forth. In treating the doings of men generically, the theorist necessarily disattends to the *specific* occasion and the *specific* individual. Yet on those occasions, just those persons within just those settings might be seeable by the parties to those settings as 'the Old Bill', 'Joe's father', or 'my friend cooking

[195]

a meal', for example, rather than as 'a man'. That they are *also* seeable as 'men' might well, for the purposes of the parties to that setting, be irrelevant. On these occasions, that these persons happen also to be men just does not figure.

I have already suggested that, for men, the doings of what one does as a man may or may not involve attention to doing 'being a man'. As a man, I may well remain blind to the fact of my maleness, in order to attend to the task of cooking a meal, riding a bicycle, or typing. We can say that, for men, the matter of their maleness is an *occasioned* matter. For it is only on occasions that a man's proper membership of the category 'man' figures as relevant to a setting and occasion. Such an occasion is where a man's 'masculinity' risks being called into question. (It is here we find the analogy with Garfinkel's 'Agnes' most apposite, for it was in those settings where her 'femaleness' was most at risk that she engaged in the most careful monitoring of her behaviour.) So, for example, if a man is asked by a female friend to hold her bag, where that bag is seeable as 'a woman's bag', then the man may make a deliberate effort to hold it in such a way as to show that it is not *his* bag, and that despite appearances (in the eyes of some possible audience) he is and remains 'a proper man'. 'Masculinity' may figure for a man if he is engaged in a task seeable by some at least as a female task: a domestic task such as ironing, for example. He may do it, but *clumsily*. Or a man's membership of the category 'man' may figure on the occasion of being called to task for being 'a typical bloody man', for example. On such an occasion it is as if all along he had been 'doing masculinity' – but hadn't been aware of it. Another example: a man may seek to display himself as a 'good feminist' by refusing to conform to some gender-specific task or role. None the less, I say, deliberately, that these things *may* figure; they may not. A man may remain blind to how he might be seen by others (and this is rather different from not caring how he is seen). Or a man may be blind to criticism (which is not the same as ignoring it). A man may see himself as 'a good feminist' yet be seen by (some) others as 'a typical bloody man'.

These, then, are *occasioned* problems – for men. Yet by treating the doings of men generically, the theorist treats them as problematic, and *abidingly* problematic for men. It is in the work of rendering masculinity problematic that the theorist achieves her *theoretical* warrant. (One could say that the theorist demands of men in their daily lives to live those lives as if under the auspices of theory and theoretical work. The theorist requires of men that they engage in a constant critical/theoretical self-examination.)[2] In accomplishing that critical perspective, the 'taken-for-granted' is constructed as rhetorical foil and occasioned contrast to the theoretical account. And in so doing, the theorist treats 'masculinity' as if it were a puzzle requiring a solution. It is logical, given that puzzlement, that the theorist is then led to ask: what sustains masculinity? As I have suggested, we can see the asking of that question as internal to the work of theorizing – work in which 'masculinity' is rendered visible as a topic of sociological inquiry, and rendered visible as *socially constructed*. Once asked, there are but two ways of answering that question: either masculinity is constructed and sustained by hidden but discoverable forces, discourses, ideologies, structures, and the like (in which case its contingent and moment-to-moment accomplishment is unconscious, the actor being unaware, and necessarily unaware, of all that he does), or else it is constructed, *bricoleur*-fashion, by the actor, and sustained by conscious monitoring and impression-management.

For purposes of clarification, it may be useful to compare the rendering visible of 'masculinity' with another category – 'Britishness'. We can talk of 'typically British' activities, things, places, interests, ideas, and so forth – and 'British' persons too, of course. What we find are normative ties between a category ('British') and a diverse set of activities, etc. Now consider those occasions on which the relevance of invoking the category 'British' might go unquestioned. For, like 'man', 'masculine', and its cognates, it is only *on occasions* that the 'Britishness' of some person, activity, place or thing is seeable as relevant. That is, there are those occasions on which no further warrant is needed for the routine invocation of the category 'British'. Think, for example, of passport and immigration controls, or of the foreigner sitting down for the first time for breakfast in a British hotel. The question, 'Are you British?' or, 'Is this a typical British breakfast?' can each be seen as relevant to those occasions. Or consider the occasion, not unfamiliar to many holidaymakers when in a foreign country, that one 'remembers' that one is 'British'. There are those occasions, when struggling to order a meal in a foreign language, for example, when one is brought up against the fact of one's Britishness. On these occasions is not what one had been doing all along 'being

[197]

(typically) British'? But of course, retrospectively, one never doubts that one really was 'British' all along, just as doubting that one is a 'man' never figures among the other doubts that a man might justifiably have. For what justification could one have for doubting that one was (really, deep down) 'a man'? (This points to differences between 'being British' and being 'a man', for one *can* readily remember situations where persons have had justifiable doubts concerning their status as 'British' citizens).

None of this should lead us to infer that I, as a 'British' person, had been consciously presenting myself as 'British' (self-consciously and deliberately wearing a straw hat and bow tie however hot the weather). No, I simply did the things I did. Until forced to notice them for some reason, I had ignored these facts about myself. (Or, indeed, I might wish to contest their factuality – and here the role of *evidence* in the establishment of the appropriateness of some category should be noted.)

Just as with 'Britishness', so with 'masculinity'. The 'rendering visible' of masculinity or of 'Britishness' – and the rendering of it in such a way as it is seeable as having been there all along, that is, as not just the product of analytical work – is an occasioned activity. Such occasion is *doing theory*.

Finally, the very diversity of things, persons, activities, places, activities, etc. seeable as 'British' or as 'masculine' serves as a warrant for the claims that 'masculinity' and 'Britishness' are social constructions. It is by adverting to the diversity of the constructional elements that the theorist is able to sustain the sense of 'masculinity' or 'Britishness' *as artefacts of social construction*. The theoretical task, so conceived, lies in accounting for that constructional work in causal terms.

As against the social contructionists, I suggest that we are in error if we consider that we have need of a *theory* of masculinity at all. The sociologist has no need to discover what is hidden or unknown and to adumbrate it in theory. For, following Wittgenstein, we can say that everything lies before us. What lies before us is the skilled gender-producing work of persons-in-the-society, of whom the theorist is one. It is this gender-producing work that requires, I suggest, a 'perspicuous representation' (Wittgenstein 1958, p. 122). This, I suggest, is the proper task of the sociologist of gender.

[198]

Notes

1 It should be noted that I am not opposed to the idea that men and masculinity be open to question. Or that I necessarily object to the conclusions purportedly entailed in 'rethinking masculinity'. My objections are of a different sort: I am objecting that these conclusions are not necessarily entailed by the arguments.

2 And this demand is not a *theoretical* but a political – or *ethical* – demand.

Part 4

COMMENTARIES

An important part of any conference is what happens between and after the papers and the workshops, and for this reason we felt that it was important to reflect this by including, in this case, three short commentaries on the debates that took place. Other commentaries on the conference have been written by Milner 1989, Jefferson 1989, Boyd & Roper 1989.

CHAPTER 13

The critique of men

JEFF HEARN
& DAVID H. J. MORGAN

When the conference was over, one of the next tasks was to write a short report on the proceedings for the newsletter of the British Sociological Association newsletter, *Network*; having done that, and having reflected upon what we had written, we thought it might be helpful to try to clarify our own position on the critical study of men and masculinities. In some ways this is an update on what we have suggested elsewhere (Morgan 1981, Hearn *et al.* 1983, Hearn 1987a, Ford & Hearn 1988), and it is also an attempt to move forward in the light of the debates at the conference.

First, we see it necessary for men to support the development of feminist scholarship in general and women's studies in particular. This is not just an abstract principle but something which involves concrete actions, including the recommendation of and use of feminist texts in teaching and research, and the vigorous institutional support for and defence of women's studies programmes, whether they be whole degrees or parts of other courses.

Second, we consider the proper focus for men interested in and concerned about gender and gender politics is men, ourselves. This particularly applies in the development of research and publication. There are a number of necessary caveats to this, including the need for men students to write required course essays about women; the obvious need to read feminist writings and scholarship and the need to study men in terms of the impact of men's power upon women; and the need in that research and writing which is collaborative with women to devise an appropriate division of labour, separation of information, and sharing of information.

Third, there is no parity between women's studies and the

critique of men. While we see women's studies as being by women, of women, and for women, the critique of men is by both women and men. While women may wish to study men critically, there is no equivalent leeway for men to study women, although we noted above that this may be appropriate under certain conditions.

Fourth, men's critique of men, ourselves, is to be developed in the light of feminism. This critique needs to be anti-sexist, anti-patriarchal, pro-feminist, and gay-affirmative. It means not just a positive academic relationship with feminism but also a positive political relationship with feminism, including men's support for feminist initiatives and political projects.

Fifth, the underlying task of the critique of men is to change men, ourselves, and other men. This involves men in both individual and collective change. It is premissed on the assumption that we learn to understand the world by trying to change it and not by trying to detach ourselves from it. Again, this necessitates concrete actions, notably self-criticism and the critical attempt to change other men, to encourage others to turn their attention to feminist scholarship, to review their reading lists, and so on.

Lastly, we see it as crucial to attend also to the longer term implications of men studying men. In particular, there is the possibility that 'good intentions' are not enough. Thus men must also vigorously support equal opportunities and similar policies at every level. We must refrain from applying for teaching and research jobs on women's studies. We also believe that men should generally refrain from applying for research grants from funds earmarked for 'equal opportunties', 'gender studies', and 'women's studies'. Instead, men might usefully apply for funds on men and gender, perhaps in collaboration with women, from supposedly non-gendered research funds. We also believe that there is a need to monitor carefully any moves towards the institutional development of studies on gender. We say this with some caution, aware that some feminists support the term 'gender studies' as an umbrella term.

We should be very pleased to hear from others, women and men, about these suggestions. We see them as first steps in clarifying men's activity in sociology in relation to feminism and women's studies. In particular, we urge men to come out publicly and institutionally in support of the continuing development of feminist scholarship, teaching, and research, and of women's studies.

Notes

This contribution is a slightly revised extract from the postscript to the report on the conference (Hearn & Morgan 1989).

CHAPTER 14

The new men's studies: part of the problem or part of the solution?

JOYCE E. CANAAN
& CHRISTINE GRIFFIN

This paper emerged from the reactions that we, and other femin-ists, had to the conference on men, masculinity, and social theory, which is where most of the papers in this book were first presented. During the Women's Caucus meetings at the conference, we agreed to provide a written summary of women's responses to the event for *Network* (Canaan & Griffin 1989). Since then we have revised our summary, at the request of the editors, for this book.

We had doubts about attending the conference and these feelings only grew as the conference progressed. We initially wrote about the conference because many of us in the Women's Caucus recognized some fundamental problems and dangers in what is now being constructed as 'the new men's studies' (hereafter TNMS). We hope that our expressed dissatisfaction might (perhaps) stir some men to question more fundamentally what their work is about and the impact it, and the proposed academic legitimation of TNMS, might have on feminism and feminist scholarship generally as well as women's studies in particular.

The phrase TNMS has been used as the subtitle of a recent edited text which includes work by predominantly male North American social scientists (Brod 1987). This approach aims to develop a critical perspective on men and masculinity, and whilst TNMS is most prevalent in the USA, it is by no means restricted to the confines of North American sociology. There is a considerable and diverse body of work by women and men which has also set out to critique dominant forms of masculinity, but which would not necessarily identify itself as part of men's studies, in its 'new' or 'old' forms.

We still have mixed feelings about including our paper in this book. We fear that, like feminist work in the past, those seeking to establish this perspective may ignore, misrepresent, or consider tokenistic what feminists, and some men, have to say about men and masculinity. However, we decided to include this contribution because we think that it is critical for feminists to understand, intervene in, question and reconstruct in our own terms and for our own purposes 'malestream' academic disciplines. It is especially important that we comment on TNMS, which explores the masculinity that so oppresses us and claims to stem from and build on feminist work. We seek to have dissenting voices present in this book because we hope that TNMS might take on some of the points that we raise.

But we do not think that it is enough for feminists to comment on *men's* work on masculinity. As men begin studying men, feminists must continue to do so, pointing out how men's analyses omit or distort certain key features of our experience with, and understanding of, men and masculinity. Indeed, one of the great contemporary myths holds that the Women's Liberation Movement (WLM) has implications only for women and that feminist research is only about women. Women have, in fact, been exploring the intersections between 'race', class, and masculinity (Brah 1988, Davis 1982). Women have also been working around and against male violence (Hanmer & Maynard 1987), sexual abuse (Driver & Droisen 1989), men's use of pornography (Dworkin 1981), links between military institutions and hegemonic masculinity (Russell 1989), and patriarchal relations in schools, workplaces, and trade unions, to name but a few. TNMS does not dispute the existence or importance of this work, but its adherents obviously feel that this work is not enough, and that men could contribute something *more* (or different) to feminist understandings of how hegemonic masculinities work. While feminist understandings of patriarchy would undoubtedly be wider if we had access to men's understandings of how they construct and transform this pervasive system of relationships, we nevertheless fear that such research might distort, belittle, or deny women's experiences with men and masculinity. Feminists therefore must be even more insistent about conducting research on men and masculinity at a time when a growing number of men are beginning to conduct apparently 'comparable' research.

For years feminists in the social sciences have been telling our male colleagues to figure out for themselves how they oppress women, and to do something about it. Men have responded to our suggestions in a variety of ways. A few men in academia have begun to build upon feminist analyses, aiming to explore how masculinity is embodied (Connell 1983), how male subjectivity is constructed (Seidler 1985, 1987, Tolson 1977), and how men's exploitative social relations with others and among themselves are constituted and might be changed (Hearn 1988, Kaufman 1987). Some men have formed men's groups, or begun developing anti-sexist programmes. We certainly welcome these critical studies of, and practical attempts to transform, masculinity.

We are, however, suspicious about the timing of the recent burst of academic activity around TNMS. The boom in conferences and books about men and masculinity would have been almost unthinkable ten or even five years ago, and it is unlikely that the BSA Sociological Theory group would have organized a conference on 'men, masculinity, and social theory'. Yet where were these men five years ago, when feminists searched in vain for more than minimal support from male social scientists, or for an organized and supportive anti-sexist male voice? Why do they all appear now, when further education and higher education are increasingly threatened both politically and financially (at least in the UK) and when areas like women's studies are becoming increasingly beleaguered? Is it a coincidence that TNMS is being constructed in the present context as a source of potential research, publishing deals, and (even more) jobs for the already-well-paid boys holding prestigious positions?

We think that this growing interest in masculinity should be placed in a historical context for another reason. There is, at present, what the Australian sociologist Bob Connell (1987) calls a 'crisis in hegemonic masculinity' which has emerged as part of a reaction to the WLM of the 1960s and 1970s. Recent feminist work suggests that there is a need to develop international links and a more sophisticated understanding of patriarchal power in relation

[208]

to capitalism, racism, and imperialism, the oppression of disabled people, homophobia, and ageism (Mies 1986, *Outwrite* 1988). This is (or can be) more than a 'list of isms'; it can be a vital means of thinking about patriarchal power in the broadest terms, as it connects with other sets of power relations. We still have a long way to go, and it has not been a smooth ride, but TNMS can draw us all back to a narrow political agenda. Radical analyses of 'race', class, age, disability, and sexuality can all be marginalized as just another set of 'variables'. These understandings, coupled with women's growing presence, if not power, in the world of waged work, means that women are becoming more visible both at local and international levels. Such visibility puts greater pressure on the privileged group of white, middle-class, heterosexual, 'western' men who must give up some of their power. This group of men feel under threat, and we wonder if TNMS is an attempt to legitimate dominant forms of masculinity in another guise. Is TNMS at least partly a response by these relatively powerful men to the demands of feminism, and other radical movements, and to the changes which the WLM has brought to so many women's lives?

Our suspicions stem partly from the tendency of the 'fathers' of TNMS to reclaim feminist work as part of TNMS 'canon'. A sub-section of Harry Brod's introductory chapter on men's studies is entitled 'A men's studies canon?'. He goes on to suggest that 'To speak of a men's studies canon is premature. The field is still too new for such grandiose claims' (Brod 1987, p. 10). Brod then proceeds to outline 'the emergence of certain figures at the core of men's studies', which include some 'women feminist theorists' presumably as distinct from *men* feminist theorists (p. 10). What Brod presents as one of the contributions of his edited collection is 'the beginning of a trend to claim certain texts as precursors of men's studies' (p. 11). He cites the work of William Whyte, C. Wright Mills, and Herbert Marcuse here, but elsewhere identifies Nancy Chodorow, Dorothy Dinnerstein, Barbara Ehrenreich, and Carol Gilligan as 'the four women's studies scholars . . . [who are] most influential in men's studies' (p. 13). Brod and his peers are careful to stress the contributions of feminist work (by women as opposed to 'male feminists'), and their support of women's studies, but it is difficult to avoid the suspicion that TNMS is being constructed as a new baby brother for women's studies.

[209]

Such suspicions are reinforced when other proponents of men's studies appear to be setting up a 'new' field of academic study which ignores some of the key critical insights about the relationship between theory and personal experience that feminist analyses have developed. Michael Kimmel argues in his recent book that analyses of masculinity must centre on 'race', class, and sexuality (Kimmel 1987). Kimmel goes on to describe group discussions during his course on the sociology of male experience, which was held at Rutgers University in Newark, New Jersey. These discussions, he argues, 'tended to overemphasize the personal *at the expense of* a serious intellectual grappling with theoretical issues' (1987, p. 288; our emphasis). Why does Kimmel use 'an uncritical dualism which separates the intellectual/theoretical from the personal' (Griffin 1989, p. 104)? Has he not learnt from feminist practice that the two are interconnected? It is not enough that adherents of TNMS and men who are interested in developing anti-sexist work simply support women's academic endeavours and political work. They need to develop strategies which start from their own experiences and relate these to a wider transformative politics which operates at the personal, ideological, and structural levels. If adherents of TNMS fail to take feminist insights on board, if they try to make men feel better about themselves without also considering the effects that their power might have on others, then we have grave doubts about the viability of this perspective.

We also wonder how much real support TNMS will give to women's studies. The wish by at least some men to set up something called 'TNMS' suggests that this support will be rather limited. We view naming as a crucial action: it provides a space in a language and cultural logic which positions a perspective relative to others. As feminist analyses have shown, at least in the west, an elite group of men have named the world from their perspective, thereby excluding or marginalizing all other perspectives (Daly 1981, Spender 1980). Given that naming provides such a striking example of patriarchal power, we could understand that men who study men and masculinity might want to construct their own name for their work. For this name must acknowledge that such studies should begin by questioning the power held by the most powerful men and recognizing the place that the process of naming has in the maintenance of this power. Connell (1987) seems to recognize these points by identifying his work as part of a 'critique of hegemonic masculinity', but this is hardly the most accessible phrase. If it has to have a name – and we are not convinced that it does because we fear that, in naming their own work, adherents to TNMS will also rename feminist work – we would prefer the term 'anti-sexist perspective'. Such a name immediately recognizes that this perspective aims to challenge the sexism of hegemonic and some other forms of masculinity.

In addition to our difficulties with the naming process, we also feel uncomfortable with the name 'men's studies'. This suggests that studies of men are complementary with those of women. As we know very well, so-called complementarity all too often results in power being wrested from the less powerful and the powerless. We recognize that 'men's studies' can literally take women's jobs in teaching and research at a time of financial cutbacks, political conservatism, and when academic institutions will be all too eager to fund less potentially controversial work in the name of 'doing something on gender'. As the cuts continue to hit, who will get the most resources? The problem here is not that anti-sexist provision for men should not exist. It should; but if this operates at the expense of feminist projects for women, without accountability or any serious attempt to challenge male power, we've had it, girls.

We think that those doing work on men and masculinity need to state how they view their perspective relative to feminism. They should 'come out' politically so that they can be aware of, and sensitive to, the ways their projects affect women and other oppressed groups. We are also troubled that some men who are given space in volumes on TNMS deny even the most fundamental feminist principle that the personal is political. In the course of his workshop at the BSA conference which provides the basis for his chapter in this book, Wil Coleman (Ch. 12 in this volume) claimed that politics and sociology should not mix. When questioned, he described his own politics, after some thought, as 'non-existent, no, wet liberal, no, just liberal'. His ethno-methodological attempt to examine how men (or women) can do masculinity; as a skilled activity is scarcely interested in challenging those skills, nor in deskilling men. Has women's work on the ways in which our personal experience serves as both the means by which we came to recognize our oppression and the means by which we fight against it been carried out only to be ignored (Taking Liberties Collective

[211]

1989)? We believe that TNMS cannot be politically liberal; it must begin with a recognition of the feminist insight that politics shapes all areas of our lives, and it must be informed by and accountable to feminist political practice.

We do not doubt that it is difficult for a dominant group to give up its power voluntarily. We wondered at the conference, and since then we have questioned if and how more male sociologists are going to take feminist critiques on board. If the role of women's studies is the liberation of women, what might be the potential contribution of a 'men's studies'? Yet we find that adherents of TNMS do not seem to be starting from this question nor always aiming to develop an anti-sexist framework. Instead, some of them begin by claiming that they are both 'critical of masculinity and at the same time sympathetic to men' (Brod 1987, p. 9). Brod does not specify to *which* men he extends his sympathy, a point which is critical to the 'movement to end sexist oppression' (Hooks 1984).

There are other men, however, whose work begins with the recognition of the need for, and the difficulties involved in, a dominant group giving up its power. For example, Bob Connell, with male and female colleagues, has been working for some years around the critique of hegemonic masculinity. Whilst Connell has not identified himself as part of TNMS, his work appears in several of the edited collections mentioned above (Brod 1987, Kimmel 1987). Connell argues that the struggles of socialism, gay liberation, and women's liberation raise many crucial issues which are 'also the business of heterosexual men, who have some specific jobs to do (e.g. in the politics of masculinity) but also ought to be involved in the general analysis of sexual politics' (1987, p. xii). Connell goes into some detail about the difficult relationship of heterosexual men to feminism and partriarchal power, since 'their collective interest . . . is broadly to maintain the existing system' (1987, p. xiii). Connell gives five possible reasons which serve 'to detach heterosexual men from the defence of patriarchy' (1987, p. xiii).

While we feel that Connell's analysis may be overly optimistic, it does at least set the critique of masculinity in the context of individual and collective political strategy. So much of TNMS operates at the relatively safer level of academic analysis. If men are interested in doing work which is critical of dominant forms of masculinity, why do their main political priorities so seldom

[212]

involve challenging the patriarchal (and racist, and capitalist) power bases in their own particular fields of work? They may advocate self-criticism or changing other men, both individually and collectively, but there is little sense that many adherents of TNMS are putting themselves or their careers (especially their careers) at risk. If they were to challenge the work of those 'Great Men' who police the boundaries of academic disciplines and control the research and teaching budgets, then we might feel more confident of their support in practice.

TNMS appears to be constructing itself as an adjunct of feminism, and particularly of academic forms of feminism. Why do TNMS texts never mention the need for men to support rape crisis centres or refuges for battered women, financially if in no other way? There is no sense of a transforming political strategy in TNMS, one in which men work together to recognize how they have oppressed women and develop strategies to change their way of action. Little attention is paid to feminist practices which have struggled to wrest control over our lives from men, both personally and in much larger systems of social relations. The focus is on feminist academic publications rather than political campaigns, such as Women against Fundamentalism, to give one recent example (Sahgal 1989).

All of these things give us the feeling that, having been cast as rebellious daughters by male academics, feminists are now being set up as mother figures, expected to provide nurturance and approval for the boys' ideas, even, or perhaps especially, when these ideas threaten our very existence. Why not take on the real 'men's studies' as identified by Dale Spender: the 'malestream' of social science research? Why not focus on that research which is still all about men, but which continues to ignore gender and masculinity? Take on the Big Boys instead of the women. Of course, such an enterprise, which feminists have always done and continue to do, and which some men have begun to do, is less likely to get jobs, research funding, and publications. TNMS looks very much like an easy option for academic men.

At best we hope that the work which calls itself TNMS is not an indication of the kind of scholarship that studies of men and masculinity might provide. But if it is, then how many feminists will be willing to write articles like this, or to attend conferences like that organized by the BSA in the future? The form that TNMS now takes is in urgent need of some profound reconstruction, or at least critical reappraisal. This is not a matter of censorship, but of political priorities and strategies. Research and teaching on men and masculinity need a radical edge if it is not to become part of the problem rather than part of the solution. We would hope that these men will begin to apply the insights of socialist Paolo Friere (1970, pp. 34–5) to their own work on men and masculinity:

> Discovering himself to be an oppressor may cause considerable anguish, but it does not necessarily lead to solidarity with the oppressed. Rationalizing his guilt through paternalistic treatment of the oppressed, all the while holding them fast in a position of dependence, will not do. Solidarity requires that one enter into the situation of those with whom one is in solidarity; it is a radical posture. True solidarity with the oppressed means fighting at their side to transform the objective reality.

CHAPTER 15

Men, feminism and power

VICTOR J. SEIDLER

Feminism deeply challenges the ways that men are and the ways that men relate. It draws attention to the power men sustained in their relationships with women and shows that what liberalism conceived of as a relationship of equality with men and women operating in different spheres is in reality a relationship of power and subordination (see Seidler 1986). Recognizing this involves more than a change of attitude on the part of men towards women, for it becomes clear that it is not simply enough to think of someone as an equal with equal respect, but it also has to do with the organization of the relationship of power that exists between men and women in relationships. It is a material issue, though there has been considerable difference about how to conceptualize the nature and character of this materialism. Feminism seems to challenge too narrow an economistic version of materialism but the extent to which feminism and feminist theory have allowed for a reformulation of Marxist conceptions of materialism is still very much an open issue.

If men have to change they have to do this for themselves, for they can no longer rely on women to 'pick up the pieces'. Men are left to explore and investigate the nature and character of their inherited forms of masculinity. The crucial point is that feminism does not simply present a theoretical challenge to the ways that men understand the world but it also presents a personal and practical challenge to who we are as men and how we relate as men both to ourselves and to others.

[215]

It was this personal challenge that men sought to meet in consciousness-raising groups, but often they were difficult situations because as men we were often so used to intellectualizing and rationalizing our experience, rather than sharing it. Sometimes these groups died after a few weeks when it was not clear what men were supposed to talk about. It was difficult for men to *share* their experience with other men because we have been brought up to treat other men as competitors in a way that makes it easy to feel that showing our vulnerability would only be used against us. It was not uncommon for many heterosexual men to say that they did not need consciousness-raising because they felt closer to women anyway, and did not find it difficult to talk to them. Often this would cover over a fear of sharing ourselves with men, a suspicion of men that had deep roots connected to homophobia and a fear of intimacy. This allowed men a certain identification with feminism while being able to disdain men who involved themselves in consciousness-raising. This allowed men to sustain a feeling of superiority in relationship to other men and also to avoid the charges of feminists who would say in the early days that consciousness-raising was simply another form of male bonding that could so easily lead to a reassertion of male power.

Rejecting masculinity

Another significant strain in the response of men to feminism has been a negation by men of their own masculinity. Masculinity was taken to be *essentially* oppressive to women and as being a structure of oppression. This touches something significant in sexual relationships, for it is a movement of denial that involves a self-rejection, often a loss of vitality and even sexuality. It is this response to feminism that was challenged in the writings of 'Achilles Heel',[1] that sought a reworking of masculinity as part of the project of men involved in consciousness-raising. In fact, this self-rejection is often because men have failed to explore the contradictions of their masculinity. Rather they have learnt that masculinity is essentially a relationship of power, so that you could only give up your power in relationship to women, and so no longer collude in women's oppression, if you were prepared to 'give up' your masculinity. This is a part of guilt and self-denial

[216]

that was not an uncommon male response to feminism. In the end it is self-destructive but nevertheless it has to be understood.

It has often meant that men, having often found no way through them, have given up these issues and concerns completely. In some cases this has possibly fuelled a kind of anti-feminist politics, a threat or fear that women are somehow out to take away men's potency, and this has fuelled the politics of the Right. The move towards a men's rights position has grown to enormous strengths in the United States, often being larger than any men's movement grouping. This is in part why it is so important to rework and rethink men's relationships to feminism.

It was an important part of the 'Achilles Heel' project in England to look for more affirming and positive visions of masculinity, and so to challenge some of the sources of guilt and self-denial that had sometimes been part of men's responses to feminism. This involves a personal and theoretical quest. It could also be that 'men's studies', as developed in the United States, is a move away from this difficult personal terrain and an attempt to deal theoretically, so that we will not need to deal more personally, with the challenges of feminism. This suspicion is partly fuelled by the strength of a positivist social science methodology within 'men's studies', which probably is related to the disciplinary strength of psychology and the ways that these issues can become 'topics' within a reworked social psychology. It is as if the claims of feminism, say, around issues of pornography, could be 'tested' so that we could know what the 'effects' of pornography are on men, whether it makes them more violent or not, and whether it influences the nature and character of their relationships with their partners. Women have grounds to be nervous about the testing of feminist claims within this kind of framework.

Of course there has to be a relationship between empirical research and feminist theory, but we have to be very careful about it. It is too easy given the struggle of social science methodologies to imagine that the causal claims can be 'neutrally tested' (see Harding 1986, Ramazanoglu 1989, Roberts 1981, Smith 1987, Stanley & Wise 1983). For what about the fact that we grow up as men within a culture that is deeply imbued with pornographic images? How does this affect us? And is this not the larger context in which these 'experiments' are taking place? At the same time it might be argued that men have to be able to set their own agendas and, if this is the way they seek to investigate these issues, it has to be left to men to be responsible for the exploration of men and masculinity. But this raises questions and issues about the challenges that feminist theory makes to different forms of social science methodologies and the ways these are marginalized by claiming that they are only relevant in the exploration of women's experience, that will inevitably be troubling.

On the other hand, what about the radical feminist assumption 'that all men are potentially rapists'? What does this mean about the conception of masculinity that underpins some feminist theoretical work? Is this something that men can challenge? If men are seen as an ontological category fixed within a particular position within a 'hierarchy of powers', what space is left for men to explore their masculinity? This is a question that feminists may wish to take seriously. It is also raised for men who would consider themselves as 'male feminists'; or, in a different way, as 'pro-feminists'. A crucial question is who 'sets the agenda' for research on men and masculinity. These are difficult issues to resolve, for it is crucial to keep in mind that it has been the challenges of feminism that have made the dominant conceptions of masculinity problematic. In this sense men's studies has to have a close relationship to feminism, while the extent to which feminism can 'set the agenda' for all studies into men and masculinity remains unclear. It is not unusual these days for men to pay lip-service to feminism and to women's struggles in their opening paragraphs, only to go on to ignore the implications of these studies for the work that they are engaged in.

It needs to be taken seriously that many men have responded to feminism by internalizing a particular conception of their masculinity as 'the enemy'. Since this masculinity was said to be 'essentially' a position of power in relationship to women, there was little for men to do but to reject their masculinity. So it seemed that to identify with feminism and to respond to the challenges of feminist theory involved an abandonment of masculinity itself. Sometimes the analogy is made, which I think is misleading, with the position of whites in South Africa, the idea that the only way that whites could abandon their privilege was to identify completely with the black struggle. So analogously it could seem that there is no point for men to work with other men, for this would be to work with the 'oppressor' and the only thing that could be justified would be to 'give up' our position of oppression.

[218]

Here again there is a resonance with an orthodox Marxist frame of mind. Just as middle-class people could 'betray their class' and identify themselves with the struggles of working-class people against capitalistic oppression, so it seems as if men can be asked to forsake their masculinity. In part it is possible to change our class position and identify ourselves within a proletarian position, though there are difficulties with this vision of political struggle. This has often involved denial of our 'education' and of our understanding of how capitalist institutions crush and distort working class life and culture. But why does an identification with feminism have to involve a *rejection* of our masculinity? If we adopt a conception of masculinity which simply defines it as a relation-ship of power, or as the top place within a hierarchy of powers, then we are tempted into thinking that it is 'possible to abandon our masculinity'. Similarly if we conceive of 'heterosexuality' as simply a relationship of power that fixed straight men in a position of power and enforces the subordination of gay men and lesbians, then it can seem that 'heterosexuality' can equally simply be abandoned. This has often gone along with the idea of sexuality as being 'socially constructed', with the implication that it can equally be 'deconstructed' and different choices made. This fosters the view that sexual orientation is in the last analysis a matter of political choice. At another level this reconstructs a rationalistic project that assumes that our lives can be lived by reason alone and that through will and determination, as Kant has it, we can struggle against our inclinations, to live according to the pattern that we have set for ourselves through reason (Blum 1981, Seidler 1989).

These are difficult and complex questions and they need to be handled with care and sensitivity. It might be that heterosexuality is a structured institution and that it enforces the conception of 'normality' that is taken for granted within the culture. This establishes important relationships of power that marginalize and, with Section 28, work to criminalize the sexuality of gay men and lesbians. It has been crucial to understand sexuality not as a 'given' but as the outcome of a series of personal relationships, so bringing out the precarious character of all our sexualities. This is part of the importance of recognising 'differences'. But it is one thing to understand the institutional power of heterosexuality and another to think that sexual orientation is a matter of 'political choice'.

In part it has been our sharp dichotomy, inherited as a defining

[219]

feature of modernity and further inscribed within a structuralist tradition, between 'nature' and 'culture', that has fostered this way of thinking, as if 'culture', in opposition to 'nature', as an outcome of reason, is within our conscious control. This is one of the difficulties with the prevailing conceptions of 'social construction' deeply embedded within the human sciences, which help foster a form of rationalism that gives us the idea that our lives are within our rational control and that through will and determination alone we can determine our lives. It forms our vision of freedom and morality which within a Kantian tradition are identified with reason.

This is part of an Enlightenment rationalism and develops a particular vision of self-determination, as if we *should* be able to control our lives by reason alone. So we begin to think that to say that our sexuality is 'natural' is either to say that it has been 'given' or that it is somehow beyond our conscious control. But this is to create too sharp an opposition. Freud helps us understand the organization of our sexuality, how it has come to be what it is. He does not thereby think that it can be 'rationally reconstructed'. For Freud change comes through some form of *self-acceptance* of our sexual feelings and desires, even if these do not take the form that we would want or even that would be regarded as legitimate within the larger society. Rather than judging these feelings and desires by external standards, we learn to acknowledge them for what they are and we learn to suspend judgement. This is part of a psycho-analytic process. It is crucial for Freud that within a rationalistic culture we learn to judge and often condemn our feelings and emotions because they do not fit in with the ideals that we have set ourselves. Part of the originality of Freud, despite all the difficulties, is his break with the idealization of culture and his recognition of the importance of validating our experience for what it is.

Similarly we cannot simply *reject* our masculinity as if it is 'wrong' or 'bad', or 'essentially oppressive to women'. This is not to say that we cannot *change* the ways that we are. What is at issue is the model of change that we inherit within our culture, and in this respect Freud is critical of a Kantian-Protestant tradition that says that we can *cut out* or eradicate those parts of ourselves, of our feelings and desires, that we judge as wanting, as if reason provides some kind of neutral arbiter or legislator for determining what is to be regarded as *unacceptable* to us. This was also part of a 1960s

[220]

inheritance, that said that our anger or jealousy was 'unreasonable' and therefore unacceptable, and that therefore it should be eradicated. It was assumed that we could somehow cut our feelings of jealousy out and behave as if they did not exist at all. Jealousy was socially and historically constructed and so equally it could be reformulated according to our wills. If we insisted on our jealousy this just showed a failure of will and determination (see Seidler 1989, Ch. 3).

Such a Protestant tradition is still very much with us in the idea of 'mind over matter', in the idea that if you take your mind off what is troubling, then the feelings of despair or sadness will somehow disappear. Because we live in a secular culture we are often unaware of the Protestant sources of many of our ideas and values. Freud and psychoanalytic theory move against this aspect of our inherited culture. It was part of the project of 'Achilles Heel' to say that you could not *reject* your masculinity, but you could work to *redefine* it. We would work to change what we are by first accepting the nature of our emotions and feelings rather than judging ourselves too harshly. This is to come to terms with the self-critical voice which too often stands in the way of our changing.

Possibly it is because the culture puts such great force on the idea of 'self-rejection' that so few men have really taken up these issues. In part it is also up to a theoretical grasp of men and masculinity to reject the idea that men cannot change and to show the ways that men can change might be an important way of un-freezing the notions that make masculinities seem unredeemable. In working towards a transformed understanding of men and masculinity we have to recognise the injuries that were done by the idea that men should be guilty *as men*. At the same time we have to take responsibility for how under-developed the theoretical grasp of men and masculinity remains and how long it has taken for men to explore more openly and honestly their relationship to feminism.

Men, power, and feminism

If we think about the question of whether feminism is in men's interests we can say that clearly at one level it is not, in the sense that it is a challenge to the power men have to make the larger society in their image. Liberal theory argues that men and women should have equal rights in society and to the extent to which women are denied these rights, the society is unequal and unjust. So it is that men have been able to support the claims of liberal feminism without having to bring into question the inherited forms of masculinity. The women's movement has gone further in its challenge to the power men have to make society in their own image. It also challenges the dominance of masculine values and aspirations which are largely taken for granted in the institutional organization of society. Feminism in its new phase presents a challenge to men's power in society and also to the sources of men's power in sustaining personal relationships. It is a challenge to the ways that both public life and private life are largely organized around the value of men's time and interests, so devaluing and failing to recognize, or giving equal value to, women's time, values and aspirations. So the women's movement has encouraged women to recognize how much they have been forced to give up in themselves in order to see themselves through the eyes of men. It recognizes the difficult tasks that women have of rediscovering their own values and relationships in the context of a patriarchal society.

So it is important to keep in view the ways that feminism remains a threat to the ways that men are, without thereby insisting that it is up to feminism to somehow set the agenda for the reworking of dominant forms of masculinity. In this context, it is quite common for men 'sympathetic' to feminism to find some kind of security in the ideas the feminism should be left to women to do, and that women should be given space to set down their ideas and projects free from the interferences of men. This is not an uncommon response but it fails to take account of the challenge that feminism presents to the prevailing forms of masculinities. Briefly, we learn to say 'the right thing' when we are around feminists; we feel that we are walking on thin ice and we learn to be careful. It is important to keep in view the ways that feminism remains a challenge to the character and organization of men's power in society, since this challenges the parallelism that can so easily be drawn when we talk about 'men's studies' in relationship to 'women's studies'. The idea that 'in the last analysis' or at some deeper level feminism is in fact in the interests of men, has to be handled with great care, for this too can foster a kind of parallelism, where it is also possible for men to assimilate certain feminist insights which they can then use against women.

It also becomes possible to give deference to feminism and to talk about the power which men have within the larger society without fully grasping the power of sociology to co-opt a feminist challenge. Even though a 'men's studies' paradigm has challenged the pervasive influence of role theory, the idea that gender exists as a pre-existing set of expectations of what 'men' and 'women' are supposed to be and do in the larger society is very current. It is easy, and the literature shows it, to fall back into a much more refined form of role theory, which allows for greater flexibility in gender expectation but loses a grip on issues of power and subordination, because this is such a dominant paradigm within psychology and the human sciences generally. It is the methodology of the social sciences, largely unchallenged, which comes to provide the legitimacy for these areas of intellectual study. The critique that feminism can make of an Enlightenment tradition and the forms of social theory and methodology that have emerged from it, tends to get lost. An empirical sociology tends to take charge and begins to set the terms in which 'gender studies' are to prove themselves as valid and legitimate.

A different approach to power is provided by recent developments in post-structuralist theory. Here we have a vision of power as all-pervasive, that can undermine our sense of the nature of interpersonal power. This insight into the pervasiveness of power can be used to question whether it is right to say that men have power in relationship to women, because it can be argued that both 'masculinity' and 'femininity' are interpolated within a particular relationship of power. This could be another support for a kind of parallelism being set up between men's studies and women's studies, because both genders are embedded or organized within particular relationships of power. We are offered the notion of identity as being articulated through particular relationships of discourses of power. This is the way that the notion of 'social construction' is conceived within a post-structuralist framework. It rejects the idea of power as a thing-like 'commodity' that some people have over others for it wants to insist that the pervasiveness of power means that all identities are articulated with particular discourses of power. In part this accounts for the difficulties which Foucault (e.g. 1976) has in illuminating gender relationships of

[223]

power. In this sense the influence of Foucault's work has tended to subvert some crucial insights into the relationship between power, identity and experience.

On the other hand, part of what is appealing in this move is that it brings out into the open the idea that men are not all-powerful in all spheres of their lives and that women are not always completely powerless or subordinate. It helps challenge the pervasive picture of a hierarchy of powers with white men sitting on the top of the pile. But this means listening to the experience of men and taking seriously the terms in which they present themselves. A structuralist framework undermines its own insight into the complexity of power by seeing experience as itself the outcome or product of particular discourses. The dialectic that exists between experience and identity and the continuous struggle that people are involved in, in trying to clarify their needs and desires, gets lost. The complexities and tensions of experience are lost as they are presented as the effects of language.

Nevertheless, the picture of the 'hierarchy of powers' so easily places woman in a position of victim, as being subordinated and oppressed, and so denies her her own activity and power to shape her own history. At one level a similar problematic can be identified within post-structuralist theory because it assumes that subjects or identities are the products or results of discourses. It tends to present people as passive. The vision of people as victims has a powerful hold within different traditions of social theory. Sometimes the theory can be part of the problem, for it can place, for instance, women in a position of subordination and powerlessness that seems impossible to break. It can create its own forms of dependency and submissiveness and it can stand in the way of women being able to empower themselves. In this sense, structuralism has found a way of talking about identities, but it has been difficult to identify the ways in which it sustains a particular form of rationalistic theory. It sees identities as being provided externally and thereby tends to reinforce a vision of women as being passive. We are back to the idea that the powerless have to be rescued or that there has to be some kind of external intervention, by the state say, to save them. Even if this process of identity formation is seen as an ongoing active process within certain post-structuralist writings, it is difficult to make sense of this because experience itself is taken to be a product of discourse.

[224]

It was an insight of the early women's movement to stress the self-activity of women and to focus on the ways that women can retain power in their lives. But this vision remains theoretically in tension with a vision that draws on the 'hierarchy of powers', as well as with a more general structuralist/post-structuralist tradition, as if we have to work for the whole structure to be turned upside down before there is going to be any movement.

Men, power, and social theory

As already noted, the dominant paradigm in much academic work on men and masculinity has in fact been provided within a revised and flexible form of social psychology. A competing conception has been provided by sociology whereby social theory has begun to talk of the social construction of masculinity, whether positivist, structuralist or post-structuralist, to point out that masculinity is not simply given or provided for by biology but is sometimes constructed within particular social relationships. Both conceptions can operate within a particular social science methodology. They can both present themselves as being 'objective' and 'impartial'. Crucially they avoid issues of method that have been acutely raised within feminist theory. It might be useful to set out some of the issues which this 'gender perspective' framework, as it is often called, tends to avoid. This begins to set the ground for a different kind of exploration of men and masculinity, which is more sensitive to historical and philosophical sources.

First, these theories avoid the tension between the experience that men have of themselves and the way they are supposed to be within the dominant culture. If they illuminate the pain and confusion that are often felt, this is put down as transitional, as part of the movement from one social role to a newly defined and more flexible social role. Second, by talking about this tension in terms of 'social construction', we undermine people's trust in their own experience, in the ways that they might come to define what they want for themselves both individually and collectively.

Third, it displaces the issue of *responsibility*, for the role, like the construction, is provided for me 'by society'. It is not anything that I can help, nor is it anything that I can be held individually responsible for. This is important for men because it is important for men to learn to take responsibility for a masculinity that is so often rendered invisible. It is also important for men to think about the dominant position of masculinity. Responsibility might well turn out to be a crucial issue for men, especially in relationships, for it can be seen that, even though men are 'responsible' in the public world of work where it can be a matter of following established rules and procedures, often in relationships men can be controlling, constantly finding fault with what their partners are doing, and feeling somehow estranged or outside of the relationship.

Fourth, these conceptions of masculinity make no sense of the contradictions within men's experience. For instance, there is little sense that it is because men identify with their reason, because of the Enlightenment identification between masculinity and reason, that they are thereby estranged from their emotions and feelings. This is systematically organized and structured. It is a matter of the way a particular dominant form of masculinity and male identity is organized. So this sets up a particular tension between what men grow up to want for themselves, for example, to do well at work, to be successful, to achieve, and their feelings for what matters most to them in their lives.

In the light of these complications, one way forward might be that we have to take more seriously the idea of sexual politics, particularly the idea that the 'personal is political', as the basis for a renewed conception of the dialectic between experience, identity and history, or of a reformulated historical materialism. Feminists have long recognized that there is no way of squaring the contradiction whereby women have struggled for an autonomy and independence which are being constantly challenged and negated within the larger society. This is a contradiction that women have learnt to live with, recognizing the importance of the support they can receive from others. In this sense it is no different from men who are struggling to change the patterns of behaviour that have been institutionalized. In both contexts we have to recognize the importance of a social movement for change, as part of a redefinition of values and relationships, so that 'the micro' and 'the macro' have to be brought into relationship. They cannot be separated off as independent levels of analysis as is often done within the human sciences.

So as men change it will have to be part of a movement for change which will transform the organization of institutional powers and the forms of personal relationships. So it is that the 'micro' cannot be separated from the 'macro', nor can they be reduced to one another. This is an important feminist insight that men are in danger of losing if they take their theoretical starting point not from within sexual politics or from within a developing male sexual politics but from within the established social scientific frameworks. It is understandable that this temptation will be strong because the movements for change have been relatively weak for men, understandably so because men have been so closely identified with prevailing relationships of power, dominance and authority. This also serves as a warning against thinking that the 'speculative claims' of feminist theory can somehow be tested against the causal claims that they seem to be making, say, in the case of the effects of pornography on men's values and behaviour. This would be for men to take the high ground of a refined positivist methodology, thinking that this is neutral and provides a secure base from which feminist claims can be evaluated.

If this temptation is to be resisted it will be because men have learnt their own complicity with the dominant forms of social theory. They have learnt to question the universality of these theories and methods, recognizing the masculinist assumptions which they carry. They are set within a rationalist framework that recognizes reason as the only source of knowledge and invalidates feelings and desires as being legitimate sources of understanding, insight and knowledge. It is a constant danger for new areas of studies, whether it be women's studies or men's studies, somehow to seek legitimacy in terms of the prevailing paradigms of scientific investigation. This is a tendency to be watched because it can easily lead to losing the crucial power and value of feminist insight.

But this is not to say that a sexual politics of masculinity will not yield new questions that might challenge some of the notions of some feminist methodologies. A study of men and masculinity will yield its own methodological concerns. These questions will not always lie within feminist theory, nor can we say in advance what they might be. They cannot necessarily be judged according to pre-existing feminist standards but if they are firmly grounded they will deepen our understanding of the sources of women's oppression and subordination. They will also illuminate the conditions and possibilities of changing conceptions of masculinity, if not also the conditions for the liberation of men.

[227]

Notes ·

This commentary is an extract from a much longer paper entitled, 'Men, feminism and social theory', part of a forthcoming text on masculinity and social theory. The full paper includes the discussion of several other questions, including the historical relationship of men and feminism, men's studies, and the 'hierarchy of powers'. Many of these thoughts were stimulated by discussions that were going throughout the conference. That it provoked such excitement and opposition can only be a tribute to the occasion and to the sense of lively exploration it helped create.

1 Achilles Heel is a men's publishing collective which produced the journal of the same name from 1977 to 1983, and again in 1987, as well as a number of pamphlets. While the political position of the collective developed over this time, it was broadly concerned with the relationship between men's sexual politics and socialism (see Achilles Heel Collective 1978, and Morrison 1980). I was a member from 1977 to 1983. The journal was relaunched in 1990.

Bibliography

Achilles Heel Collective 1978. By way of an introduction . . . *Achilles Heel* **1**, 3–7.

Adam, B. D. 1987, *The Rise of a Gay and Lesbian Movement*. Boston, Mass.: Twayne.

Akhter, F. 1986. International Centre for Diarrhoeal Disease Research, Bangladesh, UBINIG Investigative Report No. 1', *The Hygeia* **2** (1), 5–12.

Altman, D. 1971. *Homosexual: Oppression and Liberation*. Sydney: Angus & Robertson.

Altman, D. 1982. *The Homosexualization of America. The Americanization of the Homosexual*. New York: St Martin's Press.

Altman, D. 1986. *AIDS and the New Puritanism*. London: Pluto.

Ariès, P. & A. Bejin (eds) 1985. *Western Sexuality: Practice and Precept in Past and Present Times*. Oxford: Basil Blackwell.

Attali, J. 1985. *Noise: The Political Economy of Music* (Minneapolis, Minn.: University of Minnesota Press). First published as *Bruits: essais sur l'économie politique de la musique*, Paris: PUF 1977.

August, E. 1985. *Men's Studies: A Selected and Annotated Bibliography*. Littleton, Col. and London: Libraries Unlimited.

Bachofen, J. J. 1861. *Das Mutterrecht: Eine Untersuchung über die Gynaikokratie der alten Welt nach ihrer religiösen und rechlichen Natur*. Stuttgart: Krais & Hoffman.

Bachofen, J. J. 1967. *Myth, Religion and Mother Right: Selected Writings of J. J. Bachofen*, trans. R. Manheim, with an introduction by J. Campbell. London: Routledge & Kegan Paul. This work is a translation of Marx, R. (ed.) 1926. *Mutterrecht und Urreligion*. Stuttgart: Alfred Kröner.

Barker, D. L. & S. Allen (eds) 1976a. *Dependence and Exploitation in Work and Marriage*. London: Longman.

Barker, D. L. & S. Allen (eds) 1976b. *Sexual Divisions and Society: Process and Change*. London: Tavistock.

Barrett, M. & M. McIntosh 1982. *The Anti-Social Family*. London: New Left Books and Verso.

Barry, K. 1979. *Female Sexual Slavery*. Englewood Cliffs, NJ: Prentice-Hall.

Bart, P. & M. Jozsa 1980. Dirty books, dirty films, and dirty data. In *Take*

Back the Night: Women on Pornography, L. Lederer (ed.) 204–17. New York: Morrow.

Bauer, D. M. 1988. *Feminist Dialogics: A Theory of Failed Community*. Albany, NY: State University of New York Press.

Becker, H. 1963. *Outsiders: Studies in the Sociology of Deviance*. New York: Free Press.

Bem, S. L. 1975. Sex-role adaptability: one consequence of psychological androgyny. *Journal of Personality and Social Psychology* 31, 634–43.

Benard, C. & E. Schlaffer 1987. *Der Mann auf der Straße. Über das merkwürdige Verhalten von Mannern in ganz alltäglichen Situationen*. Reinbek bei Hamburg: Rowohlt.

Beneke, T. 1982. *Men on Rape*. New York: St Marin's Press.

Benjamin, J. 1980. The bonds of love: rational violence and erotic domination. *Feminist Studies* 6 (1, Spring), 144–74.

Benjamin, J. 1983. Master and slave: The fantasy of erotic domination. In Snitow, Stansell, and Thompson, op. cit., 280–99.

Benyon, J. & J. Solomos (eds) 1987. *The Roots of Urban Unrest*. London: Pergamon.

Bernard, J. 1972. *The Future of Marriage*. New York: Bantam.

Bettelheim, B. 1955. *Symbolic Wounds: Puberty Rites and the Envious Male*. London: Thames & Hudson.

Betzold, M. 1977. How pornography shackles men and oppresses women. In *For Men against Sexism: A Book of Readings*, J. Snodgrass (ed.), 45–8. Albion, Calif.: Times Change Press.

Bhabha, H. K. 1983. The other question. *Screen* 24 (6), 18–36.

Blachford, G. 1981. Male dominance and the gay world. In *The Making of the Modern Homosexual*, K. Plummer (ed.), 184–210. London: Hutchinson.

Bliss, S. 1986. Changing men's publications, *Men's Studies Newsletter* 3 (2), 4–5.

Blum, L. 1981. *Friendship, Altruism and Morality*. London: Routledge & Kegan Paul.

Blum, L. & V. J. Seidler 1989. *A Truer Liberty: Simone Weil and Marxism*. New York: Routledge.

Bouchier, D. 1983. *The Feminist Challenge: The Movement for Women's Liberation in Britain and the United States*. London: Macmillan.

Boyd, K. & M. Roper 1989. Report Back. *History Workshop Journal* 27 (Spring), 222–4.

Bradley, M., L. Danchik, M. Fager & T. Wodetzki 1971. *Unbecoming Men*. New York: Times Change Press.

Brah, A. 1988. Extended review. *British Journal of Sociology of Education* 9 (1), 115–21.

Braidotti, R. 1987. Envy: or with your brains and my looks. In *Men in Feminism*, A. Jardine & P. Smith (eds), 233–41. New York: Methuen.

Brannon, R. & D. David (eds) 1976. *The Forty-Nine Percent Majority*. Reading, Mass.: Addison-Wesley.

Bray, A. 1982. *Homosexuality in Renaissance England*. London: Gay Men's Press.

Broadwater Farm Inquiry: Report of the Independent Inquiry into Disturbances of October 1985 at the Broadwater Farm Estate, Tottenham. Chaired by Lord Gifford, QC (1986). London: KARIA.

Brod, H. (ed.) 1987. *The Making of Masculinities: The New Men's Studies.* London: Allen & Unwin.

Brod, H. (ed.) 1988. *A Mensch Among Men: Exploration in Jewish Masculinity.* Freedom, Calif.: Crossing Press.

Brod, H. 1989a. Work clothes and leisure suits: the class basis and bias of the men's movement, 1st pub. 1983–4. In *Men's Lives: Readings in the Sociology of Men and Masculinity*, M. Kimmel & M. Messner (eds), 598–605. New York: Macmillan.

Brod, H. 1989b. Eros Thanatized: pornography and male sexuality with 1988 Postcript. In *Men Confronting Pornography*, M. Kimmel (ed.) New York: Crown. Originally in *Humanities in Society* **7** (1 & 2, Winter-Spring 1984), 47–63.

Brown, C. 1981. Mothers, fathers and children: from private to public patriarchy. In *Women and Revolution*, L. Sargent (ed.), 239–67. Boston: South End. London: Pluto.

Brown, S. R. 1980. *Political Subjectivity: Applications of Q Methodology in Political Science.* New Haven, Conn.: Yale University Press.

Brownmiller, S. 1975. *Against Our Will: Men, Women and Rape.* New York: Simon & Schuster.

Bryan, B., S. Dadzie & S. Scafe 1985. *The Heart of the Race: Black Women's Lives in Britain.* London: Virago.

BSA Standing Committee on the Equality of the Sexes 1986. Teaching gender – struggle and change in sociology. *Sociology* **20** (3), 347–61.

BSA Sub-Committee on Equality of the Sexes n.d. *Sociology Without Sexism: A Sourcebook.* London: British Sociological Association.

Buci-Glucksmann, C. 1987. Catastrophic Utopia: The feminine as allegory of the modern. In Gallagher & Laqueur, op. cit., 220–9.

Cameron, D. & E. Fraser 1987. *The Lust to Kill: A Feminist Investigation of Sexual Murder.* Cambridge: Polity.

Canaan, J. & C. Griffin 1989. Men's studies: Part of the problem or part of the solution. *Network* **43** (January), 7–8.

Caputi, J. 1988. *The Age of Sex Crime.* London: Women's Press.

Carby, H. V. 1982. White women listen! Black feminism and the boundaries of sisterhood. In *The Empire Strikes Back: Race and Racism in 70's Britain*, Centre for Contemporary Cultural Studies (ed.). London: Hutchinson.

Cardozo Law Review (1989), vol. 10, nos 5–6 (Mar/Apr.), I and II, 847–1931, special issue 'Hegel and legal theory'.

Carrigan, T., R. W. Connell & J. Lee 1985. Toward a new sociology of masculinity. *Theory and Society* **14** (5), 551–604. Reprinted in *The Making of Masculinities: The New Men's Studies*, H. Brod (ed.), 63–100. Boston: Allen & Unwin. Extracts in *Beyond Patriarchy. Essays by Men on Power, Pleasure and Change*, M. Kaufman (ed.), 139–92. Toronto: Oxford University Press.

Chapman, R. & J. Rutherford (eds) 1988. *Male Order*. London: Lawrence & Wishart.

Chesler, P. 1978. *About Men*. London: Women's Press.

Chodorow, N. 1971. Being and doing: a cross-cultural examination of the socialisation of males and females. In *Women in Sexist Society*, V. Gornick & B. K. Moran (eds). London: New English Library.

Chodorow, N. 1978. *The Reproduction of Mothering: Psychoanalysis and the Sociology of Gender*. Berkeley, Calif.: University of California Press.

Cockburn, C. K. 1983. *Brothers: Male Dominance and Technological Change*. London: Pluto.

Cockburn, C. K. 1987. *Two-Track Training: Sex Inequalities in the Youth Training Scheme*. London: Macmillan.

Cockburn, C. K. 1989. Equal opportunities: The short and long agendas. *Industrial Relations Journal* **20** (3), 213–25.

Cohen, P. 1988. The perversions of inheritance: studies in the making of multi-racist Britain. In *Multi-Racist Britain*, P. Cohen & H. Bains (eds). London: Macmillan.

Connell, R. W. 1983. *Which Way Is Up?* London: Allen & Unwin.

Connell, R. W. 1985. Theorising gender. *Sociology* **19** (2), 260–72.

Connell, R. W. 1987. *Gender and Power*. Cambridge, Polity: Stanford, Calif.: Stanford University Press.

Corbin, A. 1986. *The Foul and the Fragrant. Odor and the French Social Imagination*. Cambridge, Mass.: Harvard University Press. First published as *Le miasme et la jonquille: l'odorat et l'imaginaire social XVIIIe–XIXe siècles*. Paris: Aubier Montaigne, 1982.

Cornell, D. 1985. Taking Hegel seriously: reflections on beyond objectivism and relativism. *Cardozo Law Review* **7** (Fall), 139.

Coward, R. 1984. *Female Desire*. London: Paladin.

Daly, M. 1981. *Gyn/Ecology*. London: Women's Press.

Datar, R. 1989. An elusive goal for the East End Pele. *Guardian*, 28 June, 20.

Davis, A. 1982. *Women, Race and Class*. London: Women's Press. New York: Random House.

de Beauvoir, S. 1953. *The Second Sex*. London: Cape. First pub. 1949.

Deleuze, G. & F. Guattari 1983. *Anti-Oedipus: Capitalism and Schizophrenia*. Minneapolis, Minn.: University of Minnesota Press. First published as *Capitalisme et schizophrenie*, 2 vols. Paris: Editions de Minuit, 1972–80.

Delph, E. W. 1978. *The Silent Community: Public Homosexual Encounters*. Beverley Hills, Calif.: Sage.

Delphy, C. 1977. *The Main Enemy: A Materialist Analysis of Women's Oppression*. London: Women's Research and Resources Centre.

Delphy, C. 1984. *Close to Home*. London: Hutchinson. 1st pub. in English as *The Main Enemy: A Materialist Analysis of Women's Oppression*. London: Women's Research and Resources Centre, 1977.

DeMause, L. 1984. *Reagan's America*. New York: Creative Roots.

D'Emilio, J. 1983. *Sexual Politics, Sexual Communities: The Making of a*

Homosexual Minority in the United States 1940–1970. Chicago: University of Chicago Press.

D'Emilio, J. & E. B. Freedman 1988. *Intimate Matters: A History of Sexuality in America.* New York: Harper & Row.

Department of Employment (annually). *New Earnings Survey.* London: HMSO.

Diner, H. 1965. *Mothers and Amazons: The First Feminine History of Culture,* trans. J. P. Lundin, with an introduction by J. Campbell. New York: Julian Press. Originally published, under the pseudonym 'Sir Galahad', as *Mütter und Amazonen: Ein Umriss weiblicher Reiche.* Munich: Albert Langen, 1932.

Dinnerstein, D. 1976. *The Rocking of the Cradle and the Ruling of the World.* New York: Harper & Row. London: Souvenir Press, 1978.

Dollimore, J. 1986. Homophobia and sexual difference. *Oxford Literary Review* **8**, 5–12.

Donnerstein, E., D. Linz & S. Penrod 1987. *The Question of Pornography Research Findings and Implications.* New York: Free Press.

Driver, E. & A. Droisen (eds) 1989. *Child Sexual Abuse: Feminist Perspectives.* London: Macmillan.

Ducat, S. 1980. *Taken In: American Gullibility and the Reagan Mythos.* Tacoma, Wyo.: Life Sciences Press.

Duroche, L. L. 1987a. On reading Kafka's 'Metamorphosis' as a masculine narrative. *University of Dayton Review* **18** (2), 35–40.

Duroche, L. L. 1987b. Alternative senses of male narratives: other voices/other choices. *Men's Studies Review* **4** (4), 6–7. Position paper for a workshop on Ernest Hemingway offered at the 'Men and masculinity' conference held at Trinity College, Hartford, Conn., June 1987.

Dworkin, A. 1981. *Pornography: Men Possessing Women.* London: Women's Press, New York: Perigree.

Dworkin, A. 1985. A word people don't understand. *Ms* **46** (April).

Dworkin, A. 1986. Interview in *Chicago Tribune,* 12 January, sect. 6, 3.

Dworkin, A. 1988. *Intercourse.* London: Secker & Warburg.

Dworkin, A. & C. MacKinnon 1988. *Pornography and Civil Rights: A New Day for Women's Equality.* Minneapolis, Minn.: Organizing Against Pornography, 734 E. Lake Street, Rm 300W.

Easlea, B. 1983. *Fathering the Unthinkable: Masculinity, Scientists and the Nuclear Arms Race.* London: Pluto.

Easton, S. M. 1987. Hegel and feminism. In *Hegel and Modern Philosophy,* D. Lamb (ed.), 30–55. London: Croom Helm.

Edholm, F., O. Harris & K. Young 1977. Conceptualising women. *Critique of Anthropology* **3** (9 & 10), 101–30.

Edwards, S. 1989. *Policing 'Domestic' Violence.* London: Sage.

Ehrenreich, B. 1983. *The Hearts of Men: American Dreams and the Flight from Commitment.* New York: Anchor-Doubleday.

Eisenstein, Z. R. (ed.) 1979. *Capitalist Patriarchy and the Case for Socialist Feminism.* New York: Monthly Review Press.

Ellis, A. 1980. Treatment of erectile dysfunction. In *Principles and Practice of Sex Therapy*, S. Leiblum & L. Pervin (eds). New York: Guildford.

Epstein, C. F. 1983. *Women in Law*. Garden City, NY: Anchor/Doubleday.

Erskine, H. 1971. The polls: women's roles. *Public Opinion Quarterly* **35**, 275–98.

Femiano, S. n.d. *Men's Studies Syllabi*. Northampton, Mass.: 22, East Street, Northampton, Mass. 01060.

Feminist Review 1984. Many voices, one chant: black feminist perspectives. *FR* **17**.

Ford, D. & J. Hearn 1988. *Studying Men and Masculinity. A Sourcebook of Literature and Materials*. Bradford: Department of Applied Social Studies, University of Bradford, revised 1989.

Foucault, M. 1976. *The History of Sexuality, – I: An Introduction*. Harmondsworth: Penguin.

Foucault, M. 1977. *Discipline and Punish: The Birth of the Prison*. London: Allen Lane.

Foucault, M. 1980. *The History of Sexuality*, I. New York: Vintage. First published as *Histoire de la sexualité*, I: *La volonte de savoir*. Paris: Gallimard, 1976.

Fox-Genovese, E. 1987. The empress's new clothes: the politics of fashion. *Socialist Review* **17** (1), 7–30.

Franklin, II, C. W. 1984. *The Changing Definition of Masculinity*. New York: Plenum.

Freud, A. 1936. *The Ego and the Mechanics of Defence*. New York: International Universities Press.

Freud, S. [1905] 1977. *On Sexuality: Three Essays on the Theory of Sexuality and Other Works*. London: Penguin.

Freud, S. 1925. Some psychical consequences of the anatomical distinction between the sexes. *Standard Edition* **19**, 243–58. London: Hogarth Press, 1961.

Freud, S. 1936. *The Ego and the Mechanisms of Defense*. New York: International Universities Press.

Friedan, B. 1963. *The Feminine Mystique*. New York: Dell.

Friedman, S. & E. Sarah (eds) 1982. *On the Problem of Men: Two Feminist Conferences*. London: Women's Press.

Friere, P. 1970. *Pedagogy of the Oppressed*, trans. M. B. Ramos. New York: Seasbury Press.

Gackenbach, J. I. & S. M. Auerbach 1975. Empirical evidence for the phenomenon of the 'well-meaning liberal male'. *Journal of Clinical Psychology* **31**, 632–5.

Gagnon, J. & W. Simon 1975. *Sexual Conduct*. Chicago: Aldine.

Gallagher, C. 1987. The body versus the social body in the works of Thomas Malthus and Henry Mayhew. In Gallagher & Laqueur, op. cit., 83–106.

Gallagher, C. & T. Laqueur (eds) 1987. *The Making of the Modern Body*.

Sexuality and Society in the Nineteenth Century. Berkeley, Los Angeles, and London: University of California Press.

Gamarnikow, E., D. H. J. Morgan, J. Purvis & D. E. Taylorson (eds) 1983a. *Gender, Class and Work*. London: Heinemann.

Gamarnikow, E., D. H. J. Morgan, J. Purvis & D. E. Taylorson (eds) 1983b. *The Public and the Private*. London: Heinemann.

Garfinkel, H. 1967. Passing and the managed achievement of sexual status in an intersexed person. In *Studies in Ethnomethodology*, H. Garfinkel, 116–85. Englewood Cliffs, NJ: Prentice-Hall.

Gavron, H. 1966. *The Captive Wife*. London: Routledge & Kegan Paul.

Giddens, A. 1987. In *Social Theory and Modern Sociology*. Cambridge: Polity. 52–72.

Gilroy, P. 1987. *There Ain't No Black in the Union Jack: The Cultural Politics of Race and Racism*. London: Hutchinson.

Goffman, E. 1959. *The Presentation of Self in Everyday Life*. New York: Doubleday. London: Allen Lane, 1969.

Goffman, E. 1977. The arrangement between the sexes. *Theory and Society* **4** (3), 301–31.

Goffman, E. 1979. *Gender Advertisements*. London: Macmillan.

Goode, J. 1982. Why men resist. In *Rethinking the Family: Some Feminist Questions*, B. Thorne & M. Yalom (eds), 131–50. White Plains, NY: Longman.

Gough, J. 1989. Theories of sexual identity and the masculinization of gay men. In *Coming on Strong: Gay Politics and Culture*, S. Shepherd & M. Wallis (eds), 119–36. London: Unwin Hyman.

Grady, K. E., R. Brannon & J. H. Pleck 1979. *The Male Sex Role: A Selected and Annotated Bibliography*. Rockville, Maryland: US Department of Health, Education and Welfare.

Greenberg, D. 1988. *The Construction of Homosexuality*. Chicago: University of Chicago Press.

Griffin, C. 1989. Review of Brod (1987), Kimmel (1987) and Connell (1987). *Feminist Review* **33**, 103–5.

Grossberg, M. 1985a. *Governing the Hearth: Law and the Family in Nineteenth Century America*. Chapel Hill: University of North Carolina Press.

Grossberg, M. 1985b. Crossing boundaries: Nineteenth century domestic relations law and the merger of family and legal history. *American Bar Foundation Research Journal* **4**, 799–847.

Hacker, H. M. 1951. Women as a minority group. *Social Forces* **30**, 60–9.

Hall, S., C. Critcher, T. Jefferson, J. Clarke & B. Roberts 1978. *Policing the Crisis: Mugging, the State and Law and Order*. London: Macmillan.

Hanmer, J. & M. Maynard (eds) 1987. *Women, Violence and Social Control*. London: Macmillan.

Hanmer, J., J. Radford & E. Stanko (eds) 1989. *Women, Policing and Male Violence: International Perspectives*. London and New York: Routledge.

Hanmer, J. & S. Saunders 1984. *Well Founded Fear: A Community Study of Violence to Women*. London: Hutchinson.

Hanmer, J. & S. Saunders 1987. *Women, Violence and Crime Prevention.* Wakefield: West Yorkshire Police Authority. Aldershot: Gower.

Harding, S. 1986. *The Science Question in Feminism.* Ithaca, NY: Cornell University Press. Milton Keynes: Open University Press.

Harding, S. 1987. *Feminism and Methodology: Social Science Issues.* Bloomington, Ind.: Indiana University Press. Milton Keynes, Open University Press, 1988.

Harding, S. & M. Hintakka (eds) 1983. *Discovering Reality: Feminist Perspectives on Epistemology, Metaphysics, Methodology and Philosophy of Science.* Dordecht: Reidel.

Harrison, B. W. 1985. Misogyny and homophobia: the unexplored connections in Robb, op. cit., 135–291.

Hartley, R. E. 1959. Sex-role pressures and the socialization of the male child. *Psychological Reports* 5, 457–68.

Hartmann, H. 1981. The unhappy marriage of marxism and feminism. In *Women and Revolution: A Discussion of the Unhappy Marriage of Marxism and Feminism*, L. Sargent (ed.), 1–41. Boston: South End. London: Pluto.

Haug, W. F. 1986. *Critique of Commodity Aesthetics: Appearance, Sexuality, and Advertising in Capitalist Society*, trans. R. Bock. Minneapolis: University of Minnesota Press.

Hearn, J. 1987a. *The Gender of Oppression. Men, Masculinity and the Critique of Marxism.* Brighton: Wheatsheaf. New York: St Martin's Press.

Hearn, J. 1987b, Theorising men and masculinity: specific problems and diverse approaches. Introductory paper to Symposium 'Men's responses to the feminist challenge: relationships of theory and practice', Third International Interdisciplinary Congress on Women, Women's Worlds, Visions and Revisions, Trinity College, Dublin, July.

Hearn, J. 1988, Child abuse: violence and sexualities towards young people. *Sociology* 22 (4, November), 531–44.

Hearn, J. 1989a. Reviewing men and masculinities or mostly boys' own papers. *Theory, Culture and Society* 6 (3), 665–89.

Hearn, J. 1989b. *Some Sociological Issues in Researching Men and Masculinities*, Hallsworth Research Fellowship Working Paper No. 2. Manchester: Department of Social Policy and Social Work, University of Manchester.

Hearn, J., C. Creighton, C. Middleton, D. Morgan, R. Thomas & C. Pearson 1983. Changing men's sexist practice in sociology. *Network* 25 (January), 3.

Hearn, J. & P. W. Parkin 1983. Gender and organizations: a selective review and a critique of a neglected area. *Organization Studies* 4 (3), 219–42.

Hearn, J. & W. Parkin 1987. *'Sex' at 'Work': the Power and the Paradox of Organisation Sexuality.* Brighton: Wheatsheaf. New York: St Martin's Press.

Hearn, J. & D. Morgan 1989. 'Men, masculinity and social theory': report on Sociological theory conference'. *Network* 43 (January), 6–7.

Heath, S. 1987. 'Male feminism'. In *Men in Feminism*, A. Jardine and

P. Smith (eds), 1–32. New York and London: Methuen.

Hey, V. 1986. *Patriarchy and Pub Culture*. London and New York: Tavistock.

Hocart, A. M. [1952]1970. *The Life-Giving Myth and Other Essays*. London: Methuen.

Hodson, P. 1984. *Men . . . : An Investigation into the Emotional Male*. London: Ariel and BBC.

Höfler, O. 1934. *Kultische Geheimbünde der Germanen*. Frankfurt-am-Main: Moritz Diesterweg.

Hooks, B. 1982. *Ain't I a Woman: Black Women and Feminism*. London: Pluto.

Hooks, B. 1984. *Feminist Theory: From Margin to Center*. Boston, Mass.: South End Press.

Hughes, J. 1988. The madness of separate spheres: insanity and masculinity in the late nineteenth century Alabama. Paper at conference on Masculinity in Victorian America, Barnard College. 9 January.

Institute of Race Relations 1987. *Policing against Black People*. London: Institute of Race Relations.

Jaggar, A. M. 1983. *Feminist Politics and Human Nature*. Brighton: Harvester.

James, C. L. R. 1963. *Beyond a Boundary*. London: Stanley Paul.

Jardine, A. & P. Smith (eds) 1987. *Men in Feminism*. New York: Methuen.

Jefferson, T. 1989. Conference reports. *Changes* 7 (1, February), 20.

Jeffreys, S. 1985. *The Spinster and Her Enemies: Feminism and Sexuality 1880–1930*. London: Pandora.

Jensen, A. E. 1933. Kulturkreislehre als Grundlage der Kulturgeschichte. In *Leo Frobenius: Ein Lebenswerk aus der Zeit der Kulturwende, dargestellt von seinen Freunden und Schülern*, 73–95. Leipzig: Koehler & Amelang.

Jenson, J., E. Hagen & C. Reddy (eds) 1988. *Feminization of the Labour Force*. Cambridge: Polity.

Jones, W. H., M. E. Chernovetz & R. O. Hansson 1978. The enigma of androgyny: differential implications for males and females? *Journal of Consulting and Clinical Psychology* **46**, 298–313.

Joseph, G. 1981. The incompatible menage á trois: marxism, feminism and racism. In *Women and Revolution: A Discussion of the Unhappy Marriage of Marxism and Feminism*, L. Sargent (ed.), 91–107. Boston: South End Press. London: Pluto.

Jouve, N. W. 1986. *The Streetcleaner: The Yorkshire Ripper Case on Trial*. London and New York: Marion Boyars.

Kagan, J. & H. A. Moss 1962. *Birth to Maturity*. New York: Wiley.

Kamuf, P. 1987. Femmeninism. In Jardine and Smith, op. cit., 78–84.

Kanter, R. M. 1977. *Men and Women of the Corporation*. New York: Basic.

Kaplan, E. A. 1983. Is the gaze male?. In Snitow, Stansell & Thompson, op. cit., 309–27.

Kappeler, S. 1986. *The Pornography of Representation*. Cambridge: Polity.

Kaufman, M. 1987. The construction of masculinity and the triad of men's violence. In *Beyond Patriarchy: Essays by Men on Pleasure, Power and Change*, M. Kaufman (ed.), 3–29. Toronto: Oxford University Press.

Kelly, L. 1988. *Surviving Sexual Violence*. Cambridge: Polity.

Kimmel, M. (ed.) 1987. *Changing Men: New Directions in Research on Men and Masculinity*. Newbury Park, Calif.: Sage.

Kimmel, M. (ed.) 1990. *Men on Pornography*. New York: Crown.

Kimmel, M. & J. Fracher 1987. Hard issues and soft spots: counseling men about sexuality. In *Handbook on Counseling and Psychotherapy with Men*, M. Scher, M. Stevens, G. Good & G. Eichenfeld (eds), 83–96. Newbury Park, Calif.: Sage.

Kimmel, M. & M. Levine 1989. Men and AIDS. In Kimmel & Messner, op. cit. 344–59.

Kimmel, M. & M. Messner (eds) 1989. *Men's Lives*. New York: Macmillan.

Kinsey, A., W. Pomeroy & C. Martin 1948. *Sexual Behavior and the Human Male*. Philadelphia, Pa: W. B. Sanders.

Kitzinger, C. 1987. *The Social Construction of Lesbianism*. London: Sage.

Kluckhorn, C. 1948. As an anthropologist views it. In *Sex Habits of American Men*, A. Deutsch (ed.). Englewood Cliffs, NJ: Prentice-Hall.

Lamb, M. E. & J. A. Levine 1983. The Swedish Parental Insurance Scheme: an experiment in social engineering. In *Fatherhood and Family Policy*, M. E. Lamb and A. Sagi (eds), 39–52. Hillsdale, NJ: Erlbaum.

Laqueur, T. 1987. Orgasm, generation, and the politics of reproductive biology. In Gallagher & Laqueur, op. cit., 1–41.

Lawrence, E. 1982. Just plain commonsense: the 'roots' of racism. In *The Empire Strikes Back: Race and Racism in 70's Britain*, Centre for Contemporary Cultural Studies (ed.). London: Hutchinson.

Legge, K. 1987. Women in personnel management: uphill climb or downhill slide? In Spencer & Podmore, op. cit., 33–60.

Lehman, P. 1988. *In the Realm of the Senses: desire, power and the representation of the male body*. *Genders* 1 (2), 91–110.

Leiblum, S. R. & L. A. Pervin (eds) 1980. *Principles and Practice of Sex Therapy*. Guildford, NY: Haworth Press.

Leiblum, S. & R. Rosen (eds) 1988. *Sexual Desire Disorders*. Guildford, NY: Haworth Press.

Lepenies, W. 1969. *Melancholie und Gesellschaft*. Frankfurt-am-Main: Suhrkamp.

Levinson, D. J. 1978. *The Seasons of a Man's Life*. New York: Knopf.

Lewis, C. 1986. *Becoming a Father*. Milton Keynes: Open University Press.

Louch, A. R. 1969. *Explanation and Human Action*. Berkeley and Los Angeles: California University Press.

Lowe, D. M. 1982. *History of Bourgeois Perception*. Chicago: University of Chicago Press.

Lublinski, I. 1933. *Vom Mutterrecht zum Vaterrecht: Bedeutsame Entwicklungstatsachen in ihren psychologischen, soziologischen und ökonomischen Folgen*. Berlin: F. A. Herbig Verlagsbuchhandlung.

BIBLIOGRAPHY

Lukács, G. 1972. *History and Class Consciousness: Studies in Marxist Dialectics*, trans. Livingstone. Cambridge, Mass.: MIT Press.

MacKinnon, C. A. 1979. *The Sexual Harassment of Working Women*. New Haven, Conn.: Yale University Press.

MacKinnon, C. A. 1982. Feminism, Marxism, method and the state: an agenda for theory. *Signs: Journal of Women in Culture and Society* **7** (3) 515–44.

MacKinnon, C. A. 1983. Feminism, Marxism, method and the state: towards feminist jurisprudence. *Signs: Journal of Women in Culture and Society* **8** (4), 635–58.

MacKinnon, C. A. 1986. Interview in *Chicago Tribune*, 12 January, sect. 6, 1.

MacKinnon, C. A. 1987. *Feminism Unmodified: Discourses on Life and Law*. Cambridge, Mass.: Harvard University Press.

Magnus, O. 1555. *Historia de gentibus Septentrionalibus, earumque diversis statibus, conditionibus, moribus*. Rome: J. M. de Viottis.

Mangan, J. A. & J. Walvin (eds) 1987. *Manliness and Morality: Middle-Class Masculinity in Britain and America 1800–1940*. New York: St Martin's Press; Manchester University Press.

Männer in der Geschlechterforschung. Dokumentation einer Ad-hoc-Sitzung des Soziologentages 1988 in Zürich (1988). Hennef-Wiederschall: Institut fur Sozialokologie Arbeitspapiere 8, December.

Manning, P. K. 1980. Goffman's framing order: style as structure. In *The View from Goffman*, J. Ditton (ed.), 252–84. London: Macmillan.

Marciano, L. n.d. Testimony to the public hearings of ordinances to add pornography as discrimination against women. Minneapolis: Minneapolis City Council.

Marx, K. 1964. Economic and philosophical manuscripts: third manuscript. In *Early Writings*, T. B. Bottomore (ed. and trans.), 279–400. New York: McGraw-Hill.

Massachusetts Institute of Technology Humanities Library 1979. *Men's Studies Bibliography*, 4th edn. Cambridge, Mass.: MIT.

May, M. 1987. 'An obligation on every man': masculine breadwinning and the law in nineteenth century New York. Paper given at the American Historical Association, Chicago.

McWalter, K. 1987. Couch dancing. *New York Times Magazine*, 6 December, 138.

Mead, M. 1935. *Sex and Temperament in Three Primitive Societies*. New York: Morrow.

Mercer, K. & I. Julien 1988. Race, sexual politics and black masculinity: a dossier. In *Male Order: Unwrapping Masculinity*, R. Chapman & J. Rutherford (eds), 97–164. London: Lawrence & Wishart.

Mészàros, I. 1972. *Marx's Theory of Alienation*. New York: Harper & Row.

Mies, M. 1986. *Patriarchy and Accumulation on a World Scale*. London: Zed.

Miller, D. A. 1987. *Cage aux folles*: sensation and gender in Wilkie Collins *The Woman in White*. In Gallagher & Laqueur, op. cit., 107–36.

Millett, K. 1971. *Sexual Politics*. London: Hart-Davis.

Mills, P. J. 1987. *Women, Nature and Psyche*. New Haven, Conn.: Yale University Press.

Milner, J. 1989. Whither sociology? Not this way, chaps. *Network* **44** (May), 6–7.

Minneapolis City Council Public Hearings 1983. *Pornography and Sexual Violence: Evidence of the Links*. Minneapolis, Minn.: Organizing Against Pornography. London: Everywoman.

Mintzberg, H. 1983. *Power In and Around Organizations*. Englewood Cliffs, NJ: Prentice-Hall.

Moore, S. 1988. Getting a bit of the Other: the pimps of postmodernism. In Chapman & Rutherford, op. cit., 165–92.

Morgan, D. H. J. 1981. Men, masculinity and the process of sociological enquiry. In *Doing Feminist Research*, H. Roberts (ed.), 83–113. London: Routledge & Kegan Paul.

Morgan, D. H. J. 1990. *Discovering Men*. London and Winchester, Mass.: Unwin Hyman.

Morrison, P. 1980. Our common ground . . . *Anti-Sexist Men's Newsletter* **10**. Reprinted in Hearn 1987a, 203–4, and Rowan 1987, 51.

Mort, F. 1988. 'Boy's own? Masculinity, style and popular culture'. In *Male Order: Unwrapping Masculinity*, R. Chapman & J. Rutherford (eds), 193–224. London: Lawrence & Wishart.

Moss, P. M. & N. Fonda 1980. The future prospect. In *Work and the Family*, P. M. Moss & N. Fonda (eds). London: Temple Smith.

Naser, M. 1986. ICDDRB: Healing or killing? *Dhaka Courier* **3** (1, 11 July), 4–5, 7.

Oakley, A. 1972. *Sex, Gender and Society*. London: Temple Smith.

O'Brien, M. 1981. *The Politics of Reproduction*. London: Routledge & Kegan Paul.

O'Brien, M. 1982. The commatization of women: patriarchal fetishism in the sociology of knowledge. British Sociological Association conference on Gender and Society, University of Manchester.

Ollman, B. 1971. *Alienation: Marx's Conception of Man in Capitalist Society*. Cambridge: Cambridge University Press.

Ortner, S. 1974. Is female to male as nature is to culture? In *Women, Culture and Society*, M. Z. Rosaldo & L. Lamphere (eds), 67–88. Stanford, Calif.: Stanford University Press.

Outwrite 1988. Editorial, December, 1, 4 and 5.

Palmer, R. E. 1969. *Hermeneutics. Interpretation Theory in Schleiermacher, Dilthey, Heidegger, and Gadamer*. Evanston, Ill.: Northwestern University Press.

Parliamentary Select Committee (1975) *Report from the Select Committee on Violence in Marriage Together with the Proceedings of the Committee*, II: *Evidence*, III: *Appendices*. London: HMSO.

Parmar, P. 1982. Gender, race and class; Asian women in resistance. In *The*

Empire Strikes Back: Race and Racism in 70's Britain (ed.), Centre for Contemporary Cultural Studies. London: Hutchinson.

Paton, K. 1977. Industry as a men's hut: rumbling tool power. *Peace News*, 2 December.

Pearson, G. 1983. *Hooligan: A History of Respectable Fears*. London: Macmillan.

Piercy, M. 1970. Grand Coolie Damn. In *Sister Is Powerful: An Anthology of Writings from the Women's Movement*, R. Morgan (ed.), 421–35. New York: Vintage.

Pleck, J. H. & J. Sawyer 1974. *Men and Masculinity*. Englewood Cliffs, NJ: Prentice-Hall.

Pleck, J. H. 1978. Males' traditional attitudes toward women: Conceptual issues in research. In *The Psychology of Women: Future Directions in Research*, J. A. Sherman & F. Denmark (eds), 617–44. New York: Psychological Dimensions.

Pleck, J. H. 1981. *The Myth of Masculinity*. Cambridge, Mass.: MIT Press.

Plummer, K. 1981. *The Making of the Modern Homosexual*. London: Hutchinson.

Pynchon, T. 1973. *Gravity's Rainbow*. New York: Viking.

Radio Ellen 1987. The oral vaccine trial in Bangladesh. *The Hygeia* 2, (4), 149–61 (transcript of Swedish Radio Station programme).

(RAGE) Reproductive and Genetic Engineering: Journal of International Feminist Analysis. Police raid on gene archive: News from West Germany, (1987), vol. 1, no. 1, 103–5.

Ramazanoglu, C. 1989. *Feminism and the Contradictions of Oppression*. London: Routledge.

Rattansi, A. & S. Westwood 1989. On fixity and fictitiousness: the deconstruction of black masculinity. Paper presented at the conference on Racism and the Post-modern city, University of Warwick.

Raven, H. M. 1988. Has Hegel anything to say to feminists? *The Owl of Minerva* 19 (2, Spring), 149–68.

Reed, E. 1975. *Woman's Evolution: From Matriarchal Clan to Patriarchal Family*. New York: Pathfinder.

Remy, V. 1986. Brotherhood of terror. *Split*, Midsummer, 11, 15. Reprinted in slightly abridged form in *Green Line*, November 1986, 10–12.

Rettie, J. 1988. Army hunts Tamil Tigers after Sinhalese villagers massacred. *Guardian*, 19 March, 6.

Rich, A. 1980. Compulsory heterosexuality and lesbian existence. *Signs: Journal of Women in Culture and Society* 5 (4), 631–60.

Richard, J. P. 1954. *Littérature et sensation*. Paris: Editions du Seuil.

Richards, B. 1989. *Images of Freud: Cultural Responses of Psychoanalysis*. London: Weidenfeld Dent.

Robb, C. S. 1985. *Making the Connections: Essays in Feminist Social Ethics*. Boston, Mass.: Beacon.

Roberts, H. 1981. *Doing Feminist Research*. London: Routledge & Kegan Paul.

Rodgers, S. 1981. Women's space in a men's house: the British House of Commons'. In *Women and Space: Ground Rules and Social Maps*, S. Ardener (ed.), 50–71. London: Croom Helm.

Rogers, B. 1988. *Men Only: An Investigation into Men's Organisations*. London: Pandora.

Rogin, M. 1987. *Ronald Reagan: The Movie*. Berkeley, Calif.: University of California Press.

Rossi, A. S. 1976. Sex equality: the beginnings of ideology. In *Beyond Sex Stereotypes: Readings Toward a Psychology of Androgyny*, A. G. Kaplan & J. P. Bean (eds). Boston: Little, Brown.

Rotundo, A. 1987. Learning about manhood: gender ideals and the middle-class family in nineteenth-century America. In Mangan & Walvin, op. cit., 35–51.

Rowan, J. 1987. *The Horned God*. London: Routledge & Kegan Paul.

Rowbotham, S. 1973. *Woman's Consciousness, Man's World*. Harmondsworth: Penguin.

Rowbotham, S. 1979. The Women's Movement and organizing for socialism. In *Beyond the Fragments: Feminism and the Making of Socialism*, S. Rowbotham, L. Segal & H. Wainwright, 21–155. London: Merlin.

Russell, D. E. H. 1984. *Sexual Exploitation: Rape, Child Sexual Abuse, and Workplace Harassment*. Beverley Hills, Calif.: Sage.

Russell, D. E. H. (ed.) 1989. *Exploring Nuclear Phallacies*. New York: Pergamon.

Rutherford, J. 1988. Who's that man. In Chapman and Rutherford, op. cit., 21–67.

Sacks, H. 1972. On the analysability of stories by children. In *Directions in Sociolinguistics: the Ethnography of Communication*, J. J. Gumperz & D. Hymes (eds), 329–45. New York: Holt, Rinehart & Winston.

Sahgal, A. 1989, Fundamentalism on the rise. *Spare Rib* **202**, 6–7.

Sandqvist, K. 1987. Swedish family policy and the attempt to change paternal roles. In *Reassessing Fatherhood: New Obervations on Fathers and the Modern Family*, C. Lewis & M. O'Brien (eds), 144–60. London: Sage.

Sargent, L. (ed.) 1981. *Women and Revolution: A Discussion of the Unhappy Marriage of Marxism and Feminism*. Boston, Mass.: South End. London: Pluto.

Saunders, S. 1985. Challenging patriarchy and heterosexism. Paper for Bradford Interchange conference on the Politics of Sexuality, Bradford, 18 May.

Schegloff, E. A. 1988. Goffman and the analysis of conversation. In *Erving Goffman: Exploring the Interaction Order*, P. Drew & A. Wootton (eds), 89–135. Cambridge: Polity.

Schiebinger, L. 1987. Skeletons in the closet: the first illustrations of the female skeleton in eighteenth-century anatomy. In Gallagher and Laqueur, op. cit., 83–108.

Schmalenbach, H. 1922. Die soziologische Kategorie des Bundes. *Die Dioskuren: Jahrbiuch für die Geisteswissenschaften*, Munich.

Schmidt, W. 1935. *Rasse und Volk: Ihre allgemeine Bedeutung, ihre Geltung im*

[242]

deutschen Raum; zweite, völlig umgearbeitete Auflage, 88–9. Salzburg and Leipzig: Anton Pustet.

Schurtz, H. 1900. *Urgeschichte der Kultur*. Leipzig and Vienna: Bibliographisches Institut.

Schurtz, H. 1902. Altersklassen und Männerbünde. Eine Darstellung der Grundformen der Gesellschaft. Berlin: Georg Reimer.

Schweickart, P. 1986. Reading ourselves: a feminist theory of reading. In *Gender and Reading: Essays on Readers, Texts and Contexts*, E. A. Flynn & P. P. Schweickart (eds). Baltimore, Md: Johns Hopkins University Press.

Segal, L. 1989. Slow change or no change: feminism, socialism and the problem of men. *Feminist Review* **31**, 5–21.

Seidler, V. 1985. Fear and intimacy. In *The Sexuality of Men*, A. Metcalf & M. Humphries (eds), 150–80. London: Pluto.

Seidler, V. J. 1986. *Kant, Respect and Injustice: The Limits of Liberal Moral Theory*. London: Routledge.

Seidler, V. J. 1987, Reason, desire and male sexuality. In *The Cultural Construction of Sexuality*, P. Caplan (ed), 82–112. London: Tavistock.

Seidler, V. J. 1989. *Rediscovering Masculinity: Reason, Language and Sexuality*. London: Routledge.

Shilts, R. 1987. *And The Band Played On: Politics, People, and the AIDS Epidemic*. London: Penguin.

Siltanen, J. & M. Stanworth 1984. *Women and the Public Sphere*. London: Hutchinson.

Silverman, D. 1970. *The Theory of Organisations*. London: Heinemann.

Smith, D. 1987. *The Everyday World as Problematic*. Milton Keynes: Open University Press.

Snitow, A., C. Stansell & S. Thompson (eds) 1983. *Powers of Desire: The Politics of Sexuality*. New York: Monthly Review Press.

Soble, A. 1986. *Pornography: Marxism, Feminism, and the Future of Sexuality*. New Haven, Conn.: Yale University Press.

Solanas, V. 1968. *SCUM Manifesto*. New York: Olympia Press.

Solanas, V. 1988. *SCUM Manifesto*. London: Phoenix.

Solomos, J. 1988. *Black Youth, Racism and the State: The Politics of Ideology and Policy*. Cambridge: Cambridge University Press.

Spann, O. [1914]1930. *Gesellschaftslehre*, dritte Auflage. Leipzig: Anton Meyer.

Spencer, A. & D. Podmore (eds) 1987. *In a Man's World: Essays on Women in Male-Dominated Professions*. London: Tavistock.

Spender, D. 1980. *Manmade Language*. London: Women's Press.

Stacey, J. 1987. Sexism by a subtler name? Postindustrial conditions and postfeminist consciousness in the Silicon Valley. *Socialist Review* **17** (6), 7–28.

Stanko, E. 1985. *Intimate Intrusions: Women's Experience of Male Violence*. London: Routledge & Kegan Paul.

Stanley, L. 1982. Male needs: the problems and pitfalls of working with gay men. In *On the Problem of Men: Two Feminist Conferences*, S. Friedman & E. Sarah (eds), 190–213. London: Women's Press.

Stanley, L. 1984. Whales and minnows: some sexual theorists and their followers and how they contribute to making feminism invisible. *Women's Studies International Forum* **7** (1), 53–62.

Stanley, L. 1984. Should 'sex' really be 'gender' or 'gender' really be 'sex'. In *Applied Sociological Perspectives*, R. J. Anderson & W. W. Sharrock (eds), 1–19. London: Allen & Unwin.

Stanley, L. 1990. The impact of feminism in sociology: the last twenty years. In *The Knowledge Explosion*, C. Kramarae & D. Spender (eds). New York: Pergamon.

Stanley, L. & S. Wise 1983. *Breaking Out: Feminist Consciousness and Feminist Research*. London: Routledge & Kegan Paul.

Staples, R. 1985. *Black Masculinity: The Black Male's Role in American Society*. London: Black Scholar Press.

Stearns, P. N. 1987. Men, boys and anger in American society, 1860–1940. In Mangan & Walvin op. cit., 75–91.

Stephenson, W. 1953. *The Study of Behaviour*. Chicago: University of Chicago Press.

Stoltenberg, J. 1985. Pornography and freedom. *Changing Men*, Fall.

Stoltenberg, J. 1990. *Refusing to Be a Man: Essays on Sex and Justice*. London: Fontana.

Stumpfl, R. 1936. *Kultspiele der Germanen als Ursprung des mittelalterlichen Dramas*. Berlin: Junker & Dünnhaupt.

Taking Liberties Collective 1989. *Learning the Hard Way: Women's Oppression in Men's Education*. London: Macmillan.

Tavris, C. 1973. Who likes women's liberation – and why; the case of the unliberated liberals. *Journal of Social Issues* **29**, 175–97.

Thomas, A. M. 1987. Cultural representations and personal meanings in the social construction of gender: a psychological study. PhD thesis, University of Reading.

Thurnwald, R. 1932. *Die menschliche Gesellschaft*, II: *Werden, Wandel und Gestaltung von Familie, Verwandtschaft und Bünden*. Berlin and Leipzig: Walter de Gruyter.

Tolson, A. 1977. *The Limits of Masculinity*. London: Tavistock.

Tong, R. 1982. Feminism, pornography and censorship. *Social Theory and Practice* **8** (1, Spring), 1–17.

Treadwell, P. & T. Davis. *Men's Studies Bibliography on Disc*. IBM-MS/DOS. Atlanta, Ga: 409, Oakvale Road, Atlanta GA 30307.

Turner, B. S. 1984. *The Body and Society. Explorations in Social Theory*. Oxford: Basil Blackwell.

Van Gennep, A. 1964. *The Rites of Passage*, trans. M. B. Vizedom & G. L. Caffee. London: Routledge & Kegan Paul. 1st published as *Les Rites de Passage*. Paris: Emile Nourry, 1909.

Walby, S. 1986. *Patriarchy at Work*. Cambridge: Polity.

Watney, S. 1987. *Policing Desire: Pornography, AIDS and the Media*. London: Methuen.

Webster, H. 1908. *Primitive Secret Societies: A Study in Early Politics and Religion*. New York: Macmillan.

Weeks, J. 1977. *Coming Out: Homosexual Politics in Britain from the Nineteenth Century to the Present*. London: Quartet.

Weeks, J. 1981. *Sex, Politics and Society: The Regulation of Sexuality since 1800*. London: Longman.

Weeks, J. 1985. *Sexuality and Its Discontents: Meanings, Myths, and Modern Sexualities*. London: Routledge & Kegan Paul.

Weeks, J. 1986. *Sexuality*. Chichester: Ellis Horwood.

Westwood, S. & P. Bhachu 1988. Images and realities. *New Society*, 6 May.

Wiegand, G. 1989, His-tory lessons. Men's studies gaining favor on campus. *Washington Post*, November 27, p. B5.

Williams, J. & H. Giles 1978. The changing status of women in society: an Intergroup Perspective. In *Differentiation between Social Groups: Studies in the Social Psychology of Intergroup Relations*, H. Tajfel (ed.). London: Academic.

Willis, P. E. 1977. *Learning to Labour: How Working Class Kids Get Working Class Jobs*. London: Saxon House.

Wittgenstein, L. 1958. *Philosophical Investigations*, 2nd edn. Oxford: Basil Blackwell.

Wolfram, R. 1936, 1938. *Schwerttanz und Männerbund*. Kassell: Bärenreiter.

Zilbergeld, B. 1978. *Male Sexuality: A Guide to Sexual Fulfillment*. Boston: Little, Brown.

Author index

Hartmann, H. 56
Haug, W. F. 139
Hearn, J. 3, 5, 6, 9, 16, 17, 77, 89, 96, 139, 203, 205, 208
Heath, S. 172–3
Hegel, G. W. F. 137, 139
Heidegger, M. 177–8
Hey, V. 48, 89
Hintakka, M. 8
Hirschfield, M. 112
Hocart, A. M. 49
Hodson, P. 148
Höfler, O. 52–4
Hooks, B. 56, 212
Hughes, J. 100

Institut für Sozialokologie 5
Institute of Race Relations 65

Jaggar, A. 144
James, C. L. R. 61
Jardine, A. 28–9
Jefferson, T. 63, 201
Jeffreys, S. 29
Jensen, A. E. 47
Jenson, J. 89
Johnston, J. 40
Jones, W. H. 143
Joseph, G. 56
Jouve, M. W. 34
Josza, M. 27
Julien, I. 30, 60

Kafka, F. 175
Kagan, J. 151
Kamuf, P. 28
Kant, I. 179, 219
Kanter, R. M. 85–6
Kaplan, E. A. 175
Kappeler, S. 27
Kaufman, M. 208
Kelly, L. 31
Kimmel, M. 6, 7, 10, 11, 13, 16, 17, 26–7, 30, 96, 104–5, 109, 139, 210, 212
Kinsey, A. 97–8, 104
Kitzinger, C. 186
Klagsbrun, F. 40
Kluckhorn, C. 98
Koedt, A. 39, 40

Lamb, M. 144

Lamphere, L. 41
Langsdorf, L. 139
Laquer, T. 171–4, 179
Lawrence, E. 55
Leacock, E. 40
Lee, J. 4, 10, 29, 58–9, 110, 139
Legge, K. 89
Lehman, P. 172
Leiblum, S. R. 105–6
Leonard Barker, D. *see* Barker, D. L.
Lepenies, W. 183
Levine, E. 40
Levine, J. A. 144
Levine, M. 109
Levinson, D. J. 151
Lewis, C. 143, 159
Linz, D. 103
Lonzi, C. 40
Louch, A. R. 190
Lowe, D. M. 173
Lublinski, I. 47, 51
Lukács, G. 139

MacKinnon, C. A. 26–7, 29, 31, 41
Magnus, O. 52
Malamuth, N. M. 103
Mangan, J. A. 184
Männer in der Geschleterforschung 5
Manning, P. K. 192
Marciano, L. 102
Marcuse, H. 209
Martin, C. 98
Marx, K. 111, 126–7, 130–2, 139
Massachusetts Institute of Technology Humanities Library 5
Matriarchy Study Group 40
May, M. 139
Maynard, M. 29, 33, 207
McClary, S. 177
McIntosh, M. 184
McWalter, K. 129–30
Mead, M. 111
Mercer, K. 30, 60
Merleau-Ponty, M. 175
Messner, M. 30, 96
Mészàros, I. 139
Middleton, C. 3, 203
Mies, M. 209
Miller, D. A. 183
Millett, K. 40, 48
Mills, P. J. 139
Mills, C. W. 209
Milner, J. 201

Subject index

age,
  and gender 33, 45, 46–7, 49, 105–1
agency/structure 9, 13, 87, 88, 187, 192, 193
AIDS 16, 105, 106–9, 122–3
alienation 126–7, 130–2
androcracy 43–53

bodies,
  mens 7, 127–8, 172–3, 174
body,
  commodification of 134–7
  sociology of 9–10, 134–7, 170–5

class,
  and gender 12, 30, 57, 62–3, 67, 76, 77, 78, 178–82

deconstructionism 11, 57–9, 119–22
dramaturgical model,
  and gender 186–7, 188, 191–3

epistemology,
  and feminism 28, 34
equal opportunities 72–89
essentialism 27–8, 28–9, 56, 120
experience,
  and feminism 21–2, 32, 34, 94, 153
  and masculinity 50, 215–16, 226
  and theorizing 14–15, 25–6, 121–2, 210, 211, 224

family,
  and men 50–1, 59–60, 81, 183–4
  relationships 119
fatherhood 7, 12, 50–1, 74, 81, 144, 158–9, 162–9
feminism,
  attitudes of men to 84–5, 153–9, 203
  radical 28–9, 218
  and social theory 8–9, 14
  and studies of men and masculinities 2–4, 4–6, 7, 23–31, 37–8, 93–6,

102–4, 110, 112–13, 138, 153, 204, 206–14, 215–27
feminist scholarship 21–31, 203
fratriarchy 14, 43–53, 132–4

gay men 11, 30–1, 75, 77, 106–9, 110–23
gay politics 4, 106–7, 110–23, 177, 219
gay scholarship 4, 23, 30, 110
gender,
  and sex 12, 13, 110–11, 119, 121–3, 187
  as socially constructed 9, 12, 110–14
  ideologies 152–9
  salience 10–11, 12, 146, 147–52, 158, 195–6
  theorizing 8–14

hegemonic masculinities 10, 11, 58–9, 96–7, 208–9, 211, 212–13
homophobia 77, 83–4, 107, 114, 120, 172, 180, 183–4, 216

identities 46–9, 143–99

lesbianism 31, 75, 117

marriage,
  and gender 34, 45, 155
  and sexuality 99
Marxism 14, 77, 112, 125–6, 131, 134–5, 137
masculinities,
  plurality of 96, 187
  (see also hegemonic masculinities)
men's groups,
  in sociology 2, 3, 5
men's studies 5–6, 23, 24, 26, 29, 37–8, 110–11, 206–14, 217, 222, 223

'new man' 16

[251]

Critical studies in men and masculinities

Jeff Hearn and David H. J. Morgan (editors)
Men, masculinities and social theory

David Jackson
Unmasking masculinity
A critical autobiography

David H. J. Morgan
Discovering men (forthcoming)

Jeff Hearn
Patriarchies and public men (forthcoming)

Editorial advisory board

Harry Brod (*Kenyon College, Ohio*)
Cynthia Cockburn (*City University, London*)
Bob Connell (*Macquarie University, Sydney*)
Paul Gilroy (*University of Essex*)
Jalna Hanmer (*University of Bradford*)
Jeff Hearn (*University of Bradford*)
Michael Kimmel (*State University of New York*)
Marianne Krüll (*University of Bonn*)
David Morgan (*University of Manchester*)
Mary O'Brien (*Ontario Institute of Studies in Education*)
Pratibha Parmar (*Writer and Film-maker*)
Ken Plummer (*University of Essex*)
Rosemary Pringle (*Macquarie University, Sydney*)
Lynne Segal (*Middlesex Polytechnic*)
Victor Seidler (*Goldsmith's College, London*)
Elizabeth Stanko (*Brunel University, London*)
Jeffrey Weeks (*Council for National Academic Awards, London*)
Sue Wise (*University of Lancaster*)

MEN, MASCULINITIES
& SOCIAL THEORY

DATE DUE			